THE MOZART OF
BASKETBALL

THE MOZART OF
BASKETBALL

THE REMARKABLE LIFE AND LEGACY OF
DRAŽEN PETROVIĆ

TODD SPEHR
Foreword by Digger Phelps

SPORTS
PUBLISHING

For Dražen

TABLE OF CONTENTS

Preface

DECEMBER 1985

Zagreb, Croatia

It was classic Dražen Petrović—the way the Europeans remember him. This was before he or the game he had attempted to perfect became globalized, when his stardom in Yugoslavia was growing and appearing boundless. There was the small bob of curly hair, a band on his right wrist, mouth open and tongue out, eyes darting, almost desperate to create the next play. He would move the ball from one end of the court to the other with so much speed and grace. There was something beautiful about the way he pushed the ball up the floor, as if the activity itself had not changed since he was but a small boy in the coastal Croatian town of Šibenik. It was honed. The ball could switch from one hand to the other in an instant, and with space he could leap in the air and place that ball between his legs; there being a split-second when he was suspended in mid-air, with the possibility that it could be whipped either to the right or left to an open teammate.

With his ball handling and passing there was seemingly endless showmanship, some instinctive, some deliberate, but his game was balanced by the pure fundamentals in his jump shot. Structurally, it was perfect, never strained or unbalanced. His older brother, Aleksandar, himself an accomplished basketball player, had kidded him in youth, years earlier, about that jump shot, before the spotlight had found him, and from that he had transformed himself into the best shooter in Europe. Work was not his secret as much as it was his covenant.

What followed each conversion or breathtaking pass was mass syncopated jubilation. His adorers loved him for the way that he involved them; his opponents and their fans conversely disliked him, making him as polarizing and divisive as any European athlete of the mid- eighties. He would inevitably turn to the crowd, either jumping in the air or pumping his fist, sometimes both, and be met by extreme din or silence. Whatever the situation, it was consistent; in every game that Petrović played he made the crowd feel *something*.

Nothing illustrated this point more than a European Cup contest in Zagreb late in 1985, a game between Petrović's Cibona and Simac of Italy. There was a writer watching this event; not just any writer, but one of the best in Europe, noted basketball scribe Enrico Campana of *La Gazzetta dello Sport*. The Italian paper was nothing if not a sports Bible, not only for Italy but for all of Europe, unmistaken in appearance with its pink paper and superior coverage. It had over the years sent Campana to every major tournament, every notable basketball event; and he had seen all the best players who emerged on the continent since the middle part of the sixties. There was always for Campana a special fascination reserved for Yugoslavian players. He loved to watch them play up close, for there was something special about their love for the game and the quality of performance. Campana had once begged his editor to allow him to spend a week with the legendary Yugoslav coach Aleksandar Nikolic at his training facility in Belgrade to study the bodies of the players, watch them run drills, and develop a technique that seemed exclusive. "To discover the secret about the Yugoslavian players," he pitched to his editor.

Through his work, Campana had become close with the giant personalities of the sport in Yugoslavia. They included Nikolic, Boris Stanković, and Mirko Novosel. It was Novosel who told Campana that he must come to Zagreb in Croatia and see some of the quality young players, the next generation who, too, would carry the *secret*, players who would be coming through the system, and who one day would be playing on the biggest stages.

Campana complied, and it was there that he had first spotted Dražen Petrović.

The young man stood out because of the skills with which he played, confident, so fluid, a singular flash able to pour out of those fundamentals in an instant. It had prompted a further pursuit of background information, and it led to Campana having a conversation with Petrović's mother, Biserka. What she said captivated the writer, at that point developing in him the idea that Dražen Petrović was as much a myth as he was a great basketball player. Dražen had, Campana discovered through Petrović's mother, struggled as an infant, born with a subluxation of the hips that was of great concern for the family. His legs were slow in developing, and it seemed likely that he would be different physically from the other children. "But he has a special internal force," she told Campana, "that broke the barriers."

Campana was suddenly burdened with the ultimate challenge for any journalist: writing about someone for whom he held a great admiration, and yet at the same time trying to convey to the readers that he was somewhat objective. "When I followed Dražen I did not consider myself a very balanced and honest journalist. I was a supporter," Campana said. "I looked at Dražen like my younger brother or young kid. I wished him well."

Some years passed, and now the young man had arrived at his promised bright future, composing a performance that exceeded even the pre-packaged expectations; one that was being achieved regularly in the Yugoslav league and in the international tournaments. Campana saw the performance and was immediately obligated to put it into words for his newspaper. There in his mind was the vision: the unmerciful way that Petrović was attacking his opponents, the blend of showmanship and acquired skill, the unique way with which he executed his craft.

Mozart

The name just came to him. Campana thought about it some, and it seemed to fit. Mozart had been composing music from an early age, not just writing it but doing so in a brilliant fashion, part genius, part prodigy. Petrović had been thought of as something of a prodigy, too, in his hometown of Šibenik, even then bearing an uncommon connection to his chosen path. What was before Campana and the fans was the resulting athletic life. There was an experience in watching Petrović that Campana had not felt with other players. There was little NBA coverage in Europe at that time, the occasional game beamed back from America, but it was always enough to get a taste. Campana looked at those telecasts and then looked at Petrović, and drew a conclusion: *He plays like them.* He played the American game like the Americans, Campana thought, the first European he had seen who played the game in such a way.

Ecco Petrović, il Mozart del basket.

It was too good a moniker to have not made its way into the game story, to be consumed by the masses in the following day's newspaper. So from that point, from now to forever, Petrović was to be the *Mozart of Basketball*. First in print, then to become eternal, enhancing just a small bit each of the future distance shots or between-the-legs passes to come. There was a fitting charm to it.[1]

What came with a prestigious name was a growing legend. The expectation now was to achieve greatness, a greatness that Dražen Petrović spent his brief life chasing.

---

1   Petrović heard and immediately liked the name, too, even naming his café in Zagreb—Amadeus—in its likeness.

Foreword by Digger Phelps

In 1980, I traveled to Šibenik, Yugoslavia (now Croatia), to speak at a basketball clinic. During the clinic, I watched a lot of top Yugoslavian players, but I was particularly mesmerized by one sixteen-year-old kid who could shoot the ball with precision thanks to an effortless motion.

We had an interpreter named Farouk. I asked him about this kid and he replied, "Dražen Petrović, the next great international player."

I knew from the first time I saw him shoot that he would be a great player, and I wanted him to play for me at Notre Dame. In 1982, I talked to him about coming to Notre Dame. His father was a retired Secret Police officer in Yugoslavia under President Tito.

I developed a relationship with Dražen and convinced him when they came over to the United States with the national team that he should consider visitng Notre Dame.

We played the Yugoslavian national team at Notre Dame in the fall of 1982, and after the game the media was in a frenzy because Dražen indicated in the postgame interviews that he would be coming to Notre Dame the next year. Today, that kind of news would have blown up Twitter.

Unfortunately, he didn't come that next year, because there was too much pressure on him to stay in Yugoslavia.

I saw him again at the 1984 Olympics. I told him about David Rivers, who was coming to Notre Dame as a freshman that fall. Can you imagine a backcourt with Rivers and Petrović? He could have played two years with Rivers and they would have been the best backcourt in the world, never mind the NCAA.

"All I want you to do is shoot. David will handle the ball and all the passing," I said to him.

Soon after the Olympics, Dražen signed with Real Madrid in Spain for $350,000 a year, which was $350,000 a year more than I could pay him. I was heartbroken that summer when he signed that pro contract. He was the missing piece in what could have been a Final Four season in either 1984–85 or 1985–86 for Notre Dame.

Of course, Dražen eventually came to the NBA and played with Portland and New Jersey. He was on his way to a great NBA career when he was tragically killed in an automobile accident in Germany after the European Championships of 1994.

What was his level of respect? His death was a national tragedy in his country. There were 100,000 people in the square in Zagreb for his funeral. The war stopped the day of his funeral; it was a truce in his honor.

I visited his grave in Zagreb in May of 1995 during the war. Yes, I had tears in my eyes.

Introduction

1989 EUROPEAN BASKETBALL CHAMPIONSHIPS

Zagreb, Croatia

The 1989 European basketball championships in Zagreb, Croatia, was the last tournament of its kind. It would no longer be an exclusive tournament, for once it concluded the best players were leaving to expand their careers in a way that previous generations of European players never could. Some even, for the first time, would be going to the NBA. It was the closing of the curtain for the secretive tournaments, at least to the self-proclaimed owners of the sport, the Americans. From this point forward the European players would be less of a mystery, for some of them would now be regularly pitted against the world's best, the only real true measure of determining how good these outsiders were. There was Arvydas Sabonis, Šarūnas Marčiulionis, and Alexander Volkov of the Soviet Union; Nikos Galis of Greece; and the hosts, Yugoslavia, the deepest of the European powers, with Dino Radja and Toni Kukoč, Vlade Divac, Žarko Paspalj, and Stojko Vranković, each fine international players, each still in the infancy of his time on the national team, but each giving the impression that soon he would be part of the next force of international basketball.

There was already a player on the Yugoslav national team when the likes of Divac, Kukoč, and Radja joined, a player who was three or four years older, who had already achieved what they dreamed of achieving, the figure in their lives whom they chased and whom they aspired to be like. He was as a guard the best in Europe: the best shooter, the best ball handler; certainly the one who owned at once the most flash and the most fundamentals. He seemed even to his teammates to be held in a different, higher esteem, revered among those he played with. In 1989 in Zagreb, there was a very good group of assembled basketball talent, and then above them there was Dražen Petrović.

There was something electric and everlasting about the way Petrović played in that 1989 European championship tournament. For years he had been a brilliant individual star, but the national team had seemed in varying ways to come up short, a talented team that failed to make the pieces fit. Finally, there seemed a correlation between Petrović's greatness and that of his team. His tournament numbers seem exaggerated: 30 points per game, 69 percent shooting from the field on mostly perimeter shots, the average winning margin of his team at 22 points. The final against Greece was rather informal. Petrović and his team spent the evening improvising, running, and scoring, always making eye contact after the accomplishment, winking or smiling or patting each other on the head. Few teams to that point had dominated a European competition in such a manner, which was especially noteworthy considering the rich basketball history of the Yugoslavs.

The final score was not close; Yugoslavia won by 21 points, and yet it did not even seem that close. Petrović finished with 28 points and 12 assists, yet somehow the numbers did not seem to capture the effect. He had been the tournament's best player by far, even embedded in a balanced, confident group, and it punctuated a decade that had seen him constantly climb to a new level. He had led his Yugoslav club team to the league title at the age of eighteen, won his first European Cup at twenty, and was drafted by the NBA's Portland Trail Blazers at twenty-one. He had remained in Europe even after being drafted, building upon the growing myth, there being very much a process to be played out before he was to try the greater league. Petrović had dreamed of the NBA from the time he was a small boy in Šibenik, Croatia, a time when players from Europe simply were nowhere to be found; the few who may have been good enough were always facing the internal dispute of whether to pursue an individual career—and in essence forfeit their national team commitments—knew that doing both was not permitted. By 1989 the lane was now free and open for the challenge.

There was a spectator at that 1989 European tournament taking in the games, an American man, someone from the league with a vested interest in Petrović. Bucky Buckwalter was the vice-president of basketball operations for the Portland Trail Blazers, prolific among a group of executives in the league who were entrusted with building teams. He made the trip to Zagreb, as he had to many of the other major tournaments, to see Petrović and to observe the new developments in his game. But this year there was a different hope: that Petrović might finally come to Portland. It had been three years since Buckwalter had taken him in the NBA draft, a safe selection in the third round in 1986. It was in its barest sense only a selection, for there was no commitment; while Petrović continued his career in Europe, the Blazers periodically checked on him. The season of 1989 finally presented a possibility.

Buckwalter's presence at the European championships was not an unusual occurrence. He had for the better part of the previous half-dozen years been a regular at these foreign affairs, open-minded and curious, one of the first to indulge in the out-side-the-USA form of the game. He had long been intrigued by the international flavor of basketball and its possibilities, back to when he was coaching collegiately as an assistant at the University of Utah and as the head man at Seattle University, when inter-national teams would tour. The visitors would compete admira-bly before losing, but relatively soon there came a juncture when Buckwalter would look at the individuals within these touring teams and ask himself:

Could that guy play at the Division One level?
In time, as the players got better and the teams possessed more sophistication and structure, the question changed:

Could that guy play at the NBA level?
As Buckwalter transitioned over time from the collegiate ranks to the pros, he had developed a demographic of friends within the business: Americans who had gone to Europe as players or coaches—people who became his eyes and ears for identifying the intriguing overseas prospects. To Buckwalter these friends would confirm what he had begun to suspect: the European players were measurably improving.

A man Buckwalter came to rely on heavily for information was George Fisher, a player Buckwalter recruited while an assis-tant coach at the University of Utah back in the sixties, and who would eventually carve out a lengthy playing and coaching career in France. Fisher's presence in Europe was something of a fluke: he broke his leg late in the 1966 college season and, despite being drafted by the Knicks that summer, he stayed in Utah to rehabilitate, coaching the school's freshman team. In time his leg began to heal and feel better, and once again the Knicks showed interest in signing him, as did the San Diego Rockets. But then Fisher had received a call from an Italian team named Milano. Fisher weighed the offers for his playing services, before deciding on Milano, mostly out of curiosity and for the experience. With that, he took his game to Europe. His knowledge of the European game and its leagues were limited. He remembered that Bill Bradley, the great Princeton shooter and a student at Oxford, had briefly dabbled in the Italian league, participating in a dozen or so European Cup games. What once was a curiosity would eventually turn into a lengthy playing and coaching career for Fisher, spanning well over a decade. In that time he had watched as the European game developed, in part because of the gradual influx of American talent into the club teams, and also due to the insatiable appetite of the Europeans to add more tactical sophistication, increasing the level of competition.

Teams would tour throughout Europe during Fisher's time there, made up completely of American players, and they would serve almost as auditions for the awaiting club teams. When American players were offered contracts to play, invariably they were asked to invest time in the club's development, either by assisting in the teaching of junior teams or helping the senior coaches on a strategic level, passing on knowledge learned from their rise through the American high school and college system. To their credit the European coaches were ravenous information sponges and not above instruction from outside sources—especially the proven Americans—in order to further their programs. It was very much a sports revolution. American coaches, some well-known, would in time be found in Europe in the summertime conducting clinics, teaching their methods, spreading not the game itself but the methodology, its benefits built in because they had worked at a higher level: the college game or professional. Fisher noticed a shift in the European coaches' thinking, where the focus was no longer solely on outscoring the opponent, but also *holding* them, too, defense now a growing emphasis. The teaching of skills and fundamentals elevated, and as a result so did the quality of the players.

Fisher and Buckwalter maintained steady contact throughout Fisher's time in Europe, more so when Fisher began coaching and would vacation back in the United States. The two often discussed the best players Fisher had seen: Buckwalter always asked the questions, and the answers usually were accompanied by his request for some form of evidence, either a game film or detailed report. The player that they discussed with the most enthusiasm in those early days had been Arvydas Sabonis, the great Soviet center, a player appearing at once raw and polished, reckless and majestic—a brute of a force and the possessor of a touch seemingly made for basketball.

Upon first glance at Sabonis, one would immediately notice his enormous size—7-foot-3 but *feeling* bigger—and then, when coming to terms with that, when he had the ball in his hands the fascination shifted from his size to his skills, an understanding for the game so uncommon not just for a big man in Europe, but a big man in any corner of the expanding basketball globe. He could on one possession set up on the right block for a hook shot, and on the next trail the play and spot up in transition for the three-pointer. He especially loved to leap up and swat away an opponent's shot on the game's first or second possession if possible, coming into contact with the ball at its apex, an athletic exclamation of his physical dominance, as if to show some precursor to the coming forty minutes.

What came with his enormity and growing reputation were stories to feed the myth. At seventeen, he had toured the United States with the Soviet national team in 1982, taken apart Indiana in a nationally televised game, and then outplayed Virginia's

Ralph Sampson, at the time a senior and a two-time defending National Player of the Year, before disappearing back to Europe to the club season, his exploits confined first to memory and then exaggeration. There were also the singular myths: one spectacular play from European competition that seemed to be passed around the basketball community of Sabonis grabbing a defensive rebound and in one motion firing it to the other end of the floor to a teammate streaking to the basket—a 70-foot pass with the flick of the wrist; or another, when he caught a pass in the post against Real Madrid and spun off the cheating defender to dunk with such force that he broke the backboard—both plays outlining the strength and the excesses in his game.

Fisher had first watched a then-eighteen-year-old Sabonis at the 1983 European championships in Nantes, France, and marveled at how advanced he was physically and fundamentally for a teenager, holding his own against men with far more experience and with far greater reputations. As his career slowly progressed, however, he had, in the opinion of some who followed European basketball closely, shown signs of boredom in club competition, and though his play remained at a moderately high level his intensity did not, the opponent simply not being challenging or stimulating enough for him.

He was, above all else, a player who appeared immune to the usual European stereotypes held by the American basketball people, which was to say they not only thought he could compete in the NBA, but in fact might dominate it to a degree.

On the occasions when Fisher was allowed to divert his conversations with Buckwalter away from Sabonis, they invariably talked about Petrović, at that point Europe's best and flashiest shooting guard. Fisher had coached against Petrović when Fisher was at Orthez, a French club team, and they had come up against Petrović and his first team, the Šibenik-based Šibenka team in the Korać Cup in the early eighties. Fisher thought Petrović, still in his teens, was a heady player, clearly enamored with the game, someone who seemed so sure of himself and of his abilities that it bordered on cockiness—but Fisher liked that. He thought that worked for Petrović. When Petrović's time at Šibenka was very much in its infancy, his reputation growing but his game still somewhat unproven, the floating theory that Fisher had heard was that there was a compulsive need to have the ball in his hands—that without it, Petrović's game and emotions functioned at a much lower rate. Fisher didn't see Petrović that way. If anything, Fisher instinctively felt that Petrović was the new breed of European guard, with a skill-set as a scorer and passer being so dynamic that he needed to be defended with double-teams, his teammates surely becoming the beneficiaries.

Buckwalter had seen game film of Petrović, and had even been intrigued enough by Fisher's recommendations that he made plans to travel to Europe to see Petrović play in person. The aim would be to gauge his potential readiness for the NBA. Buckwalter later estimated that he scouted Petrović on five or six occasions, between his initial discussions with Fisher and the 1986 NBA draft. Buckwalter watched him closely, and his focus had been predisposed to observe the obvious, touted qualities, the shot-making and ball handling—qualities that were celebrated and pronounced as Petrović ascended first in club competition and then with the Yugoslavian national team. Buckwalter initially anticipated that they were the elements that would most radiate in person, but he came away most impressed with Petrović's competitiveness. Every play, Buckwalter quickly noticed, had meaning and importance to Petrović, regardless of his opponent. He would leave Zagreb satisfied, convinced that the twenty-one-year-old Petrović was a potential NBA player, and saw no risk in Portland choosing him with the sixtieth selection in the third round.

That draft had carried with it a distinct international flavor for the Blazers. Buckwalter had wanted Sabonis very badly and used a first-round pick (the twenty-fourth selection) to obtain him. He also drafted Panagiotis Fasoulas, a Greek player by way of North Carolina State, in the second round. Portland and Buckwalter had been, in the lead-up to the draft, relatively secure that Petrović would be available when they selected in the third round. He was a guard, and guards at that time were the lowest form of life for the professional scouts who had entertained thoughts of drafting a European, their capabilities as athletes quite indeterminable, their chances of success deemed to be even less. Neven Bertičević, a longtime sportswriter in Croatia, remembers being told by a prominent American coach that the hardest thing to succeed at in the NBA is a guard coming from Europe; that the dynamics were vastly different and difficult to adjust to. Sabonis was exempt. He was a center, an enormous man; *that* was his determinable variable, and landing him had been the cause for a great deal of anxiety for Buckwalter, what with Atlanta lurking in the shadows, pushed by the cable magnate Ted Turner, a friend of the Soviets.[2]

Buckwalter had a clear vision and came away from the 1986 draft with three international players. It was a vision that had been sanctioned by the Blazers' owner Larry Weinberg, who was aware that even holding the draft rights to these players did not guarantee that they would end up in Portland uniforms. Weinberg was, in the eyes of Harley Frankel, the team's executive vice-president of basketball operations, a very creative and bright man, but more importantly, one who was willing and open to

---

2   Sabonis had in fact been drafted by Atlanta the previous year, but he had not been of age per the rules for international players, and the pick was voided.

trying new things in the name of helping his team. He stimulated these ideas, Frankel thought, pushing for better and more sophisticated approaches that the other clubs had perhaps been reluctant to consider. Weinberg had made his money in construction and real estate, and he, like many owners, was still attached to his businessman mentality, but in the face of that, he too could be captivated by innovation and risk. He had spoken to Buckwalter before the draft, listened to him speak of Sabonis and Petrović, and of their value in Europe, as well as of their potential should they make it to the NBA, and he had encouraged Buckwalter as a way of demonstrating his support. "In business, if you hire good people and use their expertise, then you go with it," Weinberg told Buckwalter.

"Well, nobody has ever drafted a foreign player in the first round; usually it's the third or fourth round—a throwaway," Buckwalter had answered him. "But Sabonis is a big player, and if we want him we should take him in the first round, keep his rights forever, and try like hell to get him out of the Soviet Union."

"Fine, take him," Weinberg said, giving his blessing, even as the media openly questioned this approach in the days after the draft.

Several weeks after the draft Buckwalter recommended that a small Portland contingent—featuring himself, Weinberg, Weinberg's wife, and Frankel—journey to Spain for the world basketball championships, to see Sabonis and Petrović play in person. They would take in most of their respective matches, and with some luck have the opportunity to meet with them away from the floor, make a good impression, express their interest, and promise to keep in touch for whenever one of the players would show an interest in jumping leagues.

Getting to each man was in itself a singular task, separated by varying degrees of difficulty. Petrović made himself available to them without any problems. The group found him to be a very nice young man, inquisitive about the organization and about the city of Portland, clearly a player who someday would like to test himself in the NBA, but uncertain as to when that might be. Buckwalter came away feeling confident that *one day*—these players needed to be thought of in futuristic terms—Petrović would play for Portland; his inner drive would see to that. Sabonis, however, had not been so easy to meet with. Buckwalter had to make arrangements to meet Sabonis at three in the morning one other day, in the hotel but not in Sabonis's room; instead, a private room. The meeting was known only to Buckwalter, Sabonis, and a friend of Sabonis's who acted as an interpreter. The scene was covert and secretive. There was a brief window of opportunity, so the meeting needed to be quick. Yes, Sabonis was interested in coming to Portland, he said through the interpreter, but only when given permission by the appropriate Soviet people. "Life could be very difficult for my family back home if I came without permission," he told Buckwalter. The Blazers had just entered a very complex maze, one that in the end would take nine years to exit.

Before the Portland group was to depart Spain, they were fortunate to have the opportunity to see their two picks square off against each other, as Yugoslavia had drawn the Soviets in the semi-finals. Buckwalter had, at some stage when gathering information on the two, been fascinated when he realized that not only were Sabonis and Petrović the two best players in Europe, but between them there was some very real tension, a personal rivalry—one that had emanated from their games against each other, and over time had made its way into the newspapers.

"I consider him a despicable player," Sabonis said about Petrović earlier in 1986, to which Petrović snorted back, "All the terrible things he said about me shows that he is unbalanced."

"That the Portland Trail Blazers drafted both these fellows in June," *Sports Illustrated*'s Curry Kirkpatrick wrote from Spain, "is the joke of the year on the Continent."

There was to all Petrović-Sabonis games a certain heat, a tension that seemed to be readily available to the public, as if from vapor rising off the floor. The two were so good in Europe at what they did that when their teams met there was a very real anticipation for their periodic crossing of paths within the game. Petrović was such an aggressive offensive player that it seemed his ultimate test was to be able to get into the paint and shoot his floating jump shot over Sabonis's outstretched arms. Petrović was different from many offensive players in that he was still dangerous once his dribble had ended, even finding through pump fakes or an extra step the ability to get by his defender with a dead dribble; in his games against Sabonis this would provide the closest thing to a one-on-one duel. Petrović would escape his defender, leaving him alone in the paint, a threat to shoot off either foot because he had the ability to do so. Sabonis, slightly crouched before him, would wait about a step in front of the basket, ready to time his leap with the intent to meet the ball as it travelled for the basket, the desire to bat it away, and in doing so to dominate the offensive player's mind: Europe's two best players matched up in their own private competition.

It had been noticed by some of Petrović's coaches that the games against Sabonis seemed to enable Petrović to elevate his focus almost to the point of anxiety. "Playing Sabonis was two games for Dražen," said Željko Pavličević, Petrović's coach at Cibona in 1985–86. "One to win, second to see who the best is in Europe—that was important to him." When Cibona was to meet Sabonis' Žalgiris Kaunas team in a European Cup game earlier in 1986, Petrović had been so antsy in the practice session the day before that Pavličević had kicked him out. The coach noticed that Petrović seemed distracted, and three times had asked him to concentrate. On the fourth warning, Pavličević asked Petrović to leave.

The exchange left Pavličević very angry, and early the next morning there was a tap at his office door—it was Petrović.

"Look, Coach, I am sorry for yesterday," Petrović began, hanging his head. "I was very nervous because for me it's not only a game of whose team will win; for me personally it's a big game because I wish to show that I am better than Sabonis."

Pavličević was a young coach, and after hearing Petrović's explanation he had looked at his own behavior and wondered if he had overreacted. Petrović went out and scored 44 points to Sabonis' 22, and Cibona won.

Cibona and Žalgiris had met for the European Cup title that past April in Budapest, which decided Europe's best club team, and Cibona had won by 12 points, its superior depth in the end making the difference. Neither Petrović nor Sabonis had typical evenings that game: Petrović scored just 22 points, almost half his average; Sabonis got 27, but was ejected with just over eight minutes to go for whacking Cibona's Mihovil Nakić.

The drama of the European Cup served as a backdrop for the world championship semi-final. With the Blazers' brass watching, the game not only met the hype but exceeded it considerably. The Yugoslavs controlled the game until the final minute of regulation, when a nine-point lead evaporated behind three consecutive three-pointers by the Soviets. By the time overtime arrived the momentum had changed, and the Soviets won by a point. It had been a demoralizing loss for the Yugoslavs. Petrović scored 29 points but it had been Sabonis, with 25, who had been the difference in the second half. It was a game that entered folklore due to its unusual finish and the high-level play of its leading participants. Amidst the crowd and the atmosphere were four Americans from Portland, taking it all in, the witnesses to the clear passion with which their two draftees had played. They came away absolutely delighted.

The latter part of the eighties played out and they remained Europe's best. Petrović was a dominating force in the Yugoslav league before moving to the Spanish league for the 1988–89 season, his game and personality maturing. Sabonis remained a terrific player but one with suffering attendance, numerous leg injuries costing him a portion of his prime, but he had done enough when healthy to ensure that in the moments when he did play he was a presence. The two would meet in the gold medal game at the Seoul Olympics in 1988, and by 1989 in Zagreb for the European championships, the anticipation was that they would perhaps meet again.

But that feeling was superseded by something grander: a recent ruling by FIBA would allow the participation of professionals in Olympic competition. The best Europeans could contemplate a future in America; they could come forward without consequence, with no threat of relinquishment for national team selection. For Petrović, for Sabonis, for select others, basketball was now an open playing field. The mark they would leave would prove to be everlasting.

One

THE BOY IS A MIRACLE, THE 1960s AND 1970s

Šibenik, Croatia

If, in the summer of 1964, one were to take an afternoon stroll down the banks of the beautiful Krka River, just outside Šibenik, Croatia, they would likely come across a striking, twenty-something woman named Biserka Petrović. Already the mother of a young son and pregnant with her second, she would spend hours walking up and down the river, the picturesque surroundings serving as the fiber of her very being—the place where her parents raised her. Prokljansko Jezero (Lake Prokljan) was home for the Mikulandra family, some seven kilometers outside the township of Šibenik, and even as Biserka emerged from adolescence, was married, and became a mother, she never strayed far from where her heart lay.

What came with her love for the Krka was an intimate understanding of its true treasures, and on those leisurely walks in the summer warmth she was not averse to kneeling before the stream and drinking from its pure supply. At the point where the Krka pours into the Adriatic Sea, the product is a unique

2 THE MOZART OF BASKETBALL

blend: mostly pure, clean water mixed with a hint of saltwater. Only in hindsight, when her forthcoming son Dražen was born and raised, and bestowed with stardom as one of Europe's elite athletes, would some wonder just what special elixir resided in that body of water.

Regardless of the supposed magic of the Krka, the place was already mystical for Biserka Petrović. With the waterfalls serving as a backdrop one May, on an outing with friends, she had been captivated by a young out-of-towner, Jole Petrović. "That is where we met and fell in love," she said, "right in the place where I was born." Jole was not of Šibenik, as Biserka was. He was drawn to the city by a scholarship to the Faculty of Law; what kept him there was his love for Biserka. The two would marry in 1958 and the next year, in February of 1959, they welcomed a son, Aleksandar, into the world.

Jole was greatly respected and admired in Šibenik, a man of genuine integrity. He was not fortunate enough to have been able to choose for himself a field in life to pursue—times in the former Yugoslavia had dictated that it was to be chosen for him—but it just so happened that, in rising to chief of police, he was very good at it. Born less than twenty kilometers outside of Dubrovnik, he had even as a boy displayed a serious approach to life and an appreciation for hard work (at just ten he was a regular staff member at a local restaurant). After the Second World War, it was decided for him that he would enter the police force, stationed first in Pelješac, then later Šibenik, where he rose to be second in command.

Through his work he developed an interest in criminal investigation, but his true calling was assisting those troubled few who had taken the wrong path. "When some young criminal would get out of jail, he [Jole] would want to find him a job, to employ him so that he didn't fall deeper into the abyss," Biserka would say of her husband. Jole would often wonder aloud to his wife about whether he would have been better served becoming a doctor, for his reach to help others could have stretched further, but as it was he had been forced into police work and made the very best of a difficult job.

Jole became a father to a second son, Dražen, on October 22, 1964. Shortly thereafter, he retired from police work, still relatively young but now assigned to a new task: to raise two young boys (Aleksandar was five when Dražen was born). Biserka went back to work as a librarian—her specialty was the children's section—where she stayed for seventeen years. The family resided in north central Šibenik at number 3 Petra Preradovića Street, a place they had moved to in August 1964, in anticipation of their growing family, two months prior to Dražen's arrival.

Šibenik was, thought the parents, a wonderful place to raise a young family. The locals carried with them a warm enthusiasm for life, coupled with a unique brand of pride and determination. It was said that, once honored with parenthood, the locals of Šibenik took special pride in placing their focus squarely on the next generation. "There is a tradition (in Šibenik) to give everything for the sake of the children," Biserka said. "That is the mentality. Parents are sad when a child leaves Šibenik and goes to university in Zagreb, and they remain alone. They would like to keep a child for themselves for life. I think that this is something that is characteristic for a small city, for Šibenik."

As it was, Aleksandar (known to family and friends as "Aco") and Dražen were raised in a Croatia quite different from the one in which their parents had been children. Whereas their father followed a career that he was commanded to take, the Petrović boys were children of a fresh generation. The expectations from parent to child were enhanced, and the boundaries for success were less impeded. These kids would be expected to make something of themselves. "They expected from us completely to have our own lives," said Aleksandar. "In the beginning when we were kids they would like for us to go for music, for school. They didn't push us into sport, they had totally different expectations from us. But in the end when we make our choice they followed us in our directions."

Though there was the presence of Communism when the Petrović boys were growing up in Croatia, it had been said that in these parts it was a softer brand, with room for subtle liberation, not like what was found in Russia or Bulgaria. As a result, the children of that time progressed into adolescence with a very real sense of ambition, which generally translated into athletic pursuits, for it was an avenue where there was potential for success. "Sports were the window to the world," said Neven Spahija, Petrović's closest childhood friend and neighbor. "Sports were one of the great possibilities for us to do something with our lives."

On Petra Preradovića Street, in a relatively quiet corner of the town, a good deal of the noise came from the kids on the street who were locked in athletic competition in makeshift, imaginative spaces. It was here that the Petrović boys came to play basketball, first Aleksandar, then Dražen, drawn to the game as the young, curious shadow to his older brother. The games there were tough and hard: earned, not always welcomed by the neighbors, but contests that came to be the central events in the lives of the children in the immediate area. The basket where skills were first honed sat haphazardly on a garage, held in place by a large rock, one deemed heavy enough to absorb the constant shot-taking. The playing area happened to occupy a quiet laneway, and so the temporary impediment came always in the form of a passing car, one that would stop the competition only if it were early in the contest.[3]

Beyond the street battles, Jole and Biserka Petrović had made a mild attempt at steering their sons into music early on, but it proved fruitless. Aleksandar was assigned the clarinet, Dražen the guitar. Lessons were organized and planned. One day Biserka went to the home of the teacher to pay fees, and was promptly updated on the status of her boys. Aleksandar had not even bothered showing up, instead detouring daily to a nearby playground. Dražen was at least showing up as scheduled, but when the teacher was not looking he would deviously loosen the strings on his guitar. Re-stringing would sometimes take the teacher as much time as thirty minutes, long enough for Dražen to sneak across the street to the playground. It went without saying that the Petrović boys didn't go to sleep at night dreaming of a career in music. "We saw that they didn't really like this because they had too much energy," Biserka said. "It was then that we decided that we had to stand behind our children in whatever they wanted to do. We didn't impose our opinions. We tried, but we saw that it wasn't working, and then we worked for them and stood behind them all of their lives."

It was not coincidental, merely a recurring order, that Dražen followed in step with his older brother by exiting the music lessons. His brother had been the singular source behind his early infatuation with the game. In fact, Aleksandar's early prowess in basketball had been something of an inspiration to many of the children in the local community. The older brother had developed

---

3   If it were a late critical point, or especially game point, then the general rule of the street was that the vehicle was forced to stop and wait patiently for a result, or risk the scorn of the neighborhood kids. The priority was set.

into a promising playmaking guard by his early teens, playing the game first with a childlike affection before approaching it with more seriousness as he became better around the age of twelve or thirteen, entering the cadet level. Aleksandar's increased focus on the game had led to club participation and frequent team practices. Often the younger Petrović would force his presence upon these sessions with persistence, cleverly coining excuses in an attempt to warrant his tagging along. "I will carry your bag, Aco," Dražen coaxed, snatching his brother's athletic bag out of his hand as the two made the short walk from their apartment to the gym. Once there, with time to spare before practice, the two would play. Aleksandar, older and stronger, at that point in time was far better, so he would have his way with his eager sibling. It was at this stage that Dražen was unwittingly building his own unique *need* for the sport. "If his brother had played water polo, handball, or soccer, I think that he would also have chosen that sport," Biserka said of Dražen's affinity for following Aleksandar. "His brother was his model in everything."

Once Aleksandar's practice started, Dražen would find himself shooting on an aged, well-worn goal off to the side, the early traces of an isolated paradise that he came to crave. The ball would sometimes ricochet off the rim and out onto the main court, Dražen chasing it, his eyes fixed on the ball even when there might be ten teenage boys rumbling down on top of him. "During my practice with the team he was by himself, he was not even watching us practicing," Aleksandar would say later. "He wasn't standing around, he was taking his own shots, and it was strange because it's not common that you see a kid ten of eleven years-old focus on making some basketball drills, but Dražen was. He was focused from the very beginning."

Dražen's unusual focus and maturity at such a young age was something noticed by his mother. "Even as a child, he would speak so wisely about some things that we, as parents, could only be surprised," she said. "Somehow, he was ahead of his age." At elementary school, he quickly rose among his peers to be a respected figure, smart and humorous. Around the time that his friends began showing an interest in girls, Dražen was most bashful around them, his attention happily fixed only on basketball. It was when watching her son play the sport that had quickly captivated him that she noticed a shift in personality. Off the floor he was mature and charming; on it, he became something else. "That is why I am inclined to believe that there were two men in him," she would say of her son as he grew older. "One for sport, and one for private life."

The hold basketball had on him quickly became stronger and stronger. He came to rely on these trips to practice with Aleksandar as a way to satisfy an appetite that was most rapid in its growth. Janez Drvaric coached Aleksandar on the under-seventeen Yugoslavian cadet national team that participated in the European championships in Greece in the summer of 1975 and remembered the Petrović family driving out to visit. When they arrived, Drvaric took the family to the room where Aleksandar was staying, and though Dražen had not seen much of his older brother that summer, his greeting was brief. The image of a ten-year-old Dražen Petrović saying a quick hello before bolting down the hallway, ball tucked under his arm and out to the playground in the summer heat, was not easy for Drvaric to forget.

So it was that the Petrović boys had chosen the path of sport to make their mark. That it had occurred was not totally shocking, for in the blended lineage of the Petrović and Mikulandra families there were detectable hints that led to a competitive athlete eventually making his way into the family. Jole's grandfather, from Herzegovina, stood an impressive 6-foot-7. Biserka's grandmother, meanwhile, was in the early 1900s occupied as a milk deliverer by foot, and as became her own personal tradition, according to family legend she *had* to be the first on the road each morning. It was the order of the universe. Thus the Petrović boys were inheritors of a competitive spirit.[4]

That young Dražen Petrović was able to be so active and mobile as a child was something of a pleasant surprise, for he was born with a subluxation of the hips, a condition that he had inherited from his mother (Aleksandar also suffered from the condition). It was at a three-month inspection by the local physician that it was noticed Petrović's hips were slightly off-center and not developing normally. It was a sufficient enough problem that the doctor thought dislocation seemed imminent, and instructed Biserka from that point on to wrap her son in a looser fashion, in a way that would allow proper growth and widening. At six months, the doctor recommended a belt-like device to widen the child's legs. "It was torture for all of us to look at him, but he was enjoying it," Biserka said of Dražen. "He accepted the belt, he sang, he gurgled. We were suffering more than him." By the time he was old enough to walk, Petrović had outlasted his hip problem, but the gait he strutted with throughout his life provided a subtle reminder.

Though his hips were a short-term obstacle, at the age of eleven Petrović had another potential hurdle placed in his path: a heart murmur. It had come as quite a shock to his parents and prompted them to seek the very best medical advice outside Šibenik after a local doctor suggested the child abandon his athletic pursuits for the greater good of his health. The Petrovićs took Dražen all the way to Belgrade, Serbia, to see a well-respected

---

4   Biserka also, in her youth, excelled in track. She had tremendous endurance as a result of her twenty kilometer round-trip walks into Šibenik for school.

female cardiologist who had studied in the United States. She subjected Dražen to a series of tests. "I think your son will be fine," she ultimately announced to Jole and Biserka. "This should disappear when Dražen reaches puberty." The doctor proved correct. By his early teens Petrović no longer suffered from the ailment, and continued on his determined path. Biserka would later theorize that the experience had only increased her son's desire to pursue basketball. "It would have been a disaster for him not to play sports because he had already become so deeply involved in it," she said. "It helped form him, and created greater stimulus and drive."

Though small in population and lacking a presence in the top Yugoslavian league, Šibenik had in place a solid youth basketball program which was run out of Baldekin Hall, a stone's throw from the Petrović home and the city's main basketball gym. In place was a recreational league made up of local players of varying ages. For the better ones, there were cadet (early- to mid-teens) and junior (mid- to late-teens) teams to play for, which would travel and pit themselves against better competition. It was there, on a cadet team, that Petrović and Neven Spahija, his neighbor, first played organized ball together. The two had grown close earlier in childhood, often companions in the Preradovića street battles, their homes separated by just eight doors. The window from Petrović's apartment had clear visibility to Spahija's front door, so it helped Dražen when he was trying to gain Spahija's attention, waving his arms, his intention always to play.

Spahija dabbled briefly in soccer in his youth, but quickly strayed from it and went back to basketball. The court was a place where Petrović always remained, disinterested in the pursuit of any other game, his devotion absolute.

The two friends attended a summer basketball camp at Baldekin together in 1976. Spahija at fourteen was of the appropriate age, and Dražen, eleven (turning twelve in October), was elevated based on his skill level. Even then, his play had caught the attention of the junior coaches. The boys also participated in a regional league, the third division, against players from the town and nearby villages, often older men whose bodies and maturity clearly indicated a more advanced stage. The losing scoring margins at first would regularly be in the forties and fifties, but over time the games became more competitive. The boys found themselves forced to adapt their games in this setting, the closer margins acting as a motivator of sorts, a sign of their gradual improvement. Petrović seemed to gravitate towards the competitive contests, constantly adjusting his game, displaying a superior ability to score and handle the ball.

When Petrović turned fourteen his game had developed to the point where he soon gained a reputation in the cadet and junior ranks as a player of excellent potential. Spahija remembers the day that reputation was sanctified with the words of Nino Jelavić, the man in charge of the youth teams in Šibenik. The coach spoke words that would become immortal around the small town, marking the Petrović myth in its infancy.

"The boy is a miracle," Jelavić once said.

At first, Spahija observed Petrović and then looked at the ability of the other kids in the program and could not determine why exactly his friend's future was any more promising. They all worked hard, he thought; they all played hard, they all loved the game. But in time he realized that Petrović's sacrifices to become a better player were far and above those of the other players. His desire was just that much greater and more lasting. For every Petrović action, Spahija realized, there was a wide-ranging perspective, always a plan. In a fourteen-year-old it had been a most unusual characteristic, as if he carried the thought patterns of a person much older, not unlike a college underclassman mapping out job plans even while still in school. Petrović was blessed with a very determined and narrow focus, and that would never leave him. In addition, he had been influenced and encouraged strongly by his parents, but in different ways. "He was a perfect mix between the energy of the mother and the discipline of the father," Spahija once said.

"They are completely different—completely opposite—my parents," Aleksandar said.

The motivation, enthusiasm, and unrelenting strength that young Dražen displayed came from Biserka. She had pushed for her kids to demand excellence of themselves, to be something better, and to never settle. Spahija came to believe as the years wore on that the influence of Biserka was in fact one of the most important factors in Dražen's early career. In Biserka's mind, from Jole came the self-sacrificing characteristic, a simplistic approach to life that set his son on a path to success. Jole's voice was quieter, his few spoken words carrying a different, respected weight. There was a well-known story from Dražen's teens about the time when a Šibenka basketball practice was scheduled for midday. For a mostly-adult team, there would be no conflict, but for a boy still in school there was. Jole's boy would *not* skip school for *basketball practice*. So an early-morning workout was instead arranged for Dražen.

So it was that teenage Dražen Petrović appeared destined for greatness in Yugoslavian basketball. Already the elite adolescent player in his tiny hometown, he sought out making a name for himself outside as well. The work it took to be great became a narrative almost as encompassing as his feats.

TWO

TEENAGE ASCENT, 1979–82

Šibenik, Croatia

Šibenka, the local club that represented the town of Šibenik, had its senior team promoted to the Yugoslav first division in 1979. The club had been formed just six years earlier, and in a league that boasted so many of Europe's stronger teams they were very much in their adolescence, with no real basketball tradition or establishment. The city itself instead spread its focus to other sports, such as soccer, swimming, and water polo. Initially they had competed in the third division before being promoted to second division, in part because of the contributions of Aleksandar Petrović.

Aleksandar had been a very good junior player, the possessor not of the flash of the later Petrović brother but a strong, firm player, a sound guard with a superb outside shot. He was a representative of junior national teams, and prominent enough in his junior career that he caught the attention of Mirko Novosel, the great coach at Cibona in Zagreb, and soon he was pried from Šibenka. Aleksandar was a young man deemed to have a bright enough future that he was snatched from the nest and allowed the opportunity to run with an established club. It was the type of way out that many of the neighborhood kids had dreamt of and would be motivated by. The fact that Novosel, a coach known throughout not just Europe but the entire basketball world, would take an interest in a seventeen-year-old from Šibenik proved that there was a justifiable reason for any local youth to push hard into sports.

This in itself provided a dilemma for the smaller, struggling teams in the lower divisions who were located in the smaller cities. If they were ever in possession of a young, talented player whose early career indicated promise or potentially national team representation, he was just as likely to be noticed by the bigger and more powerful clubs and lured away by the possibilities of the grander opportunity. Staying home could potentially be stunting to a player's growth. Changing teams was, under the rules at the time, forbidden in the Yugoslav league, but the governing bodies for each of the six republics had the power to overrule and allow such a transfer. It was usually done in the name of the loosely termed "best interests" of the sport in Yugoslavia and its future—an irrefutable argument. The powerful clubs would notify the federation of their interest in a certain player, thus setting in motion the act of permission to obtain him. Aleksandar Petrović, who would one day be a national team player in Yugoslavia, left Šibenka at seventeen under this premise, and years later his younger brother Dražen would do the same.

After four years in the second division of Yugoslavia, Šibenka moved up to the first league for the 1979–80 season. To survive in the second league, the club had relied on a mix of younger local talent and experienced players from the extended area, usually from nearby Zadar, to fill the roster and allow it to compete at a moderate level. It was a diverse mix of talent that was ill-timed and ill-formed. The younger players were either not fully developed or not good enough for a better level of competition; the older players were either at the end of their careers or their careers had been little more than marginal in bigger cities at better clubs with better players. It was a group of talent that simply would not be able to sustain competitiveness when exposed to the first league, and so efforts to upgrade were made.

The first move the club decided on was to pursue Zoran Slavnić, a stellar playmaking guard who was a featured member of the Yugoslavian national team throughout the 1970s. Šibenka needed Slavnić, for he gave them the assurance of a top-level player and instant credibility when they made their foray into the first league. He accepted an offer to be player and head coach. He was joined by several veterans of the Yugoslav league, players born in the late 1940s who had entered their mid-thirties—names like Srećko Jarić, Branko Macura, and Željko Marelja. For the men on the team's newly formed core their best was surely behind them, but the move presented them with the opportunity to squeeze a little more out of their careers and make a little additional money before departing the game. It was a short-term solution for a long-term goal, their presence keeping the team afloat as it hopefully grew into a mainstay in the league.

Slavnić arrived in the summer of 1979 and immediately began examining the team that he was now to lead. During that process he was told from someone within the club that at the junior level was the younger brother of Cibona's Aleksandar Petrović. Slavnić had played against Aleksandar, thought him a fine young playmaker, and was intrigued enough by the bloodlines. It drew his interest to take a look at the younger brother, fourteen-year-old Dražen. "I want to see him," Slavnić said when hearing of the younger Petrović. Slavnić soon watched a junior contest that featured Dražen just months short of his fifteenth

birthday, and on a court filled with eighteen-year-olds. Petrović played a fine game, impressing Slavnić first with his natural
instincts and then with the effort he put out when he competed.
"Dražen was not really a big talent," Slavnić remembered years
later, "maybe twenty percent of him. All of the best things came
from him working."

Slavnić asked about Petrović and was told about his excellent
potential, of how he had scored a good number of points against
not only boys his own age, but those considerably older and more
developed. Slavnić decided after observing Petrović that he would
be a good addition to Šibenka's team and offered him a roster
spot. It was quite common that some of the younger local players
occupy a position on a club team (Slavnić himself had debuted
for Red Star around the time he turned eighteen), but in most
instances they were late teens heading towards their twenties, not
mid-teens with vast physical development still ahead of them. In
Slavnić's mind, Dražen probably would not play much; it was
asking an awful lot of a fifteen-year-old to be thrown into the first
league against better and more physically imposing players, but
he would benefit greatly from the experience and from the practice sessions, in many which he would be pitted against Slavnić.
It was fortuitous for Petrović that someone of Slavnić's stature
in Yugoslav basketball had arrived to help him as he sought the
next stage. "I was in the right place at the right moment for him,"
Slavnić recalls. "His mentality was special. He was in a different
place from others."

Slavnić first broadcast his excitement about Dražen after
Šibenik played an early-season game in Belgrade. A group of
reporters surrounded Slavnić in the hallway at the old Palata
Sportova, questioning him on his presence at lowly Šibenka, and
how he planned to overcome what was sure to be a difficult season in the first division. Slavnić used the opportunity to tout his

young, hidden guard to the writers. "There is in Šibenik one boy who will be better than 'Kicha' [national team player Dragan Kićanović] and me," Slavnić told them. "He is called Dražen Petrović. Remember the name." There was something both bold and futuristic in Slavnić's words. He and Kićanović were two of Yugoslavia's finest guards in the 1970s, very much the fore-runners of the new breed of European guard. Their games had a good deal of flash to go with their substance, and the two had been cornerstones in a generation of glorious successes for the national team. Apparently, there was a fifteen-year-old from Šibenik who was going to be better than both of them.

Among the reporters standing around Slavnić that evening was Vladimir Stanković, the veteran sportswriter of European basketball. He had patiently listened to Slavnić tout the unknown kid. Stanković had never heard of Petrović. *He didn't even play tonight*, Stanković thought to himself at the time, jotting down the name anyway as Slavnić had requested, the story sure to be recalled in the event that the prophecy was delivered.

To compare a *kid* to Kićanović, still in his prime, was tremen-dously bold.[5]

Slavnić's confidence in Dražen Petrović came in large part from playing against him every day in practice. He quickly became impressed with Petrović's work ethic and ability to learn. The two would often battle at their respective offensive ends; a master-versus-apprentice scenario. Because of his age and ability to learn, Petrović was, in Slavnić's mind, improving a great deal with every passing week. His adaptation to the physical game was

---

5   In the mid-eighties, at the height of his European fame, Petrović spoke about his desire to possess a game that was the amalgam of both Kićanović and Slavnić. "Combine the best qualities of the two," he told a reporter from the Spanish journal *El País*, "would be the ultimate perfection."

far beyond most players his age, many who, because of their varying builds or ability, had less chance of surviving at that particular
level. Slavnić had remembered his own indoctrination into the
Yugoslavian league with Red Star Belgrade in the late sixties, a
team that featured its own established national team members.
He came to learn that it was a vital point in the steps toward his
future success. The daily combat against older and better players
was an environment that could not be simulated elsewhere, especially by playing against those his own age.

Petrović did not play much in that first season of 1979–80. He
appeared in sixteen regular season games for Šibenka, who would
finish eighth in the Yugoslav first division, at 9–22. But, more
importantly, away from the games he had shown great improvement in a very brief amount of time. In his second season, 1980–
81, Slavnić had given Petrović, now sixteen, more opportunity
to play. When on the floor with Slavnić, Petrović would occupy
the shooting guard position and play away from the ball. On the
few occasions without Slavnić, Petrović would be granted slightly
more freedom and play the role of point guard. He didn't shoot
much initially (he would score just 39 points in the twenty games
he played that season), but he showed assertiveness and confidence
when entrusted with the ball-handling responsibilities. Playing
against older men altered Petrović's game. In the junior ranks,
his inconsistent outside shot had been largely masked due to the
effectiveness with which he attacked the basket and finished. But
in the first league, where the opponents were bigger and stronger
and far more experienced, he couldn't pick and choose his dribble
penetrations. So Petrović worked hard at his outside shot. Even
as a teenager, he could self-evaluate and then work, an approach
that distanced him from his peers.

Slavnić viewed Petrović's development rather simplistically
over that second season. At a minimum, Slavnić thought that,

regardless of opponent or score, Petrović needed ten minutes of playing time per game; but eventually, as the season progressed and as Petrović adapted to the level of play, that number increased to the mid-teens. Šibenka was an improved team but hardly a feared one, winning twelve games to finish fourth in the Yugoslavian league in 1981, despite having rather modest talent on the roster.

Slavnić decided to leave Šibenka prior to the 1981–82 season, after two years as a player-coach. He would move to Partizan for his final club season after more than a decade as a force in the Yugoslav league and for the national team. He left behind at Šibenka two significant vacancies: head coach and starting point guard. One of those problems, that of head coach, was filled when Šibenka hired a young man named Faruk Kulenović on the same day that Slavnić left. At just twenty-nine years of age, Kulenović was younger than both the majority of the coaches in Europe and most of the core *players* in Šibenik.

The club had quickly sought out Kulenović as it became clear that Slavnić was departing. Šibenka's expectations, especially without Slavnić, were bleak and they were not given much consideration to being a serious challenger in the Yugoslav league. It was a tough league in which to have success, arguably the toughest in Europe, especially when one had to compete with such teams as Red Star Belgrade, Jugoplastika, and Partizan, perennial strengths not just in the Yugoslavian competition but in all of Europe.

Kulenović had taken the job fully aware that his team would not likely be one to compete for the Yugoslav league title. Shortly after taking over, he obtained a team statistical report from the Yugoslavian Basketball Federation that outlined the contributors from the previous year. Mindful of the absence of Slavnić, he looked for an appropriate suitor to inherit the job as the team's on-floor leader. The team was very thin with guard options, and Dražen Petrović initially didn't seem the natural candidate because of his age and lack of experience. Kulenović looked at Petrović's statistics from the previous year and came away unsure of just how much the now-seventeen-year-old could contribute.

Kulenović had a minor history with Petrović. He had been among a group of five young coaches who tutored him when Petrović was just fourteen and had been selected for a Croatian national team camp that was conducted annually by a man named Vladko Mamec. The camp was held for two weeks every summer on the island of Badija, a showcase for the top fifteen- and sixteen-year-olds in Croatia as selected by the republic's basketball federation. The camp counted the great Kresimir Cosic among its former attendees. Mamec had selected Petrović prematurely, two years younger than a vast majority of the thirty or so kids who were there, by far the youngest of the group, but by no means out of his depth. He was, Kulenović noticed, a superior player in his age group and the possessor of an unusual determination and direction for someone his age. Kulenović had also spent time with Petrović in the summer of 1980, when Petrović was fifteen, at the Balkan junior championships. Among a group of forty-five kids to start the camp, he survived to make the final team of twelve. In that brief period of time he emerged clearly in the coaches' minds as the best guard in Croatia's squad, which competed first in Istanbul and then in another competition in Bulgaria.

At the onset of the season, Kulenović began to slowly incorporate Petrović into Šibenka's rotation. Without a player-coach, Šibenka took on a more structured appearance. Petrović wanted to prove himself to Kulenović early in that season, desperate to show his abilities. Through the early rounds he was playing about twenty minutes per game at both guard spots. Petrović was very raw, his arms and legs almost spindly, but he was to his core very sure of himself and of his skills. The hours of solidarity and work had given him that. He had a knack, despite his frame, for keeping his balance and he was filled with a distinct confidence in everything he did, especially when the ball was in his hands. He did not play or conduct himself like a seventeen year-old, and he was not immune to using tricks that older and more experienced players used when off the ball. Perhaps above all else, there was a style to him. He had a mop of curly hair that grew upwards and out, socks pulled to his knees, and a distinct gait—head down, almost lost in thought, his right arm slightly swinging, his legs pushed to the outside as if he had just stepped off a horse.

Petrović's development was very much a natural progression. His early-season success generated local curiosity about his work ethic and dedication. This ultimately became a famous sidebar to the Petrović narrative, much the same way that other greats of the game were celebrated for their dedication to their craft away from the spotlight. His day would always start at six in the morning, quickly eating a banana and drinking a glass of milk before walking the two hundred or so meters to Baldekin Hall, Šibenka's home floor. Petrović was able to access the building at his choosing, since he possessed a key. He obtained it from the building's director, a gentleman named Joso Zorić, who came to be on many occasions the only other form of life in the building as Petrović toiled. The trip from the Petrović family apartment to Baldekin was unimpeded by traffic, so Dražen could get there in fewer than three minutes, ensuring that little time be wasted on the journey that could keep him away from the court.

There was regimentation to Petrović's morning workouts. He would take the ball from one end to the other, one basket to the other, as if caught in his own personal contest. There were varying degrees of speed and energy used, just like in a real game, and with each trip up and down the floor the shooting distance would increase—just as, with fatigue, so would the difficulty. Sometimes there would be chairs set up, which in his imagination would be defenders; sometimes he would work without chairs, the court now vast and the possibilities open for more creativity. Petrović would shoot layups first, before moving out to the middle distance, a place where in this stage of development was his surest shot. He would always finish with long-distance shooting, when his fatigue was pitted against the need to find additional strength in his arms and legs.

There was something alluring to him about the solidarity of this, his mother Biserka had once said. He was not bothered by the isolation or monotony that this pursuit brought; he gravitated to it. Each morning seemed compartmentalized and purposeful, part of something far grander: the need to be better today than yesterday. It was unusual and introspective—a most ambitious quality in a teenager. There were times when Šibenka would travel for a road game, and the bus ride back to Šibenik wouldn't arrive home until the wee hours. However, Petrović's schedule would not change even with fewer than four hours of sleep. Petrović would always finish his morning workout and return home after one hour, usually around 7:30, to shower and eat a quick breakfast before heading to school. School would finish shortly after midday, and he would dash home. Petrović usually dropped his school bag at the door, then bolted back to Baldekin for an early afternoon shootaround that Kulenović would hold for the Šibenka team. Kulenović would instruct the players to do individual shooting and then play mini-games among one another, one on one or two on two. The contests promoted and forced the development of individual skills in game situations; to shoot against pressure, to defend with aggression or be embarrassed.

It was here that Kulenović envisioned Petrović and his potential success as a senior player. The coach recognized that the way

Petrović dribbled when defended by much older and more physical teammates made it appear as if the ball was stuck to his hand with glue, almost an extension of his body.

In the preseason, when the players needed conditioning, Kulenović liked to put his players through the universally distressing suicide running drills, but enhanced them by incorporating dribbling. Most players would need several extra seconds running with a ball than they would when in a dead sprint; generally around thirty seconds more when sprinting while dribbling the ball, as compared to high twenties when running without it. One day at practice Kulenović timed Petrović, who ran the suicide, while maintaining the dribble, in just under twenty-four seconds, a truly remarkable display of endurance and ball control. Kulenović would allow one minute rest between suicides, and yet when the number of suicide ball sprints would get to four and five he noticed that while the other players were regressing Petrović maintained his finishing time. It was, Kulenović surmised, surely a result of all the end-to-end running that Petrović had done from a young age in isolation.

As time passed, Kulenović soon noticed that few in practice were enthusiastic about guarding the teenager, for taking the ball from him was a lost cause, and he was increasingly able to score at will. Petrović's game at that time was much more about scoring at the basket than it was later, when he became one of the world's three or four—if not *the* very best—distance shooters. His ability to put the ball on the floor against junior competition had resulted in most of his points coming from the basket area or, when fouled, at the free-throw line. It had very much molded his game to a degree where his outside shot beyond the mid-range was good, but not entirely consistent. Dražen's older brother Aleksandar would periodically visit home from Zagreb, and when the two played he would call Dražen "Stony," a good-natured name directed at Petrović's unglamorous outside shot. To Aleksandar, it appeared as if his younger brother was throwing rocks.

Dražen would return to the family apartment after the early afternoon workout for a few hours. He usually set time aside for homework or private tutoring (at the request of Dražen's father, Jole) before making one last trip to Baldekin for the main Šibenka practice in the evening, which would start at six and finish at eight. It was here that the game preparation and full-court work was done. The seventeen-year-old would somehow appear fresh and conditioned to the work load, summoning the energy to absorb the brunt of the older, tougher teammates. With three workouts a day, there was rapid evolution and growth in his game. Eventually, by sometime around eleven, when the adrenaline wore off, he would get to bed, only to rise the next day and repeat the process.

There was something almost predestined about how Petrović's 1981–82 season unfolded. With the season in its infancy, Šibenka traveled to Israel to play Hapoel in a qualification game for the Korać Cup, when one of the key players in the Šibenka rotation went down with an injury. Kulenović decided to insert Petrović into the game and the teenager played quite well in his team's loss. When Hapoel visited Šibenik for the return match the following week, Kulenović decided to start Petrović. The game did not begin well, and within ten minutes Hapoel opened a fourteen-point lead. To advance to the next round of the Korać Cup, Šibenka would need to win by more than what Hapoel had defeated them by; they were essentially chasing two deficits. Kulenović remembers that evening looking around tiny Baldekin, which seated roughly 1,500 people, and thought there must have been at least twice that in attendance. It was a gritty, tough building. When overflowing with people its atmosphere could be daunting, as if the crowd was closing in on the event itself, influencing the opposition and the officials.

Over the game's next twenty minutes it seemed Šibenka, led by Petrović, played near flawless basketball. Though later in the year there would be good wins over better teams in the Yugoslav league, Kulenović came to believe his team played its best game that particular night. What started as a fourteen-point lead for Hapoel became a ten-point win for Šibenka, with Petrović scoring 30 points while controlling the floor. The teenager had broken out.

Petrović was magnificent on such short notice, Kulenović thought. He took Petrović aside shortly after the game and told him two things: that he would be the team's point guard for the rest of the season and that he would play a lot. The coach felt it was important that the teenager be aware of the performances now being expected from him. Kulenović understood Petrović was young and that of course there would be mistakes and growing pains, but it did not deter the coach from the decision. Petrović was at first resistant to playing the point guard position, telling Kulenović that he thought it would take away from his natural tendency to be a scorer. But Kulenović spun the idea to Petrović in a way that allowed the player to see the benefits. "You will be the general on the court, Dražen," Kulenović told him. "You will decide if you will pass, or if you will shoot."

Kulenović's decision to place Petrović as the primary playmaker had come as a way to get him more involved. He noticed that when Petrović spent time at the shooting guard position he would endure stretches of inactivity, sticking to one side of the floor, away from the play while his teammates entered the offense. To offset that habit, Kulenović essentially leased a good deal of the offense to the teenager, a bold move from a coach who, like Petrović, was young and still proving himself and his worth. When Šibenka visited Cibona in Zagreb during that season, Dražen's brother Aleksandar made a point of seeking out Kulenović after the game to ask about his younger brother's progress and development. Aleksandar was curious as to why Kulenović had opted to play Dražen at the point guard position, which went against both his mentality and natural strength as a scorer. "These older guys don't want to give the ball up," Kulenović told Aleksandar. "Dražen is left in the corner watching and waiting. If I give him the ball straight away the offense is in his hands; he can make the decisions, take the responsibility." It was the type of experience that Kulenović hoped would accelerate Petrović's development.

Petrović was, even then, not like most players Kulenović had coached. Kulenović found that he was especially good at retaining information. Petrović could make a mistake, have Kulenović correct it, and he would seemingly never again make that mistake. "I can describe him as a computer," Kulenović said. "This is hard work, because a computer is a machine. When you tell him one thing he never repeats this if he made a mistake. With young players you must always repeat things, sometimes a thousand times. But he was like a computer. He watched you with his big eyes, his mouth open. I had the feeling he would open his computer, take in the information that he needs for his individual progress, and the rest he will take out. After, when it [the information] is in his head—the computer—he never did make the same mistake again."

Šibenka salvaged what could have been a poor season by finishing fifth in the Yugoslav league. Petrović's play was terrific; he averaged 16 points per game, his freedom on the court growing as the season wore on. A team that had at first not been taken seriously was suddenly winning games and earning respect. They participated in the Korać Cup, a third-tier international competition that featured some very respectable European teams, and won five of their six games in the quarter finals. They advanced to the semis, where they met fellow Yugoslav team Red Star. The first game was in Belgrade and ended badly. Šibenka lost by 16, a margin they would have to exceed in the return home game to advance to the final. Baldekin Hall was very loud, and Kulenović remembers Petrović playing with great emotion. There was a moment in the second half, with Šibenka in front and trying to hold their lead, when Petrović had been caught in a misunderstanding with Željko Marelja, the team's center. In the ensuing timeout Petrović had gone up to Marelja, yelled at him for not concentrating in such a big game and slapped him on the back. Marelja had been shocked by this. He went to Kulenović to complain, but the coach had barked at him, "Forget it!" Kulenović said. "Let's go win."

There seemed to be additional effort by the team from that point, and Šibenka ended up winning by eighteen. Their victory ensured a trip to the final of the Korać Cup. When the adrenaline wore down Kulenović looked back at that moment in the timeout, when a seventeen-year-old had challenged a teammate twice his age. "Dražen was not afraid to get in a fight with somebody who was much older," Kulenović said.

Šibenka faced Limoges of France in the final. They played a scrappy game, especially early against Limoges' zone, where missed shots were turned into second-chance opportunities. Šibenka seemed at times to have an extra body out there against the bigger, more athletic French team. They led early and controlled the first half in large part due to Petrović's passing in the half-court; he had seven assists in the first half and finished with ten. Limoges switched to a man defense and began to overrun Šibenka in the second half, and it was at that point that Petrović began to show more aggression with his own offense. Limoges sent the athletic Richard Dacoury to Petrović, who immediately tried to force the teenager to go to his left. There was one play when Limoges was threatening to put the game away, but Petrović pushed hard to the right, got Dacoury off balance, and then put the ball between his legs from right to left. He then absorbed contact from Dacoury and hit a beautiful floating shot over the helpless defender. It was a move of savvy and adjustment, certainly not one made typically by an inexperienced player, Limoges eventually proved too strong, wearing down Šibenka over the game's final ten minutes and winning by six. The disappointment of the loss was pitted against Petrović's arrival on the big stage. He scored 19 points on eight of sixteen from the field, but, more importantly, he had emerged. At seventeen years of age, it seemingly caught everyone by surprise. Everyone, that is, but himself. It was part of Dražen Petrović's plan from the very beginning, and he was only getting started.

Three

STARDOM AND A LOST TITLE, 1982–83

Šibenik, Croatia

At some point near the middle part of the 1981–82 season, Faruk Kulenović went to management and suggested some changes. Kulenović told management that in order to progress further in the Yugoslav league they needed to become more professional. He counted among his friends Indiana University coach Bobby Knight and Notre Dame's Digger Phelps, and had seen how they conducted their programs. It left him with a distinct idea of what practices should be employed to help Šibenka grow as a club. One of his suggestions had been to slowly rebuild the roster with younger players. The older players who had helped Šibenka during its first three seasons in the first league had run their course as effective players, Kulenović reasoned, and in order to build for the future they would need to be phased out and replaced with a newer generation to ensure a shot at long-term success. Management considered this, and over the season's final months that information slowly seeped back to the older players. There was resistance on their part, and ultimately management

opted to stick with their roster, thus spelling the end of Kulenović's time in Šibenka. He was replaced by a man named Vlado
Djurović, a former player who had just started his coaching career
with KK Sloboda in Tuzla.

Djurović came to Šibenik and made a point of introducing
himself to each player before the preseason started. It was an
attempt to get a reading on how the players felt about the team,
and about how it could improve. Djurović met with Branko
Macura, one of the team's better and more experienced players.
Macura insisted that with its roster Šibenka could finish no better
than fourth in the Yugoslav league. Djurović then met with the
teenage phenomenon he had heard a good deal about, Dražen
Petrović, to see how good he felt the team could be. "Top four
would be very good for us, coach," Petrović told him.

Petrović was excited by the appointment of Djurović as coach,
and sought him out early before the season for time together on
the practice floor. Petrović asked Djurović to join him for the
early morning shooting regime—the focus always on hundreds of
made shots, never about shots attempted—and Djurović initially
accepted, showing up several times, catching the ball through the
net and bulleting it back out to Petrović over and over. Petrović
also asked Djurović to meet him in the gym once he had gotten
out of school in the early afternoon. In time, the sleep-deprived
coach opted only to join Petrović for the after-school workout
while opting to pass on the dawn service, with Petrović instead
finding two or three friends to employ on a rotating roster as
rebounders.

Djurović's early interest in Petrović led him to make certain
observations about the youngster's developing basketball body
and its apparent limitations. Djurović liked Petrović's size for
a guard (he was around 6-foot-3 or 6-foot-4 and still growing,
which was above-average for a ball-handling guard) but he did

not consider him a terrific athlete. Djurović contacted a conditioning coach in Šibenik about Petrović's legs and his poor lateral movement. The coach recommended a series of stressful drills aimed at building strength in his legs and improving his mobility. Petrović quickly took to the drills with genuine enthusiasm, leaving Djurović impressed with how much work he put into an exercise that, without its use of a basketball, would leave many players bored, especially younger ones.

Djurović noticed that Petrović had very little tolerance for idle time, an impatience that extended to outside the game. When not playing or working out, he would on occasion beg Djurović to allow him driving practice around the town in Djurović's vehicle, a German Volkswagen Golf. There had been the typical element of foresight to the request: Petrović decided that on the day he would turn eighteen he would be fully prepared to obtain his driver's license.

Petrović quickly established himself at the start of the season as Šibenka's best player. He approached Djurović before the season and asked if he could remain as the team's point guard. It was a position he inherited the previous season, one to which he had initially been lukewarm, fearing that the purity—the natural, scoring style—of his game would be compromised. But once it had been put to the test and Petrović found that the ball was in his hands on every offensive possession, he enjoyed the idea of the control and responsibility. Djurović, too, liked the idea of Petrović playing the point, and afforded the teenager an uncommon freedom on the offensive end. Djurović came to believe that playing the point guard position forced, and then accelerated, Petrović's maturation against the older players.

Petrović's elevated place on the team was initially the source of some minor friction. It had been a somewhat predictable predicament considering Petrović's age and those of his teammates, many

of whom were closer numerically to their coach than they were
to him. Though most of the team's core were on the downside of
their careers, they were still competitors and contributors, and so
it became an issue of pride. Djurović remembered that he had to
make a tough decision with Srećko Jarić, once a prominent guard
in Yugoslavia, who was in his early thirties and somewhat inju-
ry-prone. Djurović limited Jarić's minutes as Petrović's increased.
Jarić was from Belgrade, like Djurović, and on one occasion when
the team played there Jarić had voiced to mutual friends displeasure over his lack of playing time. Word got back to Djurović
that Jarić was disappointed in the coach for giving an inordinate
amount of responsibility and offensive power to a teenager, and
that Djurović's decision was short on logic. Djurović created a
very strict culture within the club: no one was to challenge his
authority, and none of his players—older or younger—had the
desire to engage in verbal combat with him. The issue went unad-
dressed and remained closed.

Petrović, now in his fourth season in the Yugoslav first division, earned the respect of those within the club with his play.
He was playing a marvelous brand of ball at the offensive end.
Šibenka was two distinctively different teams when Petrović had
the ball in his hands, as opposed to any of its other guards. Most
of Šibenka's offensive possessions began with Petrović at the top
of the key, just him and his defender, Dražen almost dancing with
the ball before making a move. It was that rare instance when
there was wasted movement, for when Petrović started towards
the paint and the basket he was very direct and purposeful. He
could with a hard change of direction or a spin dribble lose his
man, his body always forward, always gaining ground and never
to the side. Because of his height, he had been able to get his shots
off without any trouble. On occasion when he picked up his dribble early, he had the unique ability to pump fake and create room,

or step through after a slight hesitation, and elevate off one foot. There was always balance to everything he did, even though his body was not yet fully developed and his opponents were often stronger.

Djurović noticed that, with the successes of the early season, Petrović possessed a healthy selfishness that was a necessary character trait of all the great players. When Djurović was young and starting his professional playing career with KK Beograd of the Yugoslavian league, he had been teammates with Radivoj Korać, a great Serbian player who was a compulsive scorer at the club level. Korać was ten years older and a revered figure, so the younger Djurović had been able to observe in his early career what made Korać great as a player. It was, Djurović soon decided, Korać's self-centered and ravenous approach. Korać had a sort of dominant approach to his own abilities when compared with others on his team, and that had led to prolific point production for an extended period in the 1960s. What was typically viewed as a negative characteristic appeared to Djurović as a separation point between the great players and the very good ones. "The big players cannot be like other normal players," Djurović said when speaking of Korać and Petrović. "They must have *something.*"

A game midway through the season confirmed this to Djurović. Šibenka was hosting on a Saturday night one of the league's weaker clubs, and mindful of an important Korać Cup game on the coming Tuesday the coach would try to rest his better players when the outcome had been decided.[6] Djurović found Petrović before the game and explained to him that he wouldn't be playing much that night. "You will play twenty minutes and no more, Dražen, because I need you to be fresh for me on Tuesday,"

---

6   The tournament coincidentally had been named in honor of Radivoj Korac, who was killed in a car accident at the age of just thirty.

Djurović said. The trip on Monday would be taxing on some of
the players, Djurović felt, as the team had arranged a three-and-a-
half-hour bus ride to Zagreb and then a flight to France.

"I agree, coach, no problem" Petrović had said when told of
the plan for his limited duty.

Petrović played well in the first half, scoring 14 points without
exerting a great deal of energy as Šibenka built a commanding
lead. Petrović excitedly came up to Djurović at the intermission.
"Hey coach, please can I start the second half? I want to score
twenty and then go out."

"Okay," Djurović answered, "but remember what I said
before. We have a big game Tuesday."

"Please coach . . ."

Petrović started the second half and made three field goals in
quick succession to get his total to 20 points. He had reached his
limit for the evening. "Dražen, you have twenty, you must come
out," Djurović said to Petrović early in the second half.

"Please coach, I want 25 points," Petrović answered, almost
desperately.

Incredible, Djurović thought, throwing his hands up. *All the
time the kid just wants more and more.*

Šibenka had a tremendous season, their rise mirroring Petrović's
as they finished first in the Yugoslav league with a 16–6 record,
edging out both Partizan and Bosna by one game. Petrović finished second in the Yugoslav league in scoring at 25.6 points per
game for the regular season. Outside the league, they once again
advanced to the finals of the Korač Cup and were defeated by

Limoges of France. Petrović carried a lingering, fortnight-old injury into the game but nothing serious enough to keep him from playing. It was obvious the injury hampered Petrović's game as he scored only 12 points, and was harassed constantly by a Limoges defense that had geared itself to slow him.

Šibenka turned its focus to the Yugoslav league championship. They were the first seed and played the eighth seed, Jugoplastika, in the opening round, a series they won in three games. In the semi-finals they came up against Red Star Belgrade, also needing three games to advance, earning their first trip to the league finals. Petrović was particularly brilliant in the first game, scoring 34 points with nine assists in a 91–88 win that protected Šibenka's home floor.

Šibenka met Bosna in the championship round. In another best-of-three series the teams split the first two games, each winning on their home floor. The third and decisive game was played in Baldekin Hall.

Bosna started the game strong, leading by 14 points just six minutes into the contest. They extended it to 19 with five minutes to play in the half. Šibenka shot poorly, which fed Bosna's transition game. They appeared sloppy and out of sync, and yet the crowd remained resilient and invested. Approximately 2,000 people packed into Baldekin Hall for the contest, exceeding capacity, many of whom stood for the entire forty minutes. It could get so loud in that tiny building that often the officials would have to dance out onto the floor to enforce a call, for their whistle had lost the battle of din against the crowd.

Petrović kept Šibenka afloat as they struggled early. He scored 14 points in the first half, and early in the second half dragged Šibenka back to tie the score. There were two plays when Šibenka drew close that seemed to symbolize Petrović's confidence. First, after hitting a short jumper from the right side he stood before Bosna's Savit Haznic, waving his arms out in front of him at head-height, one time clipping the top of Haznic's head. Haznic had been so shocked that he turned to the official, expecting a response. Then, as Šibenka pulled within two several minutes into the second half, Petrović drove to the middle of the paint, absorbed contact, and managed to launch a beautiful one-footed jump shot. Running back down the floor, he turned to Bosna's coach Svetislav Pešić, pumped his fist, and sneered. The magnitude of the game bolstered his confidence and his level of play.

Petrović would end the night with 38 points, 24 of them coming in the game's final twenty minutes, taking command when Bosna threatened to rout.

Bosna took Šibenka's best hit and yet remained close, and with twenty-four seconds to play Borislav Vučević hit an 18-footer from the left side to give them a one-point lead. On the ensuing Šibenka possession, Petrović missed a leaning jumper from the right side that was batted out of bounds, and with two seconds to go Šibenka retained the ball, down 82–81. The season came down to one possession. Zivko Ljubojevic inbounded the ball to Petrović in front of Bosna's bench, and Petrović spun to the middle, took two dribbles and launched from sixteen feet. Haznic, Petrović's nemesis for the evening and some three inches shorter, stood underneath Petrović with his arms raised, his feet never leaving the floor. Petrović over-shot it, the ball missing the rim and hitting the backboard as time expired.

Bosna invaded the floor, celebrating wildly with the impression the game was over. Ilija Matijević, one of the game's two officials, turned to the scorer's table once the shot was missed and began waving his arms. Petrović ran up to him, dodging the celebrating opposition, all the while holding up his right arm in the air and tapping it, to indicate he had been fouled. The scene quickly turned chaotic.

Matijević, surrounded by players from both sides and several fans who wandered on to the floor, called a shooting foul on Haznic. It would be the last of many calls on the evening made by Matijević, an official known well throughout the league at once for his impressive bushy moustache and also his propensity for theatrical calls. There were few games he refereed where he went unnoticed, his calls often laced with a flair for the dramatic. The game itself had been rather poorly officiated, the reins having been pulled tight from the very beginning. Matijević himself called three fouls on Bosna's first offensive possession of the game, and it continued throughout the contest, leading to a distorted tempo and numerous instances of overreacting from players who hoped to land a call.

Television cameras showed that Haznic's right hand made contact with Petrović's non-shooting arm, which caused Petrović to adjust his release. The contact was marginal—but, ultimately, was *contact*. This culminated in Matijević's foul call on Haznic that awarded Petrović two free throws. "It really was not a foul," Djurović said later. "I must be honest, it was not a foul."

The call caused much discussion at the scorer's table, and during the break Djurović grabbed Petrović by the arm to speak to him before shooting the free throws. He saw that it was not a foul and with all the bickering at the scorer's table he was sure something bad would come from a call of this nature in a big game. "Look, Dražen," Djurović said, "make one free throw and miss the other. In extra time we will win."

Djurović's reasoning was that, should the game go to overtime, Bosna simply would not be able to move past the whistle that had halted their celebrations. Djurović was confident that Šibenka would win in the extra session, with none of his players in foul trouble and with the Baldekin fans carrying them. But above all else, what concerned him was the post-match reaction that was sure to emanate from such a call. To make one and miss one and then have Šibenka run over Bosna in overtime, Djurović was convinced, would mean all was forgotten. In that scenario, the win would be *fair*.

But Petrović felt differently.

"No, coach," Petrović answered. "I will make two. I want the title."

Djurović looked at Petrović. The kid was so sure of himself that in his mind the free throws had already been made, even with a clock hanging above stating that there was no time and a scoreboard indicating a league title on the line. Petrović did not consider the consequences. He stepped to the line and made both.

There was a brief discussion among the officials before it was decided that Šibenka won, the enduring image being Petrović throwing his arms in the air when the announcement was made, mobbed by the fans. It would later be revealed that, of all the tiny people crammed into that steamy gym, there was one person missing: Dražen's father, Jole. Notoriously a fidgety, nervous type, Jole could rarely sit still while watching his boys play, opting instead for a stroll around the arena to let off some steam. It would later become a joke within the Petrović family that while the entire town of Šibenik was housed under one roof on the night of Šibenk's historic win, Jole Petrović had succumbed to the enormity of the contest. Instead, he walked the streets of Šibenik in complete solitude, pondering the game's outcome.

So it was that in just their fourth season in the first league, Šibenka had won the Yugoslav title. The man who took them there was in fact a boy, just eighteen years old.

Vlado Djurović left the arena that night elated that his team had won, but also very nervous for the coming days. Vasil Tupurkovski, the president of the Yugoslavian basketball federation, had been present for the game in Šibenik—he had even awarded Šibenka the winner's trophy on the floor after the game—and quickly decided that its ending warranted the calling of a meeting the following morning in Belgrade.

What got lost in the controversy was that Bosna was not contesting that a foul should not have been called, but that the play involving Petrović and Haznic occurred once time had expired.

The federation's meeting in Belgrade was held at ten on Sunday morning, and after two hours it was decided that Matijević's call was an incorrect one, that the foul was null and void, and so indeed were Petrović's clinching free throws. Omitting Petrović's points from the score left the final at 82–81 in favor of Bosna, and yet it did not mean that Bosna was declared champion. The game's ending had been too messy, too unwholesome, so Tupurkovski and the federation decided that there would be another game at the neutral site of Novi Sad in Serbia, to be played in the coming days.[7]

Vladimir Stanković had been covering the game, and once he was told of the meeting he traveled overnight to Belgrade to be present for the outcome. With the country slowly being made

---

7   Interestingly enough, Matijević went on the national evening news that night to defend his call. He broke down the play on film. Haznic's contact to Petrović's non-shooting hand, Matijević indeed showed, had occurred with time still remaining. It appeared that the official made the correct call.

aware of the game's dramatic ending as Saturday turned to Sunday, it was Stanković who was on hand as a decision, now anticipated, was announced. He dashed to a nearby telephone to call the Petrović home. Dražen's mother, Biserka, had climbed out of bed to answer the phone, the entire family exhausted from a night of celebration. Stanković asked if he could speak to Dražen.

"Šibenka is not champion, Dražen," Stanković said over the phone. "You will have to play another game."

"No," he told Stanković coolly, as if prepared for the outcome. "We will not be playing another game."

Djurović heard on the radio's midday news about the results from the federation's deliberation. He was now caught in a dilemma. There was considerable pressure from the outside, as the town's mayor had reached out to him and instructed that the team—at least politically—could not refute the federation's decision and that they needed to travel for the rematch and play. Team officials told Djurović it would be hard to go against the wishes of the town mayor. A local paper's headline seemed to best sum things up: "Two champions, one Yugoslavia."

Djurović was strongly opposed to playing Bosna again. That Novi Sad was selected as the site for the rematch, too, had bothered him. On that Sunday he began the process of contacting each of his players to get their thoughts, and late in the day he had contacted Petrović, the two agreeing that neither of them would be present for the proposed game.

And so the next week in Novi Sad the players from Bosna stood on the floor, their fans behind them, ready to play in a game that would decide the winner of the Yugoslav league for 1983.

The referee put the ball in the air, signaling the start of play. There was no other team in the building that night, and Bosna was awarded the title.

Four

THE NEXT MOVE, 1984

Zagreb, Croatia; South Bend, Indiana, USA

It was to be a full year before Dražen Petrović could tack on an encore performance to follow up his 1982–83 season, his arrival as a dominant player in Europe. He opted, as every young man of his generation in Yugoslavia was so obligated, to fulfill a year in the national army. Petrović took his military leave for the 1983–84 season at age nineteen, after spending his first summer with the Yugoslavian national team at the European championships. To spend a season away from competitive basketball, even at that relatively early point of Petrović's career, was an enduring exercise in patience.

Military life was something of a mixed experience for the athletes of Yugoslavia. For a select few serving, like Petrović, they were privy to limited freedom inside the army domain to practice and to work on their craft. Some others were not, first putting in several hard, intimidating months before being granted the occasional small athletic pleasure. Zoran Čutura, who would become a teammate of Petrović's first with Cibona and later with the national team of Yugoslavia, once commented that in any given year the army could field a team in the domestic league, such was the talent submerged in each annual group performing their required national service.

The young men were almost always shipped away from their hometown for duty. Petrović spent time first in Pula, Croatia, before completing his requirements in the city of Belgrade in Serbia. Many of the men serving were in fact boys—eighteen- and nineteen-year-olds—on their way to manhood. They were understandably impatient about spending a precious year of their youth stored away, taking orders from intimidating men, completing menial tasks that made little sense at the time or in the years that followed. For some the ultimate goal of each day was to get through without making eye contact with their leading officers, for it might lead to a form of menial punishment: the collecting of leaves or rubbish. The young men in their green uniforms were to do as they were told, to not argue, and not deviate at all from the tasks they were assigned. Čutura was like many in that at the time it did not seem a pleasant existence, but upon his discharge he would learn of friends who had endured far harsher treatment. Some had been stranded in snow-laden mountains, others subjected to time at the Yugoslav-Bulgarian border, places that when compared to somewhere like Belgrade seemed much worse. If nothing else, it was a life experience.

Petrović's time in the army had been better than most. He was not denied access to a basketball gym, and that enabled him to survive the year and maintain his sanity. He quickly found that he was able to establish a routine that resembled that of his earlier teenage years in Šibenik, able to gain time in the gym in the early morning, hours before reporting to duty. It has been suggested by those who watched his game closely that it was during the military year that the range on Petrović's jump shot increased exponentially, a result clearly of the time put in during isolation from competition.

While stationed in Pula, Petrović had run into his old coach at Šibenka, Faruk Kulenović, who at the time was running a basketball academy there. The coach asked Petrović about his work habits, and was told proudly that the young player's goal each week was to make 2,000 distance shots. At that time Petrović was stationed with another young Croatian named Velimir Perasović, himself a player with a bright future, not averse to long hours in the gym. Perasović quickly noted the standard his colleague set. "That was incredible how he worked; he worked like nobody before or after," Perasović said of Petrović. "He was never too tired to work, and this was the big difference for him over other players."

The two would shoot together in the morning and then return at the next possible opportunity, sometimes engaging in heated games of one-on-one or continuing to work on their shooting. Perasović had his own aspirations, but it was here that he saw there were others who shared them, too, who were working harder, and he used that to better his own career.

Even in relative anonymity there remained intrigue around Petrović, namely with which club he would continue his career. Even with Šibenka's emergence in the Yugoslav league that Petrović deemed to be his hometown club, its limited resources and aging roster could only serve his development to a point. To further advance his career, he would need to move to a bigger and better club, one better established. Within the Yugoslav league, it was the only way he could climb, and climbing was a necessary state for Petrović; the career trajectory must always be inclined vertically, and never for a moment remain stagnant.

The interest from the elite clubs naturally was there. For a time it had been thought that Petrović would choose Partizan, a powerful Serbian club. Petrović's coach in his final year at Šibenka, Vlado Djurović, traveled often to Belgrade to visit Petrović during the latter part of his military year and would often find him mixing with the Partizan players. At that time the team was coached by Dragan Kićanović, a man to whom Petrović had been compared, and who coveted an opportunity to coach Yugoslavia's next elite guard. Petrović had been given a special clearance to practice with the team, and it was a temporary departure from the regimentation of the military to be competing in drills and scrimmages. He also had been spotted at the occasional Partizan home game, and to Djurović it seemed logical that Petrović end up there.

Bosna, the team that had competed against Šibenka for the 1983 league title, had also desired Petrović.[8] There was also the expected interest from Cibona in Zagreb, the reigning league champs, already the employers of another Petrović—Aleksandar.

Among the group of interested parties was an American university, Notre Dame. Their presence in the queue for Petrović's services was traced back to head coach Richard "Digger" Phelps, and his brief, shared history with Petrović. Phelps had been introduced to the great Yugoslav coach Mirko Novosel a decade earlier. From that relationship Phelps became a semi-regular visitor to Yugoslavia to conduct clinics as the seventies played out. In addition, he helped Novosel by organizing the schedule for the Yugoslav national team that would tour the United States to play the top colleges each November. Phelps insisted to Novosel that he bring his team to the United States for exhibitions in order to further progress the program. "You have got to start playing more American teams to get the finesse game going, not just the physical style," Phelps told Novosel. "Physical *and* finesse."

---

8   They outlined their interest by giving Petrović his first car.

Phelps had an interest in the international game at a time when there was less fashion to it. He thoroughly enjoyed going to Europe in the summertime to run camps, for what awaited was a group of coaches who were like sponges. The coaches would absorb the gospel from a *name* before taking it back to their own clubs, their words now carrying with it a small sprinkle of magic dust from the Americans, the game's undisputed masters. Faruk Kulenović was one of those coaches at the feet of Phelps, and he invited Phelps to Šibenik in the summer of 1981 after taking the coaching position with Šibenka. For two days, Phelps taught offensive and defensive drills to Kulenović and his players, techniques that would be unique within the Yugoslav league.

When Phelps arrived at Baldekin Hall for the first session there was already a junior match underway. Curious to see the capabilities of the local stock, Phelps noticed a skinny teenager running up and down the floor, scoring seemingly with ease, carrying with him an overwhelming enthusiasm. "How old is this kid?" Phelps asked.

"Sixteen," Kulenović responded.

"What's his name?" Phelps asked.

"Dražen Petrović."

"Wow," Phelps answered, as if sanctifying the teenager, "he's going to be something."

Phelps would get a closer look at Petrović over the course of the two days, becoming more interested in his play after seeing him compete against older players. He pulled Kulenović aside in between sessions on the second day and asked if Petrović could shoot from the outside. "Yes, of course he can shoot," Kulenović answered. Phelps approached Petrović and asked him to stay behind at the completion of the day so he could see his shooting ability, particularly from mid-range. Phelps tested Petrović by throwing the ball in a manner that would challenge any shooter:

instead of throwing the perfect pass that could be caught at waist-height, Phelps was throwing the imperfect pass, wayward balls that forced Petrović to catch out of place and rhythm. The key, Phelps knew, was in the adjustment before shooting. Phelps demanded that he get his shot off as quickly as he could, thus raising the level of difficulty.

Petrović was unfazed by this, and he shot the ball at a very high percentage—nine for ten to finish, Kulenović remembered.

Phelps came away from the camp very excited and interested by what he had seen in Petrović, as if unearthing something potentially very special in a faraway land. Kulenović had told Phelps that Petrović had an insatiable appetite for the game as evidenced by the unusually high number of games he played—between junior and senior games locally—and also with the junior national team. "He loves to play all the time, Digger," Kulenović said.

Phelps left Šibenik, but the memory of Petrović was hard to shake, and he kept tabs on him.

Some fifteen months later, in the fall of 1982, a Yugoslavian national team featuring Petrović toured the United States to play numerous division one colleges, including Notre Dame. Petrović had just turned eighteen years old and had significantly improved since the Phelps visit; he played well in the exhibition. At times he was matched against Notre Dame's All-American guard John Paxson and fared well, scoring 13 points. Phelps watched him closely from the sidelines that evening. He came to the conclusion that what separated Petrović from most of his teammates, even at that age, was the quick release on his jump shot. Phelps thought Petrović would not only make a very good college player with his ability to shoot and create offensive opportunities for himself, but perhaps with his work ethic and ability to adjust to his environment he could be one of the first capable of taking that next step to play in the NBA. "Dražen Petrović could be a great player," Phelps told the *South Bend Tribune*. "He's going to be a super guard for their program. It's a shame he doesn't speak English, because I'd ask him to apply."

Moments after the game Phelps ventured down to the Yugoslav national team locker room and met with Petrović, informing him directly that there was strong interest on his part in signing and bringing him to South Bend. Aleksandar Petrović acted as the interpreter on that night between the two, with Phelps adamant about his feelings for the younger Petrović, that there was a place for him in the program should he choose to pursue it.

Later, at the end of the college season, Phelps ran into Kulenović at the 1983 NCAA final four in Albuquerque. "Is *he* still interested, Faruk?" Phelps asked Kulenović as the two shook hands. That summer, Phelps took his team to Yugoslavia for a series of games against the national team, and Petrović, freshly minted from his breakout season in the Yugoslav league with Šibenka, and preparing for his first major tournament as a member of the national team, once again played well.

The Yugoslavian national team, including Petrović (granted leave from the military to play), returned for a ten-game tour of American universities prior to the 1983–84 collegiate season, and was in South Bend, Indiana, to play the Irish on November 16. It was a well-played game, with Notre Dame winning by two on a late field goal by senior forward Tom Sluby. Phelps was satisfied with the victory over a good opponent so early in the year, and had come away convinced that Petrović belonged in his program. Petrović played a beautifully balanced game: 24 points and seven assists, at times the lead guard who was able to handle Notre Dame's pressure. When the game seemed to be slipping from Yugoslavia he brought them back with his scoring, having his way with the Irish guards. To Phelps, Petrović seemed seasoned and confident, certainly capable of being a very good collegiate player and potentially a professional in the NBA.

Phelps arranged for Petrović to come to his office shortly after the game, and it was there that Petrović signed a letter of intent to attend Notre Dame in the fall of 1984, just weeks after the completion of the Los Angeles Olympics. Earlier that day he visited the campus and met with a guidance counselor; the trip had gone well. Petrović, in Phelps's mind, showed genuine interest in coming to the United States to further his basketball career.

Phelps was clever in the *sell* aspect of pursuing Petrović. He was aware of the player's ambition, and sold to Petrović the possibility that at the conclusion of his time in South Bend there could be an NBA career. With his goal-setting and drive, Petrović was susceptible to such an enticing opportunity. For Phelps, the NBA in itself was not part of a car salesman's pitch. At that juncture he was, as a coach and leader of a program, ensuring two things: one, that all of his players, regardless of basketball ability, would graduate; and two, if they were good enough, he would have his better players prepared for careers in the NBA. In the three prior years, Phelps had sent eight players, with such names as Bill Laimbeer, Orlando Woolridge, Paxson, and Kelly Tripucka, to the NBA, each becoming good professionals. "It was to get him ready to play in the NBA," Phelps said about recruiting Petrović, "to know and understand what goes on defensively in this country, offensively in this country. It would have been great training for him for the next level, because I knew he was going to play in the NBA."

Notre Dame posed a realistic threat to the Yugoslav teams that pined for Petrović. Each was aware of the Irish threat to their own advances, perhaps none more than Cibona, led by Novosel. Novosel was nothing less than the sport's premier non-playing identity in Yugoslavia. He was, like Phelps, his own *name* within the sport, and thus in possession of unique influence and power. With his closeness to Aleksandar Petrović and as a contact to Phelps, he was well-informed of Notre Dame's advances. He had in his own courtship of Petrović sensed a level of reticence on the part of the player to go to the United States. "He was [turning] twenty," Novosel said of Dražen. "It was too early for him to go to America."

Novosel had at his disposal the ultimate trump card over the other competing teams when trying to lure Petrović: his starting point guard, Aleksandar. There was for Novosel a long-standing relationship with the Petrović family dating back to the fall of 1976, when he signed a seventeen-year-old Aleksandar to come to Cibona in Zagreb. It was then that he first met Dražen and in time was duly informed of the budding basketball aspirations of the boy. Novosel on occasion would jot down drills and suggestions on scrap paper for the young teenager, and they became part of his famed daily morning workouts at Baldekin. Novosel maintained sporadic contact with Petrović, sending him the occasional tutorial letter in the mail while tracking his progress in the cadet and junior levels through conversations with Aleksandar, before coaching against Petrović as he made his way up through Šibenka.

Novosel felt there had been three things that played to his advantage when recruiting Petrović. First and most obvious was the presence of Aleksandar and the overall family influence. Secondly, he would be coaching Petrović at the forthcoming Olympics in Los Angeles, the two thus being in each other's company daily. Third, and lastly, perhaps the most underrated element was that in the 1983–84 season Cibona won the Yugoslav league title (on a game-winning hook shot in the decisive game by Mihovil Nakić). Winning the league title meant that Cibona would participate in the European Cup the following 1984–85 season, allowing them to go against the best clubs in all of Europe. It would give Petrović the opportunity to consistently compete against the best players and teams outside of the NBA.

"Not only that I was playing for Cibona was the reason," said his brother, Aleksandar, on his brother's choice. "The main reason [he chose Cibona] was in the previous season Cibona became Yugoslav champion, and the possibility to play European Cup."[9]

By the spring of 1984 two choices remained for Dražen: Cibona or Notre Dame. Kulenović, through his friendship with Phelps, had come to be something of a Notre Dame representative, periodically checking in with Petrović on behalf of Phelps. He found that Petrović held his cards close to his chest. "Dražen was not so open," Kulenović said. "He was thinking probably with intensity about Notre Dame, but what he had in his mind, and how he was calculating this offer and the Cibona offer, it connected with his individual development in the future, and reaching the NBA."

Late in the spring of 1984, in a last-ditch effort to secure Petrović outright, Phelps made the decision to fly to Croatia to meet Petrović's family. "I just wanted to meet the parents and reassure them that it would be a good decision," Phelps said.

Petrović was still in Belgrade finishing up his time with the military, so Phelps was escorted by Kulenović to the Petrović family apartment. It was in the small living room that the conversation scanned over the predictable selling points: both the high graduation rate and the assurance that Petrović would be sufficiently prepared to play in the NBA by the time he was ready to graduate. "What if he breaks a leg and cannot play basketball?" Biserka Petrović asked Phelps. The coach assured her that in the

---

9   Years later, Zoran Čutura reflected that Nakić, with his winning shot to seal the league title, was a "crucial man in bringing Dražen to Cibona."

unfortunate scenario something happened that curtailed Petrović's promising career, then he would have, by virtue of a degree from Notre Dame, the opportunity to land a fine, well-paying job away from the game. This answer was met with approval from Dražen's father, Jole, who always pushed the Petrović boys in endeavors such as school and study that often seemed secondary to the leather ball.

Late in Phelps's visit, there was a phone call to the family's apartment from Zagreb. On the other end was Aleksandar Petrović. Phelps leaned forward in his chair, looking at Kulenović. "Who is it? What are they saying?"

Kulenović quickly understood the nature of the phone call. Aleksandar was inquiring about the visit, about how well it had gone, reinforcing that Dražen was as good as committed to Cibona and thus off-limits. Kulenović understood the call and it left him dejected, for it indicated that surely Petrović would remain at least for now in Europe and not move to the American college system.

Petrović had chosen Cibona. He completed his military duties in May of 1984, and on June 5 officially committed to four seasons in Zagreb. His salary would be $1,200 a month, and included use of an apartment and ownership in a local café. Upon learning of the apartment, Petrović asked specifically that it be located near Cibona's home arena. Once again he was within walking distance of a place to hold his workouts in isolation.

In the months and years that followed there was persistent belief that the Yugoslav Basketball Federation, an enterprise that was heavily interested in Petrović's choice of team, aided the final decision. To lose Petrović to an American university so early in his career was an unsettling prospect, especially when it was obvious that he was the country's next great guard, its next great *player*. They gave Petrović their blessing for him to sign with Cibona, and, in return, promised to make flexible the rule at the time that dictated Yugoslav athletes must remain in their country to compete until the age of twenty-eight. It was a rule that kept a great many athletes—of all sports—confined to Yugoslavia even when lucrative and attractive offers lay waiting outside. When the time would come for Petrović to choose to test himself outside of Yugoslavia—an inevitability, considering his nature—then it was deemed the Yugoslav Basketball Federation would not stand in his way.

Phelps soon heard of Petrović's decision. He ran into Petrović at a pre-Olympic tournament in Montreal, Canada, and made one final pitch, one final sell of the experience and the potential of the pros. "We were talking and he was just listening," Phelps said. The coach would come to surmise that Petrović had made the decision largely due to outside factors. "I think it's a case of Dražen protecting his own interests," Phelps told the *South Bend Tribune*. "He doesn't want to get his Olympic coach [Novosel] mad at him so he won't play him. Dražen was under a lot of pressure to stay home."

So it was that twenty-year-old Dražen Petrović stayed in Europe. The United States would have to wait. It was a decision that proved to be pivotal, for before he could take his game to a greater competition he would first have to conquer Europe. With Cibona of Zagreb, he would do just that.

Five

THE BEST TEAM IN EUROPE, 1984–85

Zagreb, Croatia

Dražen Petrović joined a Cibona team in Zagreb that was widely accomplished. That in large part had been the far-sighted goal of the team's coach and overseer. He had taken the Cibona job prior to the 1976–77 campaign, and with it assumed complete control of the program. In many ways his signing of Aleksandar Petrović was symbolic of Novosel's vision, for Aleksandar represented one of several teenage additions in that period. Novosel went into the assignment in Zagreb with an inclination to build the program's foundation on young players, a gutsy move in a league that was often ruled by its steadfast teams comprising key members from the strong national team.

Novosel was an excellent mentor, adept at handling young players. He had been successful coaching the national cadet and junior teams in the early part of the seventies, and their progress and success helped him land the coaching job for the senior team. That experience led him to be very specific in the characteristics he coveted when looking at younger players. He sought ambition and purposeful direction, players who were to approach practice with a level of intensity rivaling that of a game. He would learn about the players and their tendencies as he courted them. When building Cibona he stockpiled his team with strong players in their late teens and early twenties, young men such as Andro Knego, Mihovil Nakić, and Zoran Čutura, alongside Aleksandar Petrović, each of whom would at one point take his place on the Yugoslav national team.

Cibona gradually progressed in the late seventies, and by the early eighties was established as one of the top teams in Yugoslavia. It finished with nineteen wins from twenty-two games in 1981, and then seventeen in 1982, the year they won their first league title. In 1984 they once again were league champs, behind Nakić's heroics in the series with Red Star. The players believed in Novosel, and believed in the environment they played in. As the years passed, and as they remained at the top, the players for Cibona came to realize that they were part of a special club, perhaps the best structured and operated in Europe at that time, and took immense pride in maintaining that place.

Novosel was a coach unlike others in Europe at that point. Those close to Novosel would marvel at his devotion to the overall program and to each player. He was a mentor in the broadest sense, intensely involved not only with the forty game minutes, the practices, and the players, but also with the lives of the players away from the game. "He knew how to approach every other player. He didn't treat them all the same," Nakić said. "He knew what to say to each of the players to get the best out of the team, same with the national team, and I think that's why he made great success."

For Novosel, the arrival of Dražen Petrović in 1984, even with all his prior success, was something of a culmination. To the most complete team in Yugoslavia he was adding the ultimate play-making and scoring guard in Europe.

There was careful planning on the part of Novosel in culti-vating his vision for Petrović. The team, even with its established stars and national team members, would collectively welcome the younger Petrović, and with him his frenetic approach to the game. Čutura, one of Cibona's established stars, had watched Petrović at Šibenka and played enough against him to form an opinion. He saw Petrović as a player who needed to transfer his talent into quality. From Šibenka to Cibona, Čutura felt, Petrović could do that. "When you change towns and clubs, when you change teammates, when expectations rise, when you change environment completely, bad things can happen," Čutura said. "Luckily, in his case nothing like that happened. Probably because Mirko [Novosel] gave him open hands on the court and turned him into national star off the court."

The transition was made easier due to the presence of Aleksandar. He ensured that the team would be ready for his brother.

There was a healthy yet intense competitiveness between the Petrović brothers. Their playing styles were very different, and that went a long way toward them being able to co-exist as a backcourt combination. Aleksandar was very much suited to the role of point guard. He was a strong personality and very demonstrative, always talking and directing and instructing. There was something unglamorous about the way the older Petrović played, a style quite different to Dražen's. He was very purposeful with the ball, very comfortable and sensible, certainly not the risk-taker Dražen was. With time and space he was a very good outside shooter—in their younger days a surer shot than Dražen. He found that playing with Dražen did indeed make him a better player, as the defense eased off him, allowing the opportunity to catch and square himself to the basket in order to shoot.

There was a brief period of years in which they were opponents in the Yugoslav league, in Dražen's final two years at Šibenka
when the minutes were easier to come by and Aleksandar had
established himself with Cibona. The games against each other
caused a great deal of tension on the floor. "It was very aggressive," Aleksandar said. "It was a fight between the two of us."

On one occasion when Aleksandar arrived in Šibenik on the
day prior to a game, he stopped to visit the family apartment
where he grew up. When he got to the front door he was met
by the sign *No Vacancy for Purgers* (the term "purgers" reserved
in Croatia for the natives of Zagreb). The sign, of course, had
been carefully placed there by the younger, mischievous sibling. On the basketball court there was less hilarity to their
competition.

In the 1982–83 season, as Petrović rose through the ranks and
emerged as one of the best guards in Yugoslavia, part of his own
personal validation included the need to prove himself against certain opponents and players. His coach that year, Vlado Djurović,
noticed this trend and decided that Petrović's need to win and to
be the best extended beyond the normal confines of a game, and
to the mini-battles within the contest. Aleksandar most definitely
represented a mini-battle.[10]

Dražen was not the only Petrović turned on by the battle.
Aleksandar had gone to his coaches, Novosel and assistant Željko Pavličević, before their competitions and asked to be assigned
to guard his brother. "Coach, I wish to be against Dražen," he
requested.

---

10 So, too, did Zoran Slavnić, who after being Petrović's first coach at
Šibenka would then become an opponent. Petrović once tried to
embarrass Slavnić by attempting to dribble the ball between his legs as he
moved to the basket, an ambitious foray that did not pay off.

The first half of each such game became a battle both physical and verbal, a sort of backyard tussle gone public, family ties cut for forty intense minutes. Djurović remembered seeing the younger Petrović after a made basket getting in the face of his brother. *Fuck you, fuck you . . .* he whispered. At one point he committed a very hard foul on Aleksandar. The older Petrović, exasperated and exhausted from chasing around his younger and increasingly confident brother, fouled out early in the second half. Dražen had been unmerciful and finished the night as winner: 27 points and a Šibenka win.

On the bus ride home, Cibona's Mihovil Nakić rose out of his seat and walked near the back of the bus to Aleksandar, where he sat with his head down, clearly fuming at the result. "Why are you so mad, Aco?" Nakić asked. Aleksandar took a deep breath, "Dražen . . ." he said, his voice trailing off. The next day, when the game and the adrenaline was long over, Dražen sent a telegram apologizing to his older brother for how the game had played out, with his ultra-competitive behavior and foul word exchange.

Aleksandar ensured that the next matchup that season would play out differently, grinding Dražen defensively while scoring 20 points. The expletives and gestures had followed, and equilibrium was restored as Cibona won.

What was most remarkable about Dražen Petrović's first year with Cibona in 1984–85 was that a proven team, a team of talent and experience, was so willing to integrate a younger player of exceptional hype. The team managed to remain unfazed and focused. The chemistry between Petrović and Cibona of

Zagreb—player and teammates, player and city—was instantaneous. His style of high shot-taking and point totals may not have been conducive to a harmonious relationship with teammates on other teams, but the Cibona core decided early on that each was prepared to make a small sacrifice. Petrović was thought of as the final piece of their successful team, and his integration was treated as such. "Instinctively, we all recognized his ambition and his quality," Čutura said. "We all made small sacrifices for big results."

Petrović quickly established himself as a major offensive threat, his average in the early part of the season exceeding 30 points, buoyed by big games, including 45 in the first game against his former team, Šibenka. "After a few months he did special things, the offense was spectacular," Pavličević, the team's assistant coach, added. "They didn't get jealous of him. When you have several guys who fight for leadership then that is a problem, but when you have one natural leader, the best player, a great talent like Dražen, everybody accepted him as number one."

Petrović played with a different speed to his game than he had done with Šibenka. This was in part due to the upgrade in his teammates, and in part due to his body development; he seemed trimmer and quicker. What resulted was an explosive start to the season and a growing fascination from the Zagreb locals, his fame spreading quickly. Petrović was young, good looking, obviously talented, and the new leader of the best basketball team in Yugoslavia. Beyond the floor, he appeared to be a model worthy of emulation. The twenty-year-old enrolled at the University of Zagreb, as his older brother once had, to study law. His exceptional work ethic became documented and celebrated, with each game serving as reinforcement of his wholesome lifestyle, of the sacrifices it took to be great.

Indeed, in a town where the fans had already taken to Cibona, already fallen for them, there was a special adoration reserved for Dražen Petrović.

The 1984–85 season came together quickly, and the results followed. Cibona finished first in the Yugoslav league with nineteen wins from twenty-two regular season games under Novosel, and Petrović led the way with an average of just over 32 points per game. Before taking care of business in the Yugoslav league, Cibona participated in the European Cup, a competition that matched them against the winners of other European leagues. It was the elite club competition on the continent.

The Cibona players particularly enjoyed going against teams outside Yugoslavia, many of whom were bolstered with imported American players (Cibona had none). It served as added motivation. "In spite of Dražen's arrival, I would say we were not favorites in European competitions," Mihovil Nakić said. "We didn't have any foreign players, no Americans, and all the other teams from countries we played against had a much bigger budget and [more] experience in winning. We wanted to prove ourselves on the club level, to play against teams that had Americans who were considered NBA-level talent."

Cibona advanced to the final six teams (among them Real Madrid from Spain, Maccabi Tel-Aviv from Israel, and CSKA Moscow from the Soviet Union) and were well placed to advance. In the semis, they handled CSKA Moscow twice within the span of nine days, and that sent them to the final. The players later gathered in their hotel to watch the other semi-final game between Real Madrid, a team they had beaten twice during the season, and Maccabi Tel-Aviv, with the winner to be Cibona's opponent in the final. Čutura remembers that for two hours Novosel continued to insist that he preferred the opponent be Maccabi, based on simple rationale. "We have beaten Real Madrid twice already, how can we possibly do it a third time?" he told the group. But Real Madrid ended up winning, and at the end of the game Novosel rose confidently from his seat, turned to his men and said, "Real? Fantastic! It is proven that they cannot beat us." Čutura looked at the response of his teammates and decided that it had been an effective psychological maneuver on the part of the coach, and after that the team felt loose and confident.

Cibona arrived in Athens, Greece, for the final. Once there it became apparent that Petrović would be the subject of a great deal of attention even before he was to step on the floor. As the season played out it became apparent that Petrović was the target of attention and scrutiny, and the team had developed ways of coping. They became concerned with the number of local women who sought to get close to him in Athens. What resulted on the night before the Real Madrid final was that the team's physician, Dr. Ivan Fattorini, slept at the foot of the door of Petrović's hotel room, fending off women who tried to sneak in. "I have never seen anything like it," remembered Fattorini. It was a strange scene: women creeping towards Petrović's room, while one of Zagreb's most respected physicians slept in the hallway as if homeless. He was able to keep them at bay. Petrović had a full night's sleep; Fattorini got something far less than that.

There was a tremendously effervescent atmosphere in the beautiful Greek arena that housed the Cibona-Real Madrid final. An estimated 15,000 people piled in from all over Europe, many who had made the trip from Zagreb. "Everybody who was able to run, walk, or crawl in Zagreb wanted to be there," Čutura said, outlining the players' awareness that they had the backing of an enormous fan base. Some of the players noted that many people who didn't have the funds or means to be present had nevertheless managed to do so, anyway.

Dražen Petrović did not get off to a great start, making just one of his first five scoring attempts. He mentioned to teammates on the day before the game that with one side of the floor effectively cleared out, he would be able to deliver a big scoring game. Sensing this, Real Madrid sent help after the first or second dribble. Petrović did not have a big first half, but there was a key stretch in the early part of the second half—six made free throws and two field goals—which allowed him to establish his offensive rhythm. He was able to overcome Real Madrid's defensive help due to his unusual ability to remain effective even after he had killed his dribble. Petrović was unlike most guards in the European game, in that he was still effective even after picking up the ball. On the right side of the floor against Real Madrid, he stubbornly continued to take the ball past the initial defender and into the middle of the floor where the help was waiting, but he had a subtle nature to his footwork and pump fake. Petrović often gave the impression that he was coming to a complete stop, but would then gyrate his shoulders or head, exaggerating the movement, throwing the defender off balance before stepping through to release a looping shot over the *next* helping defender.

Cibona assumed control in the second half after just leading by one at intermission, a beautiful blend of Petrović's individuality and the team's depth. This was an exceptionally balanced team, with binge scoring from Petrović, and Cibona getting contributions Čutura, Nakić, Knego, and Aleksandar Petrović in the final. It was what separated them from the other top teams in Europe.

The Petrović boys enjoyed the game's final minutes, fist-pumping each made shot and playing keepings-off while wagging their tongues. It was part of the package with the brothers: excellent floor play often combined with distinct cheekiness, finding joy in informing the opponent of the beating as it was being carried out. It was the bane of many an opponent and opposing fan base, in contrast with the adoration reserved for them by the Cibona people. It was a situation that reminded Čutura of lyrics he had heard in a song by the Bosnian musician Goran Bregović: *to hate you but to worship you.* The Petrovićs were at once the top backcourt in Europe and also its most provocative; and theatrics aside, few could contend their effectiveness. Cibona ended up winning by nine, 87–78, with Dražen scoring a game-high 36 points. When he took a seat on the end of the bench in the game's final half-minute, with the result beyond doubt, a small group of photographers rushed over to his side, bathing him in flashes even as the contest played out behind them.

The next eighteen hours were something of a blur for the winners. The team spent time celebrating in Piraeus, a beautiful spot on the sea just outside of Athens, the party moving long through the night and into the next day before they slowly made their way back to Zagreb. The season was not finished. There was still business to be handled in the Yugoslav league, and the arrival back in Zagreb was just one day before the semi-final game with Partizan. Aleksandar Petrović remembers his younger brother taking the team aside at practice on the day before the game and stressing to them that though they were the champions of all Europe, there was still a job to be done at home. "It's great to be European champions," Dražen told them, "but we need to be number one at home, too."

Cibona came out in the first half in front of their fans and the game turned into a celebration. Behind Dražen's 24 first-half points they led 71–53, a staggering offensive display, a truly confident performance by a very good team. It continued in the second half, with Petrović finishing with 51 points on nineteen of twenty-nine from the field, and Cibona won easily.

Cibona swept aside Partizan and moved into the league finals, where they would face Red Star Belgrade, which finished second in the standings, just one game behind Cibona. The teams split the first two games, and in the decider it was Cibona that broke away, powered by their depth, winning by thirteen. Petrović led the scoring with 32 points (he would average just under thirty-one in the three-game series) but it had, even in the face of his offensive exploits, been a team effort, with six players in double figures.

For the second consecutive season, Cibona won the Yugoslavian league championship. The Petrović era had begun sensationally, and the consensus was that more was to follow. For an encore, Petrović delivered an individual season that would resonate unforgettably in Europe, and in the process further develop an intense rivalry with the only other man on the continent capable of taking his title as Europe's best.

Six

THE BEST PLAYER
IN EUROPE, 1985–86

Zagreb, Croatia

The Cibona team that suited up for the 1985–86 season was slightly modified but equally as talented as in the previous season. Aleksandar Petrović was gone, if only temporarily, fulfilling his military obligations before he turned twenty-seven years of age. Mirko Novosel, who was in terms of presence and control Cibona's Red Auerbach, made the decision to cut back on his coaching duties. He would hand the reigns for games in the Yugoslav league to his longtime assistant Željko Pavličević, while maintaining his presence for games in the European Champions Cup. Those close to Novosel had sensed that with all he had achieved, by the mid-eighties he was searching for a new challenge. Even with Petrović's arrival, Novosel's focus was shifting gradually away from coaching and into managerial tasks, and with Zagreb awarded the right to host the University Games in 1987, it was Novosel who had been at the forefront. Pavličević, his replacement, was at once competing against the team's high expectations and Novosel's looming shadow.

Dražen Petrović entered the 1985–86 season determined to raise his level of play, to push himself even further. There was a game very early in that season which added to the seeming excesses of the rapidly developing Petrović mythology. In the first week of October 1985, Cibona was scheduled to host a Slovenian team, Smelt Olimpija. It was a game that powerful Cibona expected to win, and in the days leading up to the game they received word that Olimpija was late registering its senior players, resulting in the basketball federation subsequently fining the team and imposing sanctions. Olimpija's regular players would be forced to miss the Cibona game and perhaps others, leaving them with little choice but to submit in their place a team of junior players. It was an awfully lopsided situation: the defending champions of Europe matched against a group of boys in their late teens, none of whom were taller than 6-foot-6.

Pavličević treated the situation with the seriousness that it warranted. He spoke to the players beforehand, and at some point it was agreed that the game and opponent presented a unique opportunity for Petrović to push the boundaries of his single-game output. "We make something good for the fans, good for us," Pavličević said. That the fans were a consideration—that the possibility of a record falling was thought of as a marketing tool to entice the locals to come—was indicative of Cibona's approach to the contest.

Petrović agreed to chase the single-game scoring record not as a way to embarrass the opponent, but, as coach Pavličević felt, because his character dictated it. It was to be a test of his capabilities. Pavličević had noticed the previous year that Petrović seemed to have no trouble summoning a high level of intensity and motivation for any opponent, a quality that he had not seen consistently in all the players that he coached. "The great players are competitive. Every practice, every game is something important," Pavličević said. "That is something that divides the very good players and the great players. There are many good players who play a good game in every five, maybe every month. But the great players always try to do their best, always, every game."

Cibona decided to rest the remainder of its core, with Zoran Čutura, Mihovil Nakić, the newly acquired Danko Cvjetićanin, and center Franjo Arapović each missing the game. It teamed Petrović with four infrequent contributors against the group of teenagers, the stage ideally set for a scoring binge.

As the game progressed, it was obvious that it was deviating from the usual realms of normal competition. Petrović was ravenous offensively. He attacked the over-matched opponent, essentially choosing *how* to score. It was Petrović in all his offensive glory but without the usual opposing resistance—his scoring total rapidly adding up. By halftime he had scored 67 points. A short while into the second half, with his total in the mid-seventies, he eclipsed the existing single-game Yugoslav league scoring record that had been held since the early sixties by Radivoj Korać. On the rare occasion that another player from Cibona *attempted* a shot, the crowd—which was not a usual Cibona crowd with its high intensity, the building less than half full—voiced a collective displeasure.

Petrović's second half pace was not the equal of his first, but it was enough to get him to 100 points, a roar that filled the sparsely populated arena as he pushed past that mark late in the second half. Cibona would eventually win 158–77, with Olimpija's overall total some 35 points lower than Petrović's who would finish with 112 points, an incredible display of energy and ability that touched on unmerciful.

It seemed perhaps more appropriate to batch his performance together with not his other high scoring games, but instead with the increasingly widespread reputation about his unique competitiveness. Score one for Petrović's nature.

There was in the execution an eerie tidiness to his final line: forty of sixty shots made from the field, including 10-of-20 three-point attempts, and he connected on all twenty-two free throws. The game seemed destined to reside in folklore as time passed, and took on a Wilt Chamberlain-like mystery: a sparse gathering of fans, no surfaced film, even the limited retaining of historical information by the Yugoslavian league of that time.

In the aftermath, peppered among the talk of Petrović's game total had been quieter talk of integrity in a game otherwise pre-packaged as meaningless and trivial. Čutura, a player of noted honesty and perspective, had not been terribly fond of the circumstances. "I was ashamed," he said, "and I still am." In the years that followed, he became friendly with one of the Olimpija players from that night, a man named Dag Kralj, and the two would on occasion reminisce about Petrović's performance. "He is still having nightmares about that game," Čutura said.

Pavličević, too, would play down the seriousness of the night. He would later cite it as an indelible example of Petrović's hunger for challenges, while at the same time making sure that the game be held in a separate, more novel esteem, one that was distant from the valued games of purpose and of winning.

The 1986 Cibona team bettered its Yugoslav league record from the glorious previous season, raising its win total from nineteen to an impressive total of twenty-one, which had once again earned them the top spot in the league. It was the height of the Petrović era in Cibona as both a player and personality: his point average moved from 32 in 1985 to 43 in 1986. With his older brother away in military service Dražen handled the ball with more frequency, and Pavličević indeed had pushed him to run more, to take more control. Novosel had given Petrović the requisite freedom the year before, but Pavličević seemed to enhance that; it was by far Petrović's best scoring season of the four campaigns he played in Zagreb. There was no reticence in Petrović's game in 1986; it was unharnessed, and with his combination of outside shooting, dynamic ball handling, and ability to penetrate, he was without peer as an offensive player in Europe.

Cibona once again participated in the European Cup, and Petrović seemed to elevate his game for those contests. The games were always very well played; the top players and top teams in a highly pressurized, motivated environment. They were unique, too. It was an opportunity to see great players or teams from one country pitted against someone they otherwise wouldn't normally see. Besides Petrović, the 1986 European Cup featured two of Europe's elite big men in Arvydas Sabonis of Žalgiris in the Soviet Union, and Fernando Martin of Spain's Real Madrid. In addition, there was a group of prominent Americans: Billy Knight, the former ABA and NBA star, who was playing for Limoges of France; Mike D'Antoni, a one-time draft pick of the Kansas City-Omaha Kings, who was with Simac Milano of Italy, and Kevin Magee, a two-time All-American at UC Irvine, who was playing for Maccabi Tel-Aviv of Israel.

It was, for Petrović, a delightful challenge to go against teams and players of such esteem. The infrequency of being matched against these teams also presented a rare opportunity to go against new defenses and schemes, and in response he seemed to raise his level of aggression. There was to be no discrimination; he scored against everyone, including 51 points against Limoges at home, which included ten three-pointers. He scored 49 points against Real Madrid, a team he especially loved to score against . . . and then 44 points against Maccabi Tel-Aviv. The presence of Sabonis eternally turned Petrović on, and he scored 79 points in two games against Žalgiris, including 44 in a heated home-court win.

There seemed a particularly entertaining element to Petrović's games against Simac Milano, the Italian team, which was led by D'Antoni. Milano was coached by an American, Dan Peterson, who had been tremendously successful in Italy, quickly acclimating to the European game and gaining a cult status. In the first phase of the European Cup that year, Milano travelled to Zagreb to face Petrović and Cibona, and Peterson was excited to coach against Petrović, to see how his help defense would stand up to a player of Dražen's offensive abilities. In the opening minutes, Petrović slipped around a screen several steps outside the three-point line, turned rapidly and launched. The shot was so pure it barely touched the net. "I was stunned by the ease with which he did this," Peterson remembered later. Petrović would go on to attempt twenty-three shots against Milano, missing just four. He would finish with 47 points as Cibona won by sixteen, a truly dominant performance. For Peterson, it was an awakening.

Peterson always encouraged his teams to help on defense before recovering back to their own man, and in Italy it had worked and been the source for much success. But against Petrović, Peterson found himself without answers. In the second half he had tried for a brief period to use height against Petrović with 6-foot-9 Vittorio Gallinari, Peterson's best defender. But that, too, had proved ineffective, with Petrović already running rampant. Peterson noticed that Petrović was imposing himself into the paint, with an aim of getting to the dotted half-circle, forcing Milano to make a choice about whether to send help or stay home on Cibona's shooters.

With single coverage, there was no stopping Petrović, his rhythm long since established.

"There are great teams in the European league," Peterson told reporters after the game, in a sentence that became famous. "But Petrović is a one-man team."

Peterson, with his American background and his tremendous success in Italy, was seen as something of a basketball savant in Europe. It was around this time that he started touting Petrović as a player of NBA potential. Such a proclamation in 1986—that a European could successfully compete in the NBA—was very much open to question. Peterson had been so enamored with Petrović that, when the *Chicago Tribune*'s Phil Hersh traveled to Italy to do a piece on Peterson in early 1986, it was Peterson who told the writer about Petrović, about his talent and his aura. Hersh decided to stay longer and write an article on Petrović and his future. He interviewed an array of people—Europeans, Americans, even Petrović—and the split opinion on whether Petrović would be an instant success in the league was a true indication of the unknown quantity the Europeans were regarding their qualifications for NBA play.

As it turned out, Hersh was on hand to document the return match between Cibona and Simac. Petrović did not play nearly as well, scoring just 20 points and shooting poorly, hounded all night by D'Antoni. "And that was just me," D'Antoni told Hersh. "What do you think would happen if he played against Magic Johnson or Isaiah [Thomas]?"

In the spring of 1986 there was a growing level of curiosity about the Europeans. In this period of basketball's international education, there was a restrained, moderate respect held for them by the Americans. Petrović's numbers—a point average of over forty, several games of over fifty points—seemed inflated, certainly less about his own greatness and more a reflection of the level of competition against which he operated. It was very difficult to translate these numbers and determine just how good he was. One indication had come in the fall of 1986, when the Yugoslavian national team toured American colleges, playing eight games in ten days. Petrović, the age of a college senior, averaged over 29 points per game. Five times he exceeded thirty points, highlighted by 35 against preseason NCAA number one North Carolina.

When looking at Petrović as an NBA prospect it was natural to assume that he would, stylistically, be the same player he was in Europe. In Cibona he was without inhibition, dribbling and shooting heavily, as much as he wanted, becoming a large part of the offense. That in itself only led to more questions. Was he good enough to warrant that style within a team? Would moves performed with regularity against lesser players be effective against better ones? Would he give up more points on defense than he produced on offense? In addition, he had self-admittedly never been pushed hard in Yugoslavia to exert a great deal of effort on defense; in the NBA that would be a legitimate concern.

Coupled with that genuine skepticism was a microscope placed over his performances, especially in international competition. Hersh interviewed Digger Phelps for his feature piece, and Phelps cited a game from the 1984 Olympics against Spain, when Petrović had trouble against defensive pressure. Later, at the 1986 world championships, Petrović famously struggled to solve the incessant ball-pressure of Tyrone "Muggsy" Bogues, a player who stood just 5-foot-3. Yugoslavia had prepared for Bogues by assigning Danko Cvjetićanin the role of mimicking him in practice, including playing without shoes, to get Cvjetićanin as low to the ground as possible. Come game-time, Petrović appeared indecisive as to how to combat Bogues. Petrović loved to rip the ball through the defender's arms when making a move, but Bogues' head was placed essentially in Petrović's chest, rendering that move ineffective. He would score 12 points in the first half but go scoreless in the second. The USA won comfortably, and afterwards Petrović was inconsolable. Dr. Ivan Fattorini, the national team doctor, remembers how he and Stojko Vranković tried to calm Petrović after the game, with little success. The expectations he had set for himself remained higher than any from the outside, including the NBA talent evaluators, and to fall on a big stage had left him hollow. "We had to stay with him because we were afraid he will jump from the window," Fattorini later said.

Petrović's answer was to continue to work. He was reaching new heights in European basketball in 1986, and though the idea of a player—especially a guard—making the successful leap to the NBA remained questionable, he was, alongside Sabonis, considered the likeliest. To combat the questions and the unknown, he would continue to push himself with his unique style and approach.

Cibona and Petrović went into the early spring of 1986 looking to repeat what was the ultimate double: to win both the European Cup and the Yugoslav league. They once again reached the final of the European Cup, this time facing Žalgiris from the Soviet Union, a game to be played in Budapest. Žalgiris meant Sabonis, and his presence along with Petrović's would vault the game to a higher interest level. Cibona controlled the early part of the game in spite of Petrović playing below his expected standards. Žalgiris switched every screen to ensure he was manned at all times, and in response he was hesitant, which went against his yearlong tear. He scored 14 points in the first half, finishing with 22, but was turnover-prone. Cibona remained in control, however, due to their balance and depth.

Sabonis was reason enough to be concerned that there was little safe about Cibona's lead. He kept Žalgiris alive with his diversity and power. Cibona didn't fear Sabonis as much as they respected his uniqueness. "Sabonis had very quick reactions, a very good body, coordination, [can] shoot the three, very smart on offense—he was like a point guard," Pavličević said. "He can play everything. Inside, no one could stop him one on one."

With just under nine minutes to go and Cibona ahead by eight, Mihovil Nakić took an outlet pass. As he reached the basket he was wrapped up by a Žalgiris player. The two exchanged shoves under the basket, then out of nowhere Sabonis arrived at the scene. He hit Nakić, perhaps not with the ultimate force of which he was capable, but surely enough. It had taken everybody by surprise, that a man so valued by his team and in such a big game had shown such poor judgment. Sabonis was ejected, taking with him 27 points, a number that would have grown with ample time remaining. His departure signaled that Cibona was safe.

It was a victory secured as much by Danko Cvjetićanin as anyone. He had joined Petrović in the backcourt prior to the season, effectively Aleksandar Petrović's replacement, and had proved with his sweet shooting stroke to be a wonderful complement. Cvjetićanin was an interesting player, a little herky-jerky, not terribly quick, but an effective scorer. Upon joining Cibona he had quickly taken to Petrović, the two drawn together by post-practice shooting games where challenges were often issued—the first to two hundred makes, sometimes five hundred, sometimes in consecutive shots made. Petrović became an example for Cvjetićanin to follow. "I noticed immediately that he dedicated every single moment of his life to being a better basketball player," Cvjetić-anin said of Petrović.

The two would combine for the signature moment of the Žalgiris final, Petrović leaping in the air on a break to whip a left-handed pass behind his back to Cvjetićanin for the lay-up. It secured a 94–82 win, in a game in which Petrović vs. Sabonis never fully materialized. Cibona's depth had been the crucial difference, and once again they were champions of Europe. Petrović emerged from a sea of people in the moments after the final buzzer, holding the trophy, his jersey ripped from his body.

The bus ride home took three days, with Cibona stopping seemingly in every town of their homeland to share their win as they made their way back to Zagreb.

The focus quickly shifted to claiming the Yugoslav league title, with little reason to believe that anyone could challenge them. Cibona first beat Red Star Belgrade and then Partizan in the semi-finals, before being matched against Zadar in the final.

Entering as overwhelming favorites, Cibona won the opener at home behind Petrović. But before the second game in Zadar, the team's management made a difficult—and unconventional—decision to rest their best player. The reason was the team's concern over Petrović's technical foul count. He had been assessed two already, and a third would result in an automatic suspension, possibly for the deciding third game. Rather than try to win on the road in the second game at Zadar, a volatile and emotional venue for opposing teams, Cibona management opted to bench Petrović and hope to take the crown at home. It was not a popular decision, a pointed lack of trust in Petrović's ability to control his own emotions, and was one that had been debated and agonized over in-house. "It was a very hard situation," Pavličević remembered.

Zadar won the second game without having to worry about Petrović, and the series returned to Zagreb to decide the league title. Cibona had not lost a home game in the Dražen Petrović era.

Zadar's coach happened to be Vlado Djurović, Petrović's leader at Šibenka for the 1982–83 season, and he sensed that Petrović would try to wipe out his team early. Djurović watched as Petrović attacked his team repeatedly in the early going. With none of his own men able to slow Petrović, he tried to get the player's attention himself. "I provoked Dražen during the game," Djurović said. "Every time when he had the ball I said to my players, 'Let him shoot, let him shoot. Don't allow [Danko] Cvjetićanin to shoot. They are better shooters than Dražen.'" With each passing comment by Djurović, Petrović became more determined to score. After baskets, he would turn to Djurović and sneer, sometimes yelling.

"Dražen wanted to beat me by himself to show me he was the best," Djurović said. "I already knew that."

Petrović's output was matched by Zadar's Petar Popović, who after a scoreless first half would go for over 30 points in the second half alone. But Popović, Pavličević felt, was only part of the problem with Cibona. "We started to play like everything is finished: spectacular for the fans, play exciting," Pavličević said. "And that, you will pay for." Zadar gained in confidence as Cibona's lead evaporated, even in an environment that had swallowed opponents for two years. By overtime, Cibona was spent. Zadar would win 111–110, becoming league champions.

Petrović appeared subdued as the final buzzer sounded and Zadar players celebrated around him. A genuine shock filled the arena.

Though no one knew it at the time (nor could anyone conceive of it), Cibona would never again get closer to the league title while Dražen Petrović was there. Slowly, the fortunes of his team were trending in a direction very different from his own, causing him to plot his next career move. What came was a historic move to the most unlikely of places.

Seven

BENDING THE RULES, 1986–88

Zagreb, Croatia

When Dražen Petrović signed with Cibona of Zagreb in 1984, the move was approved by the Yugoslavian Basketball Federation. Approval had come in part because they oversaw all player movement, and in part because there was a small threat that Petrović would follow through on his signed letter of intent with the University of Notre Dame. The Federation did not want to lose its best young player to the United States. They were the maintainers of the league and the national team, its nurturer, most heavily invested in the game's health. In the process of helping usher Petrović to Cibona it was reported that they would massage the "Twenty-eight-year rule" for him. It allowed Petrović to supersede a rule that had kept all Yugoslav athletes in the country until that age before having the freedom to explore outside opportunities.

The rule seemed by the mid-eighties to be less viable than ever before, with the increased talent emerging in Yugoslavia—a generation that promised to take their game global. As socialism softened and times changed during the eighties, it appeared that the

rule was vulnerable to being penetrated. At its core it was potentially debilitating to the development and aspirations of a generation of Yugoslav basketball players, or athletes in general, not only
in a career sense but financially, as well. The previous generation,
one that had produced a great deal of talent, had stayed home
deep into their twenties before bolting once eligible, with finally
an opportunity to make a decent living from their occupation.
There had been periodic challenges to the rule, challenges which
eventually developed cracks to be pried open. Nurko Čaušević,
one of the country's top volleyball players, had his cause for departure effectively endorsed by the local media, with an offer in Italy
waiting. He had been the star of the University Games in Zagreb
in 1987, judged the tournament's best athlete, and outside offers
proved timely. His hometown club offered no resistance as the
media pushed his case, and while in his mid-twenties became one
of the first Yugoslav athletes to form a career outside the country. By the end of the 1984–85 season, after Petrović vaulted to
another level in such a brief period of time, speculation turned to
just how far he could climb. In the days leading up to the 1985
European Cup matchup against Real Madrid in Greece, a Spanish newspaper asked him about his future. Even just months into
his twenties, the European writers were already interested in just
how far Petrović planned to rise. "I will go one day to the United
States, with the professionals," he told *El País*. "I just know that
no European player has won there. I'll be the first and nobody can
stop me. Europe does not interest me. Playing in the American
professional league is priceless to me."

In Petrović's second season with Cibona in 1985–86, amidst
the 40-point average and the developing myth, there had been
a report that he was further evaluating his future and contem-
plating leaving Yugoslavia. At that time, in order to find elevated
competition, he had two main options: to leave for another

competition in Europe, and publicly he had spoken highly of the Spanish league and the level of competition that offered; or, the less viable and guaranteed option of signing with an NBA team, a route far less likely, for Petrović preferred to wait until the age of twenty-five before making such a jump. There was on the part of the NBA teams some awareness of Petrović and his developing career in Europe, including passing interest from Boston and Houston. But no team had been more aware of him than Portland, whose Bucky Buckwalter—one of the few Americans who could advance somewhere beyond vague speculation when interpreting international players—had spent a good deal of time in Europe evaluating the talent.

The first real strike from outside had been the report of a contract offer from Real Madrid in the early part of 1986, apparently in the range of a quarter million dollars. It was a dollar figure that at least warranted the attention of Cibona and of Mirko Novosel. Novosel was without question one of the elite influences in Petrović's life and career, and he took Petrović aside after the report, sitting with his young player to discuss the matter. Between them there was much admiration, and they openly discussed the offer and Petrović's development. A decision was made between the two that Petrović would stay in Yugoslavia for the time being. A short while after, in late June of 1986, word reached Zagreb that Petrović had been taken by Portland in the third round of the NBA draft. What came with the holding of his rights had been the realization that Petrović was closer to the American league than he had ever been. Yet even if he was closer, the reality was that for Dražen and all Europeans there still remained a barrier to overcome in order to activate the dream: the "Twenty-eight-year rule" in place for Yugoslavians, and the fact that the NBA meant an automatic relinquishing of one's right to play for the national team.

Petrović was now very publicly sought after from the outside. Never one to need prodding in order to consider his future and his intentions, by 1986 it was obvious to him that he needed to further chart his course most carefully. He decided to approach the Yugoslav Basketball Federation. Later, he would pass on to *Sports Illustrated*'s Alexander Wolff what he told them. "In my home I have a contract with Portland. If you do not give me permission to play for Real Madrid, I go to the NBA and then cannot play for the national team."

For the Federation, the next step was simple: allow Petrović to pursue a contract in Spain in order to keep him on the national team. Both parties won, as Petrović in fact had no intention yet of going to the NBA.

Petrović was thus given permission to venture out and sign with the European club of his choosing, on the condition that he fulfill the final two years that he was obligated to play with Cibona. Whichever new contract he signed would take effect following the Seoul Olympics in the late summer of 1988, a wrinkle that would benefit the Yugoslav national team, for Petrović could serve them one final time before exiting.[11]

What accompanied the agreement was the creation of a new rule, the *Petrović Rule*, as he happily dubbed it to Wolff. The requirement for a Yugoslav basketball player to pursue outside offers and leave Yugoslavia was set at eight seasons of play in the domestic competition, or 120 appearances with the national team—either would suffice. Petrović, with his ambition and confidence, had buoyed a modern, impactful ruling, one that would greatly influence those who followed. Among those born three or four years behind him was a talented group chasing his standard,

---

11　The decision to allow professionals to play in the Olympics would come in 1989.

players such as Dino Radja, Vlade Divac, and Toni Kukoč, all whom were to be the first of the beneficiaries. Each of them was a superb talent later to receive outside attention and lavish offers from European clubs.

Petrović strongly believed that going to the Spanish league would provide him the best competition available to serve his development. Unlike the NBA, going to the Spanish league didn't require guesswork, for he had played numerous times against Real Madrid in the European Cups of both 1985 and 1986, in addition to games against the Spanish national team. In being the marquee attraction and best player on the two-time defending European Cup winner, he was of course in a commanding bargaining position. He and Novosel chose a Spanish agent named Jose Antonio Arizaga to represent him, to help him field offers, and Arizaga was in the initial process instructed to deal primarily with two clubs, Barcelona and Real Madrid. Though Real Madrid had been most aggressive in their pursuit of Petrović (an offer in February of 1986 was followed by another in May), it seemed Petrović's preferred home was Barcelona. Just days after scoring 47 points against them in a European SuperCup game in early October of 1986, Petrović told a Spanish news outlet that they were the best club in Spain, one certainly capable of winning the Spanish league championship, not just in the current year but in future years. They would be an ideal choice for him. The Spanish newspapers did as they were obligated to do; they prematurely united them. "PETROVIĆ TO BARCA IN '88," one headline cried.

The interest was mutual, as Barcelona maintained steady contact with Arizaga and a tentative agreement was reached, though it was one that remained unsigned. Then something unexpected occurred. There was a call to Arizaga's office one morning, the same day that the newspaper headline ran, and on the other end was Salvador Alemany, Barcelona's chief executive officer.

"Mr. Arizaga, I am sorry," Alemany began. "I am very sorry. I must speak with you about Dražen."

"What has happened?" Arizaga responded, suddenly uncertain.

"We can't take Dražen. My team is very interested, but there is bad blood. Our coach [Aíto García Reneses] is unsure about this," Alemany said.

Arizaga was taken aback. With that, Barcelona officially backed out of the deal. Arizaga put the phone down and sat there shocked, wondering now which direction he should take. Minutes later he placed a call to Ramon Mendoza, the president of Real Madrid.

"Are you still interested in Dražen Petrović?" was how Arizaga opened the call.

"Sure. Is it possible?" Mendoza replied.

Of course it is possible, Arizaga assured Mendoza.

"It was a very easy operation," Arizaga would say years later. In a matter of minutes, one door closed for Petrović, and another opened. The formalities were sorted quickly. One afternoon Petrović had been a missed proposition to Real Madrid; the following he was in the airport in Madrid, flanked by Novosel, signing a four-year deal worth just over $900,000, a sum that Arizaga remembered as close to what Barcelona had been willing to pay.

Real Madrid now had in its possession the most attractive, most exciting player in Europe, certainly the one who generated the most buzz. The club happily paid Cibona a fee of $225,000, before then parting with $80,000 to the Yugoslav Basketball Federation. The contract would commence two years from the signing, in October of 1988, the same month Dražen Petrović would turn twenty years old.

In the final two years with Cibona there remained some of the magic, some bullying in the regular seasons, but both campaigns ended in disappointment. The Yugoslav league was changing, becoming stronger. The strong teams, able to hold on to their talent as it matured, were able to build and sustain themselves as Cibona descended. There seemed something special about the core of players coming through during the period. Vlade Divac, Aleksandar Djordjević, and Žarko Paspalj spearheaded a contender at Partizan Belgrade. Dino Radja and Toni Kukoč led Jugoplastika. Cibona perhaps had never been stronger, even on the back of two European Cup titles, with Aleksandar Petrović returning for the 1986–87 season after a year in the military. Essentially, the 1987 team was an amalgam of the 1985 and 1986 team: the former had contained Aleksandar Petrović and the latter Danko Cvjetićanin, and together, under new coach Janez Drvaric, the 1987 version of Cibona figured to remain dominant. They went undefeated in the regular season, winning all twenty-two games, with Petrović averaging 37 points (including a 59-point game against Bosna) and there appeared to be no team capable of unsettling them at the top.

Although there had been massive disappointment at the collapse the prior season against Zadar in the finals, the consensus was that Cibona would be hungrier this time around. But in the semi-finals they came up against a Red Star team that was growing in confidence. The teams had met in the final game of the regular season, and there had been talk among the Cibona players about possibly playing at a lower gear in order to manipulate the final standings (a Red Star win would have eventually meant a semi-final alignment of the Belgrade rivals Partizan and Red Star) but in the end Cibona had resisted, and they beat Red Star on their own floor rather easily. Through two games in the semi-finals they were tied, and in the third game Red Star went into Zagreb and beat Cibona. It was dramatic, the underdogs gaining more and more in confidence as the game wore on, staying close and then snatching it late. It had been a repeat of the Zadar loss one year earlier. With that, Petrović's season was over. Twenty-five straight wins (including postseason) were followed by two losses, and it had been enough to finish the season. As with most Cibona losses during that period, it was accompanied by genuine shock.

In 1987–88 Cibona presented an overhauled team, one considerably younger and vastly different from the teams of the mid-eighties, there being less certainty about their chances. Petrović ensured that they would remain a contender, and his 37-point average helped Cibona to seventeen wins, the league's second-best record. But once again they failed in a bid to return to the Yugoslav league finals, losing to Partizan Belgrade and Divac in the semis, the season once again flaming out at home.

The cracks had been forming since 1986, even though the gaudy regular seasons had patched over and concealed things before the postseason provided full exposure. To those within the group, the feeling was that with Novosel's less frequent coaching presence the replacements, though good coaches, had not sufficiently been nurtured to take over the head position. Novosel had sort of lingered, like a shadow, but he had also been largely involved in other endeavors outside the game, and his role with Cibona had taken a backseat.

The 1988 loss, with Petrović heading to Spain, with Novosel set to leave, with the roster equal parts young and old—it all signaled the end of an era. Petrović was joining Real Madrid, one of the enemies from the glory years, and that reality was harsh and difficult to digest.

That Petrović had ended up with Real Madrid seemed against some natural order, at least in the mid-eighties in European basketball, where the player and the team had gone against each other in big contests. Petrović seemed to save both his most potent offense and *venom* for the Spanish club. There was a game early in Petrović's time with Cibona, the first round of the European Cup in December of 1984, which first presented to Real Madrid the notion of Petrović as an enemy. It was played in Zagreb, and the crowd immediately sensed its importance, rising for the first real test for Cibona in the Petrović era. It was one of the charms of the Zagreb crowd, the energy always seemingly in tune with the level of the opponent—the better the team the more invested they became and the more value they were to Cibona. The game was tightly contested in the first half, well played and tough, but in the second half Petrović broke free, opening up on the right side of the floor and becoming relentless in his dribble attacks. He was brilliant in that game, his first signature performance for Cibona, with 44 points in the win. The final minutes were essentially devoted to playing keep-away with his dribble, much to the anger of the opponent. It was one of the first of the classic Petrović performances of the mid-eighties, when it wasn't just the points but the effect on the crowd. Each basket was followed by his demand that they join him, raising their level and thus *his*— the type of effort where an extravagant nickname like *Mozart* seemed appropriate. His celebration was its own performance art alongside his basketball ability.

Petrović had not just scored and exhorted the fans, but made the opposition aware of his performance, too. The twenty-year-old was still not fully mature, armed with youthful invincibility and a joy in the act of tormenting the opponent as the action was being carried out. "He used to play with Madrid players' minds very easily," remembered Spanish journalist Juan Escudero. "[They] were nullified by the curse or the spell of Petrović." Zoran Čutura remembered Petrović matched against Alfonso Del Corral, a player who would often test himself defensively against Petrović. When Petrović approached him on the dribble, Del Corral had crouched low into his defensive stance, pulled his shorts up, and stuck his rear-end down. Del Corral had been so driven by the matchup that he screamed at Petrović, "Vamos amigo!" but by mid-sentence Petrović had danced by him and into the paint for an easy score. "It was sudden death," Real Madrid's assistant coach Clifford Luyk said. "At least here in Europe, there was no one here defensively who could go one on one against him."

When the Real Madrid players convened in the locker room after their defeat to Cibona and Petrović, the tension among the players was much less about the loss than it was about what the players believed was poor conduct by Petrović in the moment immediately following the final buzzer. According to some of the Real Madrid players and coaches, Petrović and his brother Aleksandar spat at Fernando Martin as the teams left the floor. "He spit on them," Luyk said. "He and his brother Aleksandar, they were spitting at Martin. I was there." A number of Real Madrid players confided in members of the Spanish media about the incident, which had not been visible on the game's television broadcast. From that point Petrović was no longer merely a feared opponent, but to the writers he was the *Black Beast*, or *Cyclone Petrović*, or *Syndrome Petrović*, as if his presence demanded they stretch their journalistic creativity. Any contest that brought Petrović to Spain, whether it was with Cibona or with the Yugoslavian national team, seemed to carry with it a pre-packaged heat.

The names derived by the media were on some level justi-fied, for it seemed to symbolize the concurrent streams of Real Madrid's helplessness against Petrović's burgeoning greatness, each individual game summoning within it a storyline of its own. But come 1988, he was no longer a periodic visitor to Madrid. Instead, he now belonged to them. And what would ensue was a season of two distinct characteristics: splendid basketball, and in-house tension.

Eight

JOINING THE ENEMY, 1988–89

Madrid, Spain

Dražen Petrović's 1988 arrival in Madrid not only carried with it the tension from the prior matchups, but stylistically there was something compelling about the fit. With Cibona, the team was built around him and his singular creations. He was not only Europe's most devastating and rounded offensive player, but his teammates had also benefited, learning to move *with* him. Even when Petrović seemed focused on taking his opponent, his teammates moved with purpose, for despite his penchant for putting the ball up he could also in an instant whip a pass to them for the score. In Zagreb, most possessions started with Petrović. In Madrid, they didn't play basketball that way, with their successful teams of the eighties built on multiple contributors.

Petrović's style had been openly discussed following his final game against Real Madrid before he was to join them, at the 1988 Korać Cup. It had been one last strike, one last reminder, 47 points and the eternal satisfaction that in his four years in Cibona they had never truly found an answer for him. "With us he will change," Real Madrid head coach Lolo Sainz told Ignacio Torrijos of the *Blanco y Negro*. "There is no other way."

Petrović was told of this and in response told Torrijos, "It will be a lot different when I put the baskets in their favor next season." A seamless integration into Real Madrid's style, as had been the case with Cibona four years earlier, was thought to be unlikely.

Petrović arrived in Spain a short while after the 1988 Seoul Olympics and moved into an apartment in La Vaguada. It was in the northern part of Madrid, not far from where the team practiced, and populated with a good number of the team's players. Petrović loved the city but during the season spent a great deal of his time away from basketball and the team, holed up in his apartment. Often he was with his girlfriend at the time, Renata Cajić, or his parents when they visited.[12]

Petrović made the decision not to keep a telephone in his apartment, which resulted in him being isolated from the outside. Quique Villalobos, one of the team's younger players and also in his first year on the team, lived two buildings down from Petrović. If there was a practice time change or anything of note that needed to reach Petrović, Villalobos would take the call at his house, bolt from his own apartment and head down to Petrović's, where he would pass on the message. On occasion Petrović would invite him to stay, and the two would sip on soda and chat.

Villalobos considered Petrović to be a nice person, friendly, but also distanced. He didn't allow anyone to get too close to him while in Madrid. Part of it, Villalobos felt, was the language barrier, as at first Petrović's Spanish was limited, but grew exponentially in a very brief amount of time. Over the season, he became

---

12 Famously, both made a special trip to be present with Petrović to celebrate the New Year in Madrid, but he opted instead for a session in the gym. It made for a quiet celebration.

quite fluent. It was common for a majority of the team's players to go out after a game and enjoy a late dinner, as the custom dictated in Spain, but Petrović generally stayed away from that scene. "He stuck to himself a little bit more; he wasn't going out," said Johnny Rogers, the only American on the team and who would become, with Villalobos, one of the few in Madrid who befriended Petrović. "In Spain it's very normal to go out to dinner, have some drinks. Dražen wasn't like that."

With Petrović and his history with Madrid there promised to be several unsettled teammates. The history of his prior perceived disrespectful behavior from the Cibona days left Petrović distanced from the team. There were essentially two clusters within the playing group: the established players and the new players, the latter whom Petrović was closer. He became most friendly with two players, Rogers and Villalobos, but even then there was distance. Clifford Luyk, the team's assistant coach who would often work with Petrović on an individual basis, decided that Petrović's distancing from the team was in part because of his past, but far more because of his future. "Let's say he was in transit, as in at the airport," Luyk said. "He was in transit from Croatia to the NBA. It was a stopover in Madrid. I don't think he ever thought about being here more than one year, so all his intentions that year were to be a standout, score a lot of points, and get a good NBA contract."

Luyk often worked with Petrović on his shooting before practice, while the other players were getting treatment from the trainer. Petrović insisted on wearing a tattered, well-worn vest that was packed with weights Luyk remembered as totaling around seven kilograms. "It had pockets all the way around with small cement bricks," Luyk said. "It looked like what the police wore, like a bulletproof vest. It was discolored, and it must have been over ten years old that he came from Yugoslavia with." Luyk would stand underneath the basket as Petrović shot with his aged vest on, several hundred from the mid-range before stepping out to behind the three-point line. Soon, Luyk noticed that Petrović had little interest in shooting from the European three-point line of just over twenty-two feet but instead, from further out, suspiciously a lot like the NBA distance which extended out to almost twenty-four. "Dražen, shoot from closer in, at our line," Luyk would bark during the workouts.

"No," Petrović answered, smiling. "This makes it more difficult."

Luyk marveled at Petrović: the definition in his calves, the amazing stroke with which he shot the basketball, and the steely determination. He saw a young man who was looking at something beyond this season in Madrid. He was looking toward the NBA.

It was rather coincidental, then, that the NBA itself would pay a visit to Madrid in the fall of 1988, with the city hosting the second McDonald's Open championship and bringing with it a taste of the American league. The competition was seen as the league's initial reach toward globalization, a cross-pollination between enterprises of varying styles. The first tournament was in Milwaukee the previous year, with the Bucks playing host to the Soviet Union national team and Italy's Tracer Milan. It was, commissioner David Stern said at the time, entirely likely that it would be a competition with a far greater significance outside the United States than it would be within it. He was right. The Soviets traveled and played without Arvydas Sabonis, and the Bucks took care of both teams with uneventful and relative ease.

Stern had the foresight to recognize the reach of basketball, with its ability to excite and to overcome languages, and so the second version of the Open had two major points of attraction that differed greatly from the first. One, it would not be played before an audience that was accustomed to NBA basketball, so it would be taken overseas and thus be more celebrated. And two, it would feature the Boston Celtics, who in any country were a form of basketball royalty. They were the world's most well-known and successful team, headlined by the incomparable Larry Bird. The Celtics were just one year removed from their last finals appearance and two years from the last title. Bird was flanked by the universally identifiable quintet of Kevin McHale, Robert Parish, Dennis Johnson, and Danny Ainge, and their presence in Madrid was a rare treat. They were joined in the four-team tournament by the hosts, Real Madrid; the Yugoslavian national team, which just weeks earlier had competed in the gold medal game at the Seoul Olympics, and Scavolini Pesaro, an Italian team. Scavolini was chosen by Real Madrid as an opening game opponent, a sort of manipulation of the schedule, presumably a win away from meeting the Celtics in the final.

Even with the attendance of the Celtics, the tournament itself was not without its idiosyncrasies, ones that seemed to define the innocence of the experiment. One member of the Celtics' front office received a frantic call from Madrid on the morning the team was to fly out. The person on the other line was requesting that they bring *nets*. Dozens of European reporters, anxious to be present at an event that, in their opinion, was transcendent and revolutionary, showed up unannounced and without media credentials. And the games were played under a murky amalgamation of NBA and international rules. The tournament was less about fluency and more about the foray, the continued globalization, and if consumer reception and enthusiasm was the measure of its palatability then it was tremendously successful.

Real Madrid beat Scavolini Pesaro in the opening contest, overcoming an early deficit before pulling away. Petrović was determined to be brilliant on this international stage, and he pushed and panted his way to 34 points and seven rebounds.

There had been 10 assists, too, and two in particular stood out. Early in the first half Petrović led the break and then suddenly leapt into the air, putting the ball between his legs before flipping it with his right hand to a teammate for the dunk. In the second half he had repeated the move but with his left hand, leaping and whipping the ball again to a teammate for the layup. It was the type of move, Villalobos came to realize as the season wore on, that Petrović would be more apt to try when the game's outcome was somewhere beyond secure, when it was time for the fans to take with them something lasting. It was also a pass that fueled, especially to the Americans, the idea that the best way to describe Petrović at that point was to compare him to Pete Maravich. As a player with a beautifully innovative nature, Maravich had never been one to overlook the opportunity to make a show out of a fast break.[13]

Real Madrid won by twelve and waited as Boston completed the formality of beating Yugoslavia. No one in Madrid minded the pre-ordained result, for the *Celtics in Madrid* was in itself an experience to be savored.

The opportunity to play Boston excited Petrović. He had at various times over the years told reporters that, alongside his brother Aleksandar, the basketball figure he most idolized and was heavily influenced by was Bird. Celtics games and those of various other attractive NBA teams would be funneled through the European networks (in Šibenik it was through an Italian station) in the early eighties as Bird's career was lifting. Petrović, like many other players of his generation, would devour these telecasts that seemed so far away, the level of play so very good and perhaps unattainable. He loved the idea that he could test himself against

---

13 Coincidentally, his career was essentially ended by a knee injury in 1978 while throwing the very same pass Petrović was attempting.

an NBA team. Even in an exhibition setting nothing would be held in reserve, for there would be plenty of basketball people watching, waiting to see how he would respond.

The final itself contained little in the way of revelations. Petrović seemed, perhaps with the excitement of the game, to be anxious—a little frantic—with the ball in his hands, the determination as always to generate the offense. The Madrid crowd accompanied Petrović as this anxious force, riding the contest's every singular turn. They had quickly taken to him, proving to be a forgiving group considering the continued torment he had provided as an opponent.

Boston paid Petrović the ultimate compliment and assigned Dennis Johnson to guard him. Johnson was by 1988 aging as a player, but there was no doubting he was one of the elite defenders of his generation. He was a player of nearly unmatched anticipation, and quite capable of embarrassing the ball carrier with his deceitful poke-aways. His lunges for the ball didn't appear sharp, but because of his uncommon wingspan the ball would pop backward as the offensive player thrust forward, the ball dutifully waiting for Johnson to pick up. Petrović had watched Johnson and seen countless players fall victim, and he was in the early going most protective of the ball. He would draw three quick fouls on Johnson, a small measure of effectiveness. Boston's coach Jimmy Rodgers then turned to the younger Brian Shaw, a rookie guard. Shaw was a confident young player, Petrović's equal in quickness, and he brought energy. He would meet Petrović as soon as Real Madrid gained possession, pushing his body up against him. There was a play in the second half that seemed revealing: Petrović spun to his left, only to be cut off by Shaw; he spun back right and Shaw recovered to meet him before he passed the ball off. The spin dribble had been so effective for Petrović in international play that he was surprised to see an instance when it was not. Shaw had been the antidote, but perhaps it was a necessary revelation to Europe's best guard that work still needed to be done before jumping leagues. It was a situation not dissimilar to the previous year's McDonald's Open, when Milwaukee's Paul Pressey had stymied the great Soviet guard, Šarūnas Marčiulionis, rendering him ineffective and holding him to 4-for-15 shooting from the field.

There were moments of dash for Petrović, a quick spurt in the third quarter as Real Madrid stayed close, but there were also stretches when he was unaccounted for. He would finish with 22 points, but they came with difficulty, needing twenty-eight shots to get there (6-of-16 from the field, 8-of-12 at the free throw line). There were contradictory conclusions taken from the game. Petrović played well against a very good NBA team. He had been comfortable and aggressive against them. But it also showed him that he still had a ways to go, that the European competition could aid him only to a degree, and that for his game to continue to grow and develop he needed to be tested against better players. Not only were there no Larry Birds or Dennis Johnsons in Europe, there were no Brian Shaws to defend him.

The true display of the disparity between the basketball worlds came when Bird and his team simply accessed a higher gear when it was deemed necessary. Real Madrid flirted and stayed close, but Bird came to a point where he decided the outcome needed to be finalized. His 12 assists seemed to carry as much weight as his 29 points. He and his team did just enough to make it a comfortable fifteen-point win, at 111–96, and with that they had won the tournament as expected. Jack McCallum, the great basketball writer for *Sports Illustrated*, wrote about a moment of hilarity when Bird accepted the winner's trophy. The presentation wasn't made on the floor, but instead at the top of the arena, up in the balcony, where Prince Felipe, the son of King Juan Carlos, was waiting. McCallum watched as Bird trudged up the stairs to get the trophy. "The Prince does not come down," a local told McCallum. "Larry Bird goes up."

As the 1988–89 Spanish league season commenced, Real Madrid quickly showed they were capable of winning it all, even if internally it was a team that was neither harmonious nor close. For that they were not in the minority. Teams were comprised of individuals, the individuals have egos, and Real Madrid had players with requisite egos. From the season's infancy there was an interesting dynamic within the squad that gained a seemingly endless amount of attention from the media: the relationship between Dražen Petrović and Fernando Martin. There was an expectation that there be tension. Martin was the team's figurehead, the clubhouse leader, as much their identity as anyone, and the team's most decorated player of the decade. Petrović was the showy newcomer. There was an obvious history of heated battles in very big games, incidents that had become part of the legend. The reporters and those who followed the team closely quickly came to the conclusion that the two would never be close.

During the 1988–89 season there was not a single explosive moment that characterized the tension between them; instead, it was a steady, gradual stream of words that leaked out and was trumpeted by the Spanish writers. The two received an almost tabloid-like coverage. The team was winning and so it provided a nice contradictory element, the two having their every on-court move interpreted and molded by the writers. A magazine report early in the season claimed that Martin had grown to dislike the flashy way in which Petrović threw his passes. Another suggested Petrović was over-passing to Martin in the post as a way to appease him. Staff from the Portland Trail Blazers visited Madrid in December of that season to view Petrović, and he had hit for 42 points against Juventus. It was written later that some of his teammates, namely Martin, hadn't been impressed with a shot total (twenty-seven attempts) tailored seemingly for the eyes of the Blazers and no one else. It was mostly a series of minor "infractions" with a residual build-up as the season played out.

The writers seemed to push the angle. After one particular game in which Petrović scored a great many points and Real Madrid had won, a reporter from the *El País* newspaper asked Martin if that had bothered him. "Yes," he had answered, "because Madrid is not used to that." Martin grew tired of being asked about the state of his relationship with Petrović. By season's end he was telling the reporters that it was a non-story, that not every set of teammates will be close. He often pointed out to scribes that they were only interested because Petrović was a star and would have no interest in him not getting along with a reserve who played very little. (It was an indirect admission.) Petrović was less vocal, even coy when questioned about his relationship with Martin. He preferred to continue through the season without incident, head down, working towards the greater goal while keeping to himself.

Real Madrid remained an efficient team, somewhat top-heavy in its reliance on the starting group, but truly a contender in the Spanish league. Petrović led the team in scoring, Martin in rebounding. Together they were flanked by José Biriukov, a terrific shooter, and Rogers, the American with NBA experience. They had been locked with Barcelona in a battle for the league's best record, and in the end Barcelona won out, as Real Madrid finished with twenty-nine wins from thirty-six regular season games. Though Petrović had been prolific enough to cause a jolt to the playing group, his game had indeed been watered-down post-Cibona, toned and more matured. He was playing with less inhibition and abandon, but was certainly a better player. He finished the season with averages of 28 points on 54 percent shooting from the field, to go with four assists. He had enhanced development by filtering out some of the flash in a more disciplined environment; less was more, and it was arguably his best professional season to that point.

As league runner-up the prior year, Real Madrid participated in the Winner's Cup, in addition to the Spanish league. They played well enough to reach the final in March 1989, when they were matched against Snaidero Caserta, an Italian team. Snaidero was led by the great Brazilian Oscar Schmidt, a compulsive scorer on the international level, a player who in the eighties had become among the best players outside the NBA. He was not a glamorous player, but he was an excellent shooter who seemingly had little trouble getting his shot off despite an unusual release that saw him hold the ball above his head for a split second and then aim the ball. It helped that he was quite tall for an outside shooter, 6-foot-8, and he could stretch any defender out on the perimeter, forcing the opposing player to extend. Any game featuring the presence of both him and Petrović opened the possibility for unusually high individual scoring, and between them there was mutual respect. Schmidt had seen and played against Petrović and had heard about his legendary work ethic, a narrative that gained momentum as Petrović became more well-known. Schmidt himself had seen the similarities to his own practice habits. Going against Schmidt in such a big game ensured that Petrović would bring something additional.

Prior to the game, Johnny Rogers noticed that Petrović was particularly maniacal about the contest while preparing at the team hotel. He already knew who was to officiate the game, even while obsessing over his own responsibilities, trying to ensure that the result would play out as he desired. It was a characteristic that Rogers and others had noticed in Petrović throughout the season. Rare was the statistic that didn't stick in his memory: he knew every team's win-loss record, who led in individual statistical categories, even the upcoming schedule complete with dates and starting times. He also had a knack for retaining his own statistics—both during and after the game. To Petrović, basketball was not only a sport that he played; it was something that consumed him.

Petrović began the game aggressively, and it was evident early on that with his outside shot clicking he had the advantage against Snaidero Caserta. Villalobos watched him closely over the course of the game as he answered every Snaidero Caserta burst with his own offense. He watched the confidence that seemed to increase within Petrović as the game went on. It provided a strange comfort for Villalobos: that even in this giant arena, with a tight score and tension, Petrović was going to score and Real Madrid was going to win. It was one of those rare foregone conclusions, with a game hanging in the balance, when all that was required was to get the ball to Petrović and he would find a way to score. "With Dražen you always have the feeling that, 'OK if we go to a tight game, we're always going to win,'" Villalobos said. "His confidence, his everything, he had so much confidence in himself and you could see this confidence was hitting us too. If we're on the court and we're in trouble, give the ball to Dražen and he's going to score."

It was the type of game Petrović believed was within him every time he played, and that if he delivered it in the Winner's Cup final that it would be remembered. In the end he took thirty shots, made twenty (including eight three-pointers) and finished with 62 points. It was enough to overshadow Schmidt's 44. The two men combined for 106 points as Real Madrid won in over-time, 117–113.

Real Madrid had won, and yet the mood of the team was not that of celebration, but instead was surprisingly glum and unenthusiastic. Clifford Luyk looked around at his team and thought, "We are not celebrating like we should." There was division in the locker room: those who were amazed at what Petrović had done, and then those who did not endorse the number of shots it took for him to amaze them. Some of the team's longer-tenured players had not appreciated Petrović's heroics, viewing it as individualistic; a gross undertaking for one man to essentially pit himself against five, even when the result was what they all had desired. It was the raw essence of Petrović's ability in the European game that he was capable of such a dominating performance. "He was a killer," Dino Radja once said. "The only guy I know who was able to beat somebody by himself." And yet it had exposed the friction that lay beneath the surface of the team throughout the season. "That was just very disappointing," Rogers said later of the scene in the locker room. "Dražen and I never really talked about it, but I know he was affected by it also. I came from the perception that you do whatever it took to win, and he did that. I didn't care if he shot every time down, he was the best option. That was critical. That might have damaged some of the chemistry. It was already fragile, but that probably damaged whatever chemistry there was."

Lost amidst the post-game drama was that Martin had played with a badly broken right thumb, an injury that only he and the team's physician were aware of. Martin had been prideful in his approach to the injury, concealing it as best he could. He insisted on playing, and whatever treatment was needed could wait until the team returned to Spain. It was a gutsy effort, but one largely unnoticed. "He really made an effort to play that game with a broken finger," Villalobos remembered. "And nobody really recognized that effort."

Real Madrid reached the Spanish league finals, and Barcelona was waiting for them. It was the matchup that everyone wanted, the league's two best teams from the beginning of the campaign. Since the forming of the *Asociacion de Clubs de Baloncesto* (ACB) some five seasons earlier these two teams had combined to win all five titles, squaring off against one another in three of those years. They were to the Spanish league in the eighties what the Lakers and Celtics had been in the NBA, the domination never shifting outside of their exclusive grasps. The year 1989 brought with it the dynamic of Petrović. He had not been part of the on-court history, but the teams had clamored for his services in 1986 until Barcelona opted out, adding another element to the matchup. Barcelona fired off the first grenade before the series began, with their head coach Aíto García Reneses talking to the reporters about how Petrović was eternally protected by the referees. *Bula* was the word the coach used to the writers, a Spanish term to describe the act of Petrović fooling the officials into making a call. It was, thought Luyk, the ultimate gamesmanship. "I think that was a determining factor in the outcome of the Spanish league," Luyk said. "He [Reneses] was a determining factor. It was his strategy to eliminate the Dražen effect."

The opener was not close. Barcelona won by twenty-five and was simply dominant. Real Madrid was without Martin, who had a sore back, and played seemingly without spark. Between the first and second games the team gathered for a meal at their hotel;

the mood was somber. They had been embarrassed in the first game, shamed, their confidence low with another game on Barcelona's floor before heading home. Villalobos looked around the room and remembered that mood, especially the look on Petrović's face. He thought it was unusual that even a man with Petrović's confidence seemed so flat emotionally early in the series. But then the door to the hotel restaurant flung open, and through it walked Martin and his towering presence; he was carrying his gym bag. "Dražen turned around," Villalobos said. "From a sad face came a big smile."

Martin looked around at his teammates. "I didn't get out of bed to lose this game," he told them, and immediately the mood in the room changed.

Martin gutted it out through twenty-seven minutes and Petrović scored 37 points in the second game. Real Madrid won in Barcelona by seven. The teams then split the next two games (with Petrović scoring 42 and hitting eight three-pointers to avoid elimination in the fourth game) to set up the decider in Barcelona. It would be a bizarre fifth game. Barcelona won by eleven, with six players reaching double-figures and Petrović scoring only 14, but the main story following the game was the officiating. Real Madrid committed forty fouls to just eighteen by Barcelona. All five of its starters were disqualified by fouls, in addition to one reserve. They were forced to play the final half-minute with four men on the floor. There was a thirty-second span in the second half with four minutes left when Real Madrid's two best players were wiped from the contest. Martin was first, whistled for his fifth foul when trying to seal his man in the paint. Petrović then contested a pass at the top of the key, making slight contact with the wrist of the passer, promptly receiving his fifth. The whistle blew and there was a brief moment of shock, with Petrović turning to the referee with a half-smile before deciding better of a confrontation. Barcelona's crowd was in nirvana.

The locker room was quiet in the game's immediate aftermath, the echo of celebration out on the floor seeping in as Real Madrid pondered where it had gone wrong. There was a genuine feeling in the post-game interactions with the media that something was taken from them, with Sainz and several players voicing displeasure at just how poor the officiating had been. They felt the opportunity to fight fairly for the league crown was denied to them. Real Madrid had not played particularly well, and yet at the half they had been within two and were down just four with ten minutes to play, before it began to fall apart. Petrović's game had been distorted by the early foul trouble, and he never found a sustained rhythm, with his point total near his lowest of the season.

In the days that followed, one of the game's referees, Juan Jose Neyro, received death threats over his officiating, threats coming from those who had been upset with Real Madrid's loss. The calls had been answered at various times by him, his wife, and his daughter. Neyro felt obliged to take his case to the papers, defending his officiating performance to them, and encouraging the Real Madrid organization to re-watch the film in order to see the game that he saw.

Neyro's involvement in the deciding game, and the claim that he was being fingered as the official who had been hardest on Real Madrid, was the topic for some internal discussion. In the game's post-mortem there was a line of thinking that Neyro had been purposeful in his calls, that there was a deeper meaning to his focus on calling the game tightly for Real Madrid and for Petrović. Those who had been around the club for a significant period of time pointed to a September 1986 exhibition in Puerto Real in Spain between Cibona and Real Madrid as the origin point, a game in which there had been an incident between Petrović and Neyro away from the play. The incident was not captured by the television cameras (one of the announcers on Spanish television claimed that Petrović spat on Neyro) but it had seen Petrović ejected, upset at not getting a foul as he drove aggressively to the basket. By the time the 1989 season came, the two crossed paths again in Spanish league play, and it was Neyro who ejected Petrović from a midseason game with Joventut. In the aftermath of the finals, it surfaced again as a potential catalyst for the way the decider was officiated. "Problem with Petrović?" Neyro queried when the writers began to circle. "No." Petrović's Spanish agent, Jose Antonio Arizaga, was friendly with Neyro and remembers talking with the official long after the furor of the fifth game died down. "I am a referee first," Neyro told Arizaga, insisting that the prior incidents had no influence on how he called a game.

In any case Real Madrid and Petrović came up short in their quest for the league title. It had, overall, been a mixed season. He had certainly improved his game, but there was off-court theatre to accompany it, seemingly taking on equal or greater importance. The 1989 Eurobasket soon arrived, and that soothed the pain of Real Madrid's disappointing end to the season.

By the summer of 1989, Dražen Petrović was through one season of his four-year contract with Real Madrid. He was fast approaching his twenty-fifth birthday, and as his sport was about to experience a global shift, Petrović's next sudden move would not only shock the organization that held his rights, but prove to be the biggest chance he would ever take. He was about to jump to the NBA.

Nine

GUESSWORK TO GET HIM HERE, 1986–89

Europe; Portland, Oregon, USA

In the months after the Portland Trail Blazers took Dražen Petrović in the third round of the 1986 NBA draft, Bucky Buckwalter realized the team had something of a dilemma: the team owned the rights to several very good but ultimately un-NBA-tested players who were stored away in Europe with limited means of direct communication. Petrović and Arvydas Sabonis would continue on with their careers in Europe. Portland, not present, would be left to make sense of their status through periodic word-of-mouth updates and the occasional VHS game tape. Once Petrović's draft rights were held by Portland, Buckwalter sought the help of an American coaching in France named Kenny Grant to track and occasionally gauge Petrović's interest in coming to Portland. "How else would we know," Buckwalter thought, "if these players are seriously considering coming to the NBA?" Unlike George Fisher, who first planted the seed of intrigue with Buckwalter for Petrović, Grant's assignment was essentially the next step. He would be enlisted to check in with

Petrović, talk to him about his future and about Portland, and get an idea of how soon he planned on testing himself in the United States. The Blazers would then act based on Petrović's level of interest.

From Grant's vantage point, the gradual changing of opinion toward the European players and this sudden desire to claim their rights was nothing if not inevitable. But, he thought, teams weren't drafting players and then wondering if they were good enough to play—they were drafting them and then being met with the dilemma of, *"Now how do we get them here?"* Grant already held a strong interest in Petrović when Buckwalter reached out to him, having long enjoyed his game, and he was curious as to whether there was serious consideration on Petrović's part in leaving Europe to join Portland, now that they owned his draft rights. Fully aware of Petrović's work ethic and focus, Grant wondered why such a driven young man had not taken the opportunity to come to the Blazers, a team that through the middle part of the eighties had fielded strong offensive units, ones that could use such a prolific scorer. In the preparation stages of his association with Petrović, Grant asked one of his players at the time, Ratko Radovanović, a teammate of Petrović's on the Yugoslavian national team, to get Petrović's thoughts on the NBA. "Talk to Dražen," Grant said to Radovanović. "See if he's interested in the NBA. I don't know why he's not there."

Radovanović had the opportunity to speak with Petrović at the Yugoslavian national team camp in preparation for the basketball world championships in Spain, just weeks after the 1986 draft and with the excitement of a possible future in the NBA still fresh. Petrović told Radovanović that, yes, joining Portland in the future was a possibility, but not now.

Later that fall Grant flew to Zagreb for a meeting with Petrović and his family on the eve of the 1986–87 club season.

When Grant arrived at the apartment of Petrović's parents, he looked across the street and saw a basketball gym. *That's appropriate*, Grant thought. The meeting went well, Grant and Petrović sipping espresso and discussing the Blazers and the future, the conversation never straying far from basketball. To Grant, Petrović seemed a private but very driven person, interested and excited in the possibilities but wary of the obstacles it would take for him to come to the NBA and be successful. There was no doubt he wanted to go to the higher league at some point, and testing his skills was always important to him. It had been Petrović's goal to not merely compete with the best but to take his place among them, a mindset that separated him from other early European players who had considered making the jump in the late eighties.

What loomed over Petrović and all of Europe's best players was the unknown that came with jumping leagues and continents. He seemed stranded somewhere between the conventional wisdom that European guards couldn't cut it in the NBA, and the less-heralded possibility that, with his flash and charisma and hard-headed determination, he could break through and make it, becoming a *good* NBA player. He may have been to the European evaluators of talent the equal of or, to some, greater than, Sabonis, but to the NBA people he was, as a perimeter player, a far less guaranteed and unknown proposition. The narrow ideals that at the time were attached to European players—exclusively shooters, weak defenders, lacking the requisite physical toughness—seemed to describe Petrović, but he had combated those generalizations with his self-confidence and unique flair that provided an additional dimension not possessed by the typical European backcourt player. The comparison to Pete Maravich seemed to differentiate—and in some instances, validate—Petrović when described by the American writers.

112 THE MOZART OF BASKETBALL

Sports Illustrated's writer Alexander Wolff saw plenty of Petrović as the eighties progressed, and was one of the few American writers who seemed to have a legitimate feel for the heartbeat of the European game. He, too, had seen some elements of Maravich in Petrović. Wolff was assigned by his magazine to do some work in Rotterdam, Netherlands, for the 1988 European Olympic qualifying tournament, in part to do what he called "some pre-Olympic story to see who could possibly beat the United States" and partly to see Petrović, who was to be the subject of a feature piece by Wolff. With Petrović, like Sabonis, there was something almost mythical about the great European players at that time; the tales of their greatness were passed almost exclusively through word of mouth from one basketball person to another, and the opportunity to delve deeper into the Petrović narrative provided a unique angle to Wolff. Wolff was excited to see Petrović play, and what he saw in Petrović at Rotterdam that he did not see in other European guards was inventiveness, a daring creativity that revealed the sheer joy of the player. "Dražen was the first guy in Europe whose game was flash and dash," Wolff said. "Frankly, that's what beguiled me about him."

Wolff nabbed Petrović for some quiet time in Rotterdam, the two getting together in Petrović's tiny hotel room. "It was full of gym bags and open suitcases," he remembered. Quickly, Wolff found the role of interviewer and interviewee reversed: Petrović was curious about the basketball universe and the place he could possibly occupy within it, and asked questions about the NBA and particular players, about what it would take to get there and *make it*. There was certainly part of him, Wolff believed, that was peering beyond his glamorous European athletic existence and to the NBA.

Kenny Grant, too, was in Rotterdam, and met once again with Petrović for the semi-annual temperature check. Petrović had just finished his fourth year with Cibona, and Grant sought to learn more about the Real Madrid deal that was about to commence.

To Grant there was a touch of irony in the fact that he was having this conversation with Petrović in Rotterdam, with the Blazers lurking somewhere in the background crossing their fingers with hopes Petrović would jump to them. Grant remembers looking around at that pre-Olympic tournament for European countries and thought it a mini-landmark. He noticed for the first time not the presence of the occasional American scout or NBA team executive hidden in the crowd, but instead a sizeable contingent of Americans there to observe and learn. Chances were, they would leave with a name or a lasting impression. In Grant's mind, the NBA's gradual interest in European talent had come with a touch of ignorance. Front-office types would be captivated by players while not knowing their names or their backgrounds, having trouble estimating exactly how they would measure fundamentally or athletically against the NBA talent. The ceiling for the very good European players was most hard to decipher due to the competition and the vast physical disparity, and what resulted was a mini-boom for lifers like Grant—Americans who were educated about the foreign leagues. Suddenly their expertise was required.

Bucky Buckwalter had also been in Rotterdam and planned to travel on to Seoul for the Olympics, where he was set to meet with his prized imports, Sabonis and Petrović. That Sabonis would be healthy enough to play in Seoul was a miracle in itself. Soviet authorities granted him permission to rehabilitate his Achilles (which had twice ruptured) in Portland, and he was eventually pivotal in helping take down the United States in the Olympic semis. John Thompson, the Americans' coach, openly questioned just who exactly had benefitted from the rehab, especially when Sabonis had no plans to play for Portland anytime soon. He then led the Soviets past Petrović and the Yugoslavs in the gold medal game.[14]

Portland and Buckwalter kept a close eye on Petrović during his season in Madrid and made sure he was present for the European championships in Zagreb in the spring of 1989. A local newspaper reported that Petrović had already committed to a trip to Portland as soon as the tournament was over, to begin negotiations on a contract. It forced Petrović to address the report on the day of the championship game against Greece. He was increasingly interested in Portland once he was informed that Terry Porter, a rising point guard with the Blazers, had signed an offer sheet with Denver. Very well versed on Portland's roster even from the other side of the world, Petrović knew Porter's departure could open a door for him.[15]

Buckwalter met with Petrović in Zagreb and once again pushed for him. "We are in need of a guard who can shoot," Buckwalter told him. "You have grown in your game. You can help us immediately."

"He was ready to play," Buckwalter said. "We kept trying to get that message across to him."

One month prior to the Eurobasket, basketball's governing body, FIBA, ruled that professionals would be able to compete at the next Olympics in 1992. The vote was 80-percent in favor (the United States, in what has become forgotten historically, resided

---

14 Buckwalter had been left uneasy post-game when it was revealed that both Petrović and Sabonis were randomly chosen to provide samples for drug testing together in a side room. Well aware of their genuine detest for one another, Buckwalter paced the hallway for an hour hoping they would emerge without incident. Eventually they did, arm in arm, smiling, the tension eased when Sabonis sent out for a six-pack of beer so the two supposed enemies could bury the hatchet.

15 Portland eventually matched Denver's offer.

in the minority). Though most of the attention was directed at the prospect that the Games would feature NBA players, the reverse current would prove to be just as strong: the best European players could now jump to the NBA and not forfeit their national team eligibility. Previously, players such as Petrović and Sabonis, Vlade Divac, and Šarūnas Marčiulionis, stars on the powers that were Yugoslavia and the Soviet Union, were under pressure to avoid the NBA at risk of not representing their country. The medal chances of their homeland at any international competition depended on their presence. Marčiulionis soon signed with Golden State. The day after the Eurobasket, Divac boarded a plane in order to attend the NBA draft, where he was taken by the Lakers. And Alexander Volkov, a fine forward from the Soviet Union, signed with Atlanta. All indications pointed to Petrović soon joining them.

"This is my dream," he told reporters.

Perhaps the most convincing piece of evidence that Petrović was looking to jump came by officially hiring Warren LeGarie as his agent during the Eurobasket. LeGarie was a unique agent, bright, multilingual several times over. Compared with his contemporaries, his clientele was internationally flavored and unique to the business at a time when the outsiders were less desired by the general American basketball community.

In the eighties, LeGarie had an interesting demographic of clients. His stars were outweighed by his share of borderline players, types who were in and out of the league and had little in the way of guarantees—players who *needed* Europe as a back-up plan. He had a growing reputation as a relentless agent, one who would fight hard for his players, in part because they needed someone to fight for them and their security. LeGarie had, like others who manage to find success in athlete representation, benefited a great deal from his own foresight: nameless assistant coaches could one day become head coaches; European players, vastly improving and in the right environment, could be a commodity; and American players could leave NBA offers on the table and accept terms from eager, wealthy European clubs. This vision led to a measure of power within his finite corner of the business. Roger Newell, who provided statistical reports to a significant portion of the NBA and who was the son of the great coach Pete Newell, was an acquaintance of LeGarie's and had sat with him at many college games. He estimated that LeGarie's office hours surely must have started between four and eight in the morning, because it seemed the rest of the time he was out meeting an executive no one had heard of, or flying out to Europe to meet with a player who existed exclusively on his radar, such was his ravenous and thoughtful approach.

LeGarie represented the first western European to play in the NBA, Fernando Martin, who had signed a one-year deal with Portland the same summer that Petrović was drafted in 1986. Though one of Spain's elite players, in Portland Martin was anonymous and went without a definitive opportunity. The team was neither willing nor able at that point to deal with the unique needs of a foreign player, especially one who wasn't contributing. That lone season in Portland did not go well. There were persistent problems in communication between Martin and the coaches, and at times the organization didn't know if they were dealing with Martin or the friend who was helping him acclimatize to Portland, a Spaniard who happened to speak English. He appeared in only twenty-four games before returning home, both sides being left rather disappointed.

LeGarie was determined to learn something from the Martin experience. When representing foreign players, he found that the pitch to management wasn't a difficult one. It certainly didn't hurt fan interest to have a difference-maker or someone unique—an identifiable novelty with the talent and ability to contribute to the team. What *was* difficult, LeGarie realized, was getting the coaches to buy in, partly because they suspected management's signing of a foreign player to be more a marketing decision than a basketball one. When a coach overcame that hurdle, then there was the issue of communicating effectively with the player. There were late-game situations, the knife's edge where instruction was critical, and there was general concern about whether someone with limited English could first understand that instruction and then execute it on the floor. George Fisher, in his dealings with American executives and coaches, heard of this train of thought and did not subscribe to it. He had, in fact, experienced a reversal of this as an American coaching in Europe. He quickly discovered that the language that truly mattered was *basketball*, with its universally distinguishable words building the bridge between coach and player. "There aren't twenty-five ways to say 'pick and roll,'" Fisher said.

LeGarie remembered well his first encounter with Petrović. He was in Madrid to see his client, Johnny Rogers, a teammate of Petrović's who had played minimally for Sacramento and Cleveland before turning to Europe. Real Madrid had just returned from a road game, and LeGarie was scheduled to meet with Rogers at the building where the team practiced. LeGarie arrived early and was greeted by the gentle, rhythmical thud of a basketball out on the practice court. He followed the sound before finding Petrović, alone, a toned figure lathered in sweat. LeGarie was not a stranger to the degree of stardom experienced by Petrović. He thought highly of the youngster's future prospects. The two began to chat in Spanish while LeGarie waited. Soon, LeGarie found himself in the ultimate role that would endear him to Petrović—rebounding for him, catching the ball as it repeatedly came through the net, and then firing it back out, Petrović waiting with hands up and mouth open, ready to repeat the process. A friendship was conceived in that almost predestined setting.

The two would speak periodically throughout the season, sometimes directly, sometimes through Rogers. LeGarie sensed Petrović's growing interest in leaving behind his pact with Real Madrid to join the NBA. He made preliminary contact with the Blazers about Petrović to get the ball rolling. Portland quickly started to prepare a legal team that would attempt to, first, make sense of Petrović's contractual rights, and then seek a way to free him to join the Blazers. The team's owner, Paul Allen, asked his lawyer, Allen Israel, to lead the legal efforts to get Petrović. Israel was briefed on the situation: Portland owned Petrović's NBA rights for three years, that he wanted to join the team, and that he was under contract with Real Madrid.

Israel obtained a copy of Petrović's contract with Real Madrid from LeGarie and agreed that there was a clear provision that stated the contract could be bought-out for US $200,000 per remaining season. Real Madrid countered by producing a document that they claimed was Petrović's contract, which had no buy-out provision. Israel asked Petrović about it. "That is a forgery," he told Israel flatly.

Israel reached out to Gary Bettman, at the time the NBA's general counsel, and others in the NBA legal department to argue that Petrović had a clear right to buy out his contract with Real Madrid. Portland should have been permitted to negotiate and sign him to a Uniform Player Contract for the 1989–90 NBA season, Israel argued. However, Bettman was bound by a deal between the NBA and the ACB Spanish league that was first conceived during the McDonald's Open basketball tournament in October of 1988 and finalized in February of 1989. The document was signed by NBA commissioner David Stern and the CEO of the ACB, Eduardo Portela. It effectively prohibited either league or any team in either league from negotiating or attempting to negotiate with a player who was under contract with a team in the other league. In essence, the NBA was by force of this agreement oddly aligned with the interests of Real Madrid and not that of Portland.

Under that provision, neither Portland nor any of its attorneys could represent Petrović. So Israel, based in Seattle with the law firm Foster Pepper, contacted his partner at the Portland office, Ken Roberts, about the Petrović situation. Roberts suggested to Israel that they enlist the help of Portland attorney Nick Goyak, who, Roberts pointed out, had a thread of commonality with Petrović: he was of Croatian descent and his parents were born in an area some fifty miles from Šibenik, Petrović's hometown.

Roberts reached out to Goyak. "Nick, I understand you have Yugoslavian background," he began. "We can't represent Dražen. Would you be interested in representing him?"

Goyak enthusiastically accepted.

Goyak was an ideal choice on several accounts. He spoke Croatian, which at that time was a significant factor with Petrović's English still developing. He was also a self-confessed basketball junkie, a close follower of the Blazers, and well aware of Petrović and his exploits in Europe. He quickly found it to be an unusual case that required an unusual tactical approach. Customarily in matters that involved an international party such as Real Madrid, the case would be sorted out in a federal court. However, a friend of Goyak's who was a litigation specialist suggested that they take it to a state court in the county where Portland was located. This meant Goyak would not have to formally notify Real Madrid of what was occurring, just merely make an attempt to do so. He called the Real Madrid offices and spoke to a woman whose English was non-existent. Goyak also didn't speak Spanish, so the call was short. He then faxed the club some basic information and proceeded on to the courtroom, pitted against no opposition.

In late July of 1989, Petrović brought suit in an Oregon state court against Real Madrid, the ACB, the NBA, and the Portland Trail Blazers. The lawsuit sought Petrović's release from his Real Madrid contract and an injunction that would prohibit the Spanish club from interfering with any subsequent negotiations that Petrović would have with Portland. Goyak submitted to the court an English-written copy of Petrović's Real Madrid contract, dated October 27, 1986, that Goyak insisted had a clearly stated buy-out clause that was valid under both Spanish and United States law.

The nature of the case led to a bizarre courtroom scene. With the involved parties located in Portland, New York, and Madrid, three local lawyers were quickly engaged to represent the NBA, ACB, and Real Madrid. However, none of these lawyers had much familiarity with their clients or their cases by the time they convened in a courtroom some week or so after the lawsuit was filed. When the judge asked to be briefed on the situation, none of the lawyers seemed to know all of the facts or completely understand their clients' positions. "I can't rule anything if no one knows what is going on," the judge said.

Israel was sitting in the courtroom that day, a bystander watching all this unfold. He raised his hand, explained who he was, and that he understood the case and would be able to make sense of it. "Yes," the judge answered to Israel's offer to explain. "Please tell me what is going on." The judge listened as Israel described the disputed and undisputed facts, and explained the legal position and desired outcomes of each party with great detail. The judge asked the lawyers representing the other parties what they thought of Israel's explanation, with each claiming that it was comprehensive and fair. The judge was satisfied and decided to grant a temporary restraining order that would allow Petrović to start negotiating with Portland.

"This," Goyak told the *Associated Press*, "is a very important victory for us."

However, it proved only a temporary victory. The judge specifically reserved making a final decision on the case. Furthermore, he made clear his doubts that the court actually had jurisdiction over the ACB or Real Madrid, because neither party had any contact with the State of Oregon. This was potentially a fatal flaw in Petrović's case. The ACB and Real Madrid held all the cards, it seemed, and Petrović and Portland were stuck.

Petrović had been in Europe for the summer while the legal case was being carried out. He took a brief trip to Portland immediately after the Eurobasket, where he worked out for Portland's head coach Rick Adelman at Portland Community College. Petrović then flew back to Zagreb from the United States, and a short while later was visited by Lolo Sainz, the coach at Real Madrid. Sainz was aware of Petrović's visit to Portland and made the trip to Zagreb to remind his player that he was still expected to fulfill the three remaining seasons of his contract in Spain. Sainz was disappointed in the lack of communication from Petrović after the season. Sainz had gone to Zagreb expecting that Petrović would ask for a financial increase but quickly saw that the player's sole objective now was the NBA.

Where Sainz failed, the team's president, Ramon Mendoza, felt he could succeed and flex his managerial muscle. He requested a meeting with Petrović on *his* turf, in Madrid. The two met near the end of July, days before the team was to reconvene in preparation for the 1990 season. The message was essentially the same as Sainz's. It reinforced the remaining years on the contract, even reminding Petrović of the handwritten note the team had asked him to compose after a December visit by Portland, one that stated he would stay and fulfill his contract.[16] According to a report of the meeting in the *ABC* paper, after twenty minutes Petrović told Mendoza that, yes, he would reluctantly stay.

Petrović remained in Madrid. When not participating in his team's preseason camp under new coach George Karl he was holed up in his apartment, a very public uncertainty arising about whether he would be there when the season opened. He showed up on the first day of practice as he had been asked. He was warmly received by the fans on that annual introduction day, a reception that was not duplicated by the local media, which daily was documenting the situation. To them he was no longer a man but a *serpent*. His newspaper caricature, which always accompanied a Petrović story, suffered a makeover. It became more exaggerated and unflattering with each passing day: his ears pushed out, lips overly supple, his mouth always open, a handsome man gone ugly.

The Blazers decided it would be important for someone to be there in Madrid for Petrović, to spend time with him and provide support. So they sent Brad Greenberg, recently hired as director of player personnel. Greenberg was in his mid-thirties, a former scout and assistant coach for various teams, a friendly sort who the team was sure would connect with Petrović on a basketball level and thus a personal level. Greenberg, asked to go to Spain on short notice, scurried to organize a passport and left in a matter of days. He arrived in Madrid and found access to Petrović rather easy. Within several days a routine was established: taxi

---

16 That document drifted its way into court, but Goyak pointed that it was not the official contract, and it never became a factor.

from his hotel to the Real Madrid practice gym, sit alone in the seats while Petrović participated in workouts, and then arrange to meet Petrović. It was a strange scene: Petrović, in Madrid colors and in sports terms their *property*, being watched by Greenberg, a representative of the poacher. In time Real Madrid sought to limit the access, and the club closed off practice to outsiders.

Greenberg spent fewer than two weeks in Madrid and was exposed to the type of stardom that was afforded to Petrović as a European athlete. He had gone to Madrid and initially seen the situation as most others had: by coming to the NBA, Petrović would be fulfilling a dream he had long carried with him. But upon his arrival and spending time there, Greenberg had reshaped those thoughts, looking at Petrović and his life there and concluding that this leap was indeed a very big one. *He could be the best player in Europe for another ten years and make all the money he wants*, Greenberg thought to himself. He was impressed by the ambition and risk that Petrović showed by wanting to test himself in the NBA, when there was a clearly defined comfort zone in Europe.

Greenberg made several attempts to meet with Ramon Mendoza, and was denied each time. The first came through the Spanish agent Miguel Ángel Paniagua, and then through a member of the ACB league. Greenberg's presence in town had long moved past being a secret. In one of the local papers there was a photo of him with Petrović, the two walking down the street, with Greenberg in shorts, enjoying the spoils of Madrid in August. Amid the clutter of go-betweens and mixed messages was a story that Greenberg never came to verify but would come to be a source of amusement. "There's a man from Portland here to meet with you," one of Mendoza's assistants told their boss. Mendoza bristled. "There is no man from Portland, just a man in shorts."

Shortly before leaving Madrid, Greenberg learned that Mendoza had once again spoken with Petrović in his office. It left Petrović despondent over his chances of leaving for the NBA. Mendoza was apparently relenting, but only a short way: he was now willing to free Petrović after the 1990–91 season, which would end the contract one season early. That was still two years away, and Petrović would be twenty-six by then. "Is there a document, Dražen?" Greenberg asked.

"Yes," Petrović answered.

"Is it signed by Madrid?" Greenberg pressed.

"No," Petrović answered. "But I trust Mendoza. He has been like a father figure to me."

"If you want assurance, Dražen, that this will be carried out as they say, it needs to be signed," Greenberg said.

Somewhat desperate to have something to go back to Portland with, Greenberg finally met someone from Real Madrid, a gentleman named Miroslav Gorgic, a Yugoslavian who was a trainer with the soccer team but who had befriended Petrović during the year. "Here," Greenberg thought of meeting Gorgic, "is finally an opportunity to speak with someone at Real Madrid who has an interest in Dražen's career and is willing to listen to me." He went into the meeting with a measure of optimism but left in a different frame of mind. "I left there thinking it was almost like a warning: 'Get out of town man, you're messing around with the wrong people,'" Greenberg said later. "He wasn't friendly and he didn't threaten me, but I left there thinking that wasn't exactly a way to smooth things over."

Greenberg stopped by Petrović's apartment on his way to the airport. It seemed the dream was gone; at least Petrović's mood suggested so. With much legal ground to be made up, Greenberg left town with uncertainty. That same day, Warren LeGarie flew in.

In Portland, Petrović's attorneys struggled to find a legally compelling basis for the Oregon Court to assert jurisdiction over the ACB and Real Madrid. But then a most fortunate thing happened. Goyak had gotten wind that a representative of Real Madrid—who happened to also be employed by the ACB—was on his way to Portland to meet with their lawyer. When the gentleman stepped off the plane and was walking across the runway, a process server served him with the complaint. The basis for Oregon jurisdiction, with that single act, was now indisputably established. This changed the legal landscape of the case completely. The five parties negotiated a settlement and final agreement in August, and Petrović's contract with Real Madrid was subsequently bought out.

Petrović did not show up for practice with Real Madrid that same day. A team employee went to his apartment building, obtained keys from the concierge and accessed the residence. All he found was a hand-written note. Petrović was already gone. He had boarded a flight to the United States with his girlfriend, Renata Cajić, and LeGarie. The three were headed to Portland, to a new world and a new beginning.

Dražen Petrović was, finally, a member of the Portland Trail Blazers.

Ten

FINDING HIS PLACE, LATE 1989

Portland, Oregon, USA

Rick Adelman was unproven as a head coach on the professional level. He had been a member of the Blazers on its
inaugural team in 1970, which ensured that he was eternally
accepted in the Portland community. He was an unspectacu-
lar player, his better years coming in those dark early days on
those infant, easily-beaten Blazers. His tenure in Portland was
one of five teams he would play for in seven seasons. By the
age of twenty-eight Adelman was out of the league as a player,
vaguely aware of his next move and hardly a picture of financial security from his playing days. He bartended and dabbled
briefly in the athletic sneakers business with Converse before
taking a head coaching job at Chemeketa Community College
in Salem, Oregon, some forty miles from Portland. He worked
hard to build the program there, self-taught in the nuances of
recruiting and developing chemistry on teams that had constant player turnover, where the coach usually had one season
to make it all work.

Adelman won 80 percent of his games at Chemeketa, an outstanding record that reflected well on the coach, for he was the one constant as the years and players passed. After six years he was offered an assistant coaching position with the Blazers by Jack Ramsay, a man who gave to the sport a fluid and exceptional world champion in 1977. Adelman beat out another young aspiring coach, George Karl, for the position and benefited greatly from working under Ramsay, one of the game's renowned strategists.

By the mid-eighties, the Blazers were a team stranded in the middle of the road, certainly not good enough to neither contend nor sink into the draft lottery, and ties were severed with Ramsay in 1986. For a period Adelman had not known where he stood, but Ramsay's replacement, Mike Schuler, decided to keep him. It proved a seminal moment at which a lifeline emerged when he easily could have been washed away back to the collegiate ranks.

Schuler was named the NBA's Coach of the Year in his first season of 1987, and then in his second led the Blazers to fifty-two wins. Schuler had taken the team's most talented player, Clyde Drexler, a beautifully athletic talent, and given him ownership over the shooting guard position. Ramsay had been non-committal about Drexler as a full-time starter, splitting him with Jim Paxson, a pure shooter. But under Schuler, Drexler was given more freedom and more minutes, and he responded with averages of 27 points, roughly seven rebounds, and just under six assists, making him one of the three or four best shooting guards in the league.

Portland was building itself no longer in the image of Paxson or Kiki Vandeweghe, associates of the Ramsay regime, but with Drexler and an unusual cast of obscure draft finds and castaway talent. There was point guard Terry Porter from Wisconsin-Stevens Point, and small forward Jerome Kersey of Longwood College; and at center was Kevin Duckworth, who hailed from

Eastern Illinois and who had been brought in for failed first-round choice Walter Berry. The 1988 team under Schuler came together very quickly, playing a very hard, exciting brand of basketball, and seemed to be building something. But the 1989 season started poorly and eventually succumbed to bloated expectations. It was a season Schuler did not survive, and Adelman was allowed to finish the season at the helm.

The team did not finish well under Adelman, and yet the franchise offered him a one-year deal and a fresh start, in essence an audition to right a talented but underwhelming ship. He was an in-house choice, and by some description a Blazers lifer with ties to the franchise's infancy, to Ramsay, and to the promise of the Schuler years.

The initial contract offered little in the long term but Adelman saw it as an exciting opportunity with the team's core entering their primes. Petrović's attorney and friend Nick Goyak remembers being at a luncheon prior to the 1989–90 season where Adelman made a presentation to the group. He outlined definitively how many minutes each of his star players would receive each game, even before the season had started. It was a pre-packaged rotation. As Adelman broke down the players' distribution, Goyak wondered what that meant for the incoming Petrović.

Adelman was acutely aware of Petrović and the team's courtship of him. He was fond of Petrović as a person and had publicly acknowledged his skills when Portland was finalizing arrangements to obtain the player. But his place in Adelman's rotation was uncertain.

Petrović's preseason was derailed before it began. He experienced back pain while working out in Zagreb in the summertime, and it was alarming enough that Dr. Ivan Fattorini, who had treated Petrović while with Cibona and also the Yugoslav national team, left his vacation early to take a look. When he found Petrović, the player was lying flat on his back in the apartment, with limited mobility. Fattorini called Dr. Robert Cook, the Blazers' team physician. "You need to put Dražen on the first plane to Portland," Cook said.

"If there is a big problem then it should be operated on before he goes anywhere," Fattorini insisted.

"Don't do anything," Cook reinforced. "Send him here."

Petrović and his brother Aleksandar immediately flew to Portland. It was there where Cook examined Petrović, performing a minimally invasive procedure to relieve what Cook believed to be sciatic nerve irritation. Within ten days, Cook estimated, Petrović would be fine. However, a fortnight later Petrović was working out at a local community center when he felt twinges in his back. The pain persisted for two days before Petrović decided to call Goyak. "Nick, I am having a problem with my legs," he said. "I am not feeling my legs very well."

Goyak placed a call to Dr. Calvin Tanabe, a leading neurosurgeon. Tanabe joined Cook to make a more thorough examination, and the two concluded that some disk fragments needed to be removed from Petrović's back. However, once on the operating table, the two found a cyst containing fluid that was pressing on a nerve root in his back. It was causing the persistent discomfort. This revelation had come as a pleasant surprise, and it was deemed there would be no long-term damage.

On the first day of his first NBA training camp, Petrović sat on the sidelines watching his new teammates. The scene was eerily similar to ten years earlier, in Šibenik, when a young teenager—one so sure of himself—waited anxiously for an opportunity.

Petrović's back healed and in the end it cost him all of training camp and the exhibition season, save for Portland's finale. He entered his first NBA season vastly underdone physically, and in the early part of the regular season he played little. Petrović's place within the Portland rotation was not fully established. There was some thought by the Portland brass that he could be used both as a back-up point guard and shooting guard, but time eventually revealed he was far more effective off the ball as an offensive player than he was handling it. That in itself was a revelation. For years in Europe, Petrović had been the primary ball-handler on every team that didn't feature his brother Aleksandar, the offense resting purely on his creativity. Portland, with Porter and Drexler, did not need Petrović the creator. Instead, from the driving ability of Porter and Drexler, they needed a spot-up shooter, one who could force the defender to stay home and open driving lanes for his teammates. What resulted was the realization that Petrović would need to transform his game—less dribbling, more movement without the ball, better use of screens, primarily to catch and shoot—in order to best contribute to his new team. In part, too, it was to maintain survival in the elevated league of stronger and more athletic opponents.

Petrović was, the coaches agreed, a very smart and observant player. He did not need to be told of his new requirements, having altered his workouts to feature an emphasis on the elements that now would be the central focus of his offensive game.

Petrović himself had looked at his situation and decided that there were four main obstacles as he began his NBA career: three of them, the language barrier, the cultural differences, and homesickness, could be addressed and repaired with time. But the other, the adjustment from being a star in Europe to being a role player in the NBA, was something that needed immediate acceptance. He came to the Blazers with a definite understanding of their personnel and make-up. Portland assistant coach John Wetzel remembers Petrović sitting in the locker room sometime during training camp, alone with the three coaches, and being surprised at how well Petrović knew the Portland franchise and its roster, as well as its hierarchy. "My immediate reaction was, 'He knows what's going on,'" Wetzel recalled.

Petrović was competing with another rookie, Byron Irvin, for minutes behind Drexler at shooting guard. It was not an envious position—that of backing up an NBA star. In his introductory press conference, Petrović told reporters that with twenty minutes of playing time he could be effective and could help Portland. Playing exclusively behind Drexler, without any leftover minutes as a back-up point guard, suddenly made that number seem less likely. Drexler infrequently slid to the small forward spot, for Portland was very balanced there, with Jerome Kersey and Cliff Robinson, a talented rookie. And Adelman had settled on Danny Young as Porter's back-up at point guard. Young was a secure player, certainly not spectacular and not comparable to Petrović as an offensive force. But as an on-ball defender he could be effective, a disruptor with quick feet and active hands, and as an offensive player Young was safe and careful with the ball. Most importantly, Adelman trusted him.

Petrović's desired on-court goal of twenty minutes, eventually lowered to fifteen, seemed to be hard to conceive when considering his abbreviated season preparation and the secure, talented Adelman rotation. Petrović felt he needed minutes to prove himself as an NBA player; finding them consistently was a task unto itself.

What became apparent for Petrović was the realization that, for all he had accomplished in Europe and in the international tournaments, it essentially counted for little when contesting for playing time. There was with his signing a certain excitement: for even though he was sight unseen to the Portland followers he indeed was still a celebrated figure, with periodic articles tracking his status during the three years since being drafted in 1986. Numbers and awards were the standard measure for Petrović the European player; there was no denying he was a good player, but just *how good* remained the unanswered question, for this was not a player from a large division one university who could be seen regularly on national television. He was, instead, among a group of the first European NBA settlers, so he was as much as anything unknown. The variables for his success were larger and more complex than those of an American kid from the college system.

There was a section of the basketball community that was aware of his feats—those few purveyors of the European game outside the United States—and what came with Petrović's scant early-season minutes were questions and puzzlement. The man who would field those questions was Dwight Jaynes, a Blazer beat writer with the *Oregonian* who had written with depth about the team's pursuit of Petrović. November 1989 signaled the start of a ritual that would last for one-and-a-half seasons for Jaynes: the phone was likely to ring at the oddest of hours, and the caller usually would be a journalist from Europe.

"What's wrong with Petrović?" the voices on the line would ask Jaynes. "Why is he not playing?" Jaynes would explain what he knew about the situation—about Petrović's absence in training camp and about the logjam at the guard positions. His explanation was always met with genuine confusion on the other end of the line about why the finest European guard of the eighties was not playing.

Jaynes and the other writers in turn would ask Adelman in the season's infancy about Petrović, with interest about how he would fit into the team. Adelman preached patience to them in an effort to quell the inquiries. He missed all of training camp, Adelman would repeatedly tell them, one that would have been immensely beneficial to him from a teaching standpoint. He needs to get in better shape, into *game* shape, the coach stressed as November continued. "That's the thing I'm most gratified about," Adelman told the *Oregonian*'s Kerry Eggers. "Here's a guy who has had tremendous honors overseas and a lot of publicity, but he has never grumbled or complained to me about his playing time. He just keeps working hard."

There was something novel about the arrival of central and eastern Europeans in the NBA. These players were not coming to become stars or replace the league's name; instead, it was a voyage of belonging and surviving. The group that joined the league was proud, each of the players accomplished, each especially aware of the brief history of the Europeans who had tried before them. With the beginning of the 1989–90 NBA season there were both national and local stories in the papers about the group, the articles pushing the usual angles of a player living out his dream and of the adjustments, both in game and daily lifestyle. The group consisted of three Yugoslavs: Petrović, Vlade Divac, and Žarko Paspalj; two Soviets, Šarūnas Marčiulionis and Alexander Volkov, and a Norwegian player, Torgeir Byrn, who would play only three games before departing. There was something special about not only their presence in the NBA, but their willingness to surrender successful careers in Europe, where even though there was a significant drop in competition they enjoyed financial spoils and status.

There was a mild attempt at integration in 1985–86, when Georg Glouchkov of Bulgaria joined the Phoenix Suns, one year before Fernando Martin's brief stint with Portland. The Suns appeared willing to integrate Glouchkov, going to great financial lengths to secure him. They reportedly spent close to half a million dollars on his contract, not including the transfer fee to the Bulgarian league and the cost to then hire a translator. At first, communication seemed to be Glouchkov's main obstacle, but as the season wore on he gained a good deal of weight (a combination, it was theorized, of fast food and steroids) before falling out of favor with coach John MacLeod. He returned to Europe after one season.

Petrović was all too aware of the prior failures. He spoke to the *Oregonian* around the time of the 1988 Olympics about his reasons for not yet coming to Portland, and there was legitimate concern on his behalf about repeating the failures of Glouchkov and Martin. "I didn't want to go because I wanted to play," Petrović said of his previous moments of entertaining the idea of coming to Portland. "I didn't want to sit down like Fernando Martin and Georgi Glouchkov." For all the European entrants of 1989–90, the respective tales of Martin and Glouchkov always lurked in the background.

Among the early interest in the new European players, the consensus by basketball people seemed to be that Golden State's Šarūnas Marčiulionis, a guard from Lithuania, was the most NBA-ready of the entrants. The most noticeable indicator was his body—he was 6-foot-5 and a robust two-hundred pounds, with thick thighs and toned arms. His teammates marveled at the strength in those arms, especially in the wrists and hands, with his uncanny ability to *snatch* the ball as opposed to stealing it from the offensive player. His rise in basketball in the Soviet Union was in fact very different from that of his countryman, Arvydas Sabonis's, whose stardom seemed assured at an earlier age.

Marčiulionis came of age at the 1987 European championships in Greece as a twenty-three-year-old, and then had followed that up the next year in Seoul at the Olympics as the Soviets won the gold medal. Sabonis was injured entering Seoul, and though a physical presence had not played as well as many expected. However, Marčiulionis's play assured the Soviets a victory. He was the best player on the floor in the gold medal game against Yugoslavia, better for longer stretches than Petrović, and more impactful and sustained than Sabonis. In international play, opposing teams would try to defend him with height, but he welcomed the challenge with his drives generating contact, allowing him to develop a physical style of play that served him well in the NBA. He didn't have Petrović's outside shooting ability or offensive compulsion, but he was the possessor of the same type of fearlessness and confidence, the elements that separated them from their contemporaries.

Marčiulionis was highly thought of by the Americans, in some instances touted by them in part because his characteristics did not fit the pre-conceived notions that had been established about European players. He had benefited greatly from the Soviets' harmonious relationship with Ted Turner, and, by extension, the Atlanta Hawks. Marčiulionis starred in the summer of 1987 in four Pro-Am games on a mixed Soviet-Hawks team, and then a year later, in 1988, had played exceptionally well in three exhibitions for the national team against Atlanta. His style translated well.

It was Marčiulionis, not Petrović, who was rated by Marty Blake, the NBA's long-time chief of scouting, as the best player outside the United States prior to the 1989–90 season. For Marčiulionis and Petrović, the challenge would be playing against quality opposition every night, and so there was during the early judgment period a need for them to prove themselves. In Golden State, Marčiulionis found minutes in Don Nelson's hybrid system; for Petrović, Portland was more difficult.

Petrović approached his foray into the NBA as if it would define him. There was suspicion from friends that Petrović was highly driven to do something that no one else had achieved, that being the first European to have success in the league was important and everlasting to him. Goyak grew close to Petrović over the course of that rookie season, and noted that his disinterest in anything not related to his basketball career was total. There was rarely any conversation of any depth about another sport. There would be times when Petrović would speak with Goyak on the phone and he would be out of breath, having just finished a stint on the exercise bike in his apartment (even on game days). When Goyak spoke to Petrović about whether he would purchase a home in Portland or one of the neighboring suburbs, Petrović quickly changed the subject. "Buying a house is a distraction," Petrović often said. "I don't have time for that."

"He wanted to be the best he could be," Goyak said. "He was obsessed with making it."

Petrović was frugal by nature, largely in part, Goyak thought, because what arrived with money were potential distractions, a deviation on the march toward his lifelong goal. He loved cars, but didn't purchase one because a local Jeep dealer had given him a Cherokee—or "Che-*ro*-kee" as Petrović said in the commercial he did in return. In quieter moments, he spoke to Goyak of a dream he had of owning a speedboat and one day driving it along the Adriatic Sea. There were many dealers in the Portland area, Goyak informed him, but once again Petrović had resisted. "Only after I retire," he would emphasize, the implication always that relaxing was to be enjoyed only *after* all goals had been met.

One of the central figures in Petrović's life during his initiation in Portland—and someone who understood the goals that Petrović set for himself—was his girlfriend, Renata Cajić. It was Cajić who helped encourage Petrović to chase his NBA dreams over the summer of 1989, when the Madrid situation was cloudy and unknown. "She was very big in this, pushing him to challenge himself and go to the highest level," Warren LeGarie said of Cajić. A beautiful young woman with a sweet nature, she and Petrović began dating in 1986, and she quickly became a positive influence in his life. Whether in Europe or the United States she was never far from Petrović, even spending extended time with him during his rookie season, while juggling studies as a speech therapy student in Zagreb. With the help of Goyak, the young couple acclimated to Portland by being introduced to a group of Yugoslav families in the area. Within the circle of friends, they quickly became well-liked. "She was a delightful personality," Goyak said of Cajić. "They were a very attractive couple."

Cajić helped provide stability off the floor for Petrović when his on-court fortunes were still very much undetermined. With the 1989–90 season underway, the goal of playing and contributing appeared to be an arduous one.

Playing in the NBA was difficult enough. Cracking Portland's rotation, however, would prove to be the toughest opponent of Petrović's career.

Eleven

TRANSITION GAME, 1989–90

Portland, Oregon, USA

By mid-December 1989, Dražen Petrović gradually began to move in a direction his motivation could tolerate, supplanting Byron Irvin as the back-up shooting guard behind Clyde Drexler. Each of the early contributions was seen as a mini-milestone, with his first real significant performance coming in a December game against Houston, when Petrović scored 14 points in nineteen minutes. Afterward, Adelman spoke about the coaching staff's encouragement of Petrović to look for more of his shooting. "That's what he needs to give us to be effective," Adelman told reporters.

One of the initial challenges as Petrović began to gain more minutes was the increased pace of the new league. He was hesitant with his shooting, initially uncertain that he would have enough time to release. The nightly assignment was to play against bigger players who were quicker and faster with their reactions than his European opponents, and Petrović needed time to adjust. The coaches felt that he was passing up shots upon catching the ball, shots he should be taking. The uncertainty had led him to be holding the ball, dribbling into trouble, and either ridding himself of it or forcing a shot, hurting his usefulness. In discussing this, Adelman told the *Oregonian*'s Kerry Eggers that, for players less athletic than their opponents a split-second could be the difference between a clean shot or being left with nothing. Adelman felt that with Petrović's shooting ability and learning capacity, he could be successful in the mold of former Blazer Jim Paxson, a player of similar athletic capabilities who consistently found the required space to shoot the ball.

Petrović was a self-generating offensive player in Europe and the transformation in basketball from a creator to rhythm shooter was, he found, not easy. His natural inclination was to put the ball on the floor and create. In Europe, Petrović was practically unguardable, especially when a side of the floor was cleared for his approach. His offensive rhythm was often self-induced. However, in Portland, the coaches quickly preached to him the importance of developing the ability to catch and shoot, the rhythm no longer his to create. When he worked his way into the rotation, Petrović quickly noticed that most of his offensive opportunities were as a result of a teammate's penetration: a Drexler, a Terry Porter, a Danny Young—drive and kick to the open shooter. He began to work very hard on catching and—*boom,* as he called it—shooting. It was a reprogramming of his thinking; to ready himself to shoot the ball before the ball found him.

Petrović had always been very analytical of his own craft. He began working on ways to get open, to better use screens and find spots on the floor where he could be effective. He developed confidence as the months progressed, using his consistent rotation cameos to develop into a scoring reserve. He told reporters that with a minimum fifteen minutes of playing time he expected himself to generate at least 10 points. "That's very good production,"

Petrović told the *Statesman Journal.* "I scored 62 once, and I have that mentality that I can score."

There was a steady increase in Petrović's minutes and numbers. In December he played ten minutes per game for just under 5 points per game. In January he was up to thirteen minutes and over 7 points, and in February he came to fourteen minutes per game and an average of just under 9 points. Drexler missed a series of games that month and Petrović responded well to the additional time. He registered 22 points at Charlotte, 15 in each of two games against Cleveland, and Indiana. He remained a reserve in Drexler's absence, but he was playing more, and it was the first sustained patch of success in his NBA life.

There was something confirming about that stretch to Petrović; it gave him confidence in the face of his changing game. In the stretch of the season after the All-Star break he became a very good reserve: 9.7 points per game, 49 percent from the field and 50 percent from the three-point line, all in just fourteen minutes per game. He averaged 12 points on 56 percent shooting in fifteen minutes of playing time for the month of April, numbers that placed him among the best reserves for scoring in the league and easily the most efficient at his position. Petrović, with increased playing time, had shown an ability to quickly find spots where he could get off clean shots, and his percentages reflected that.

Being encouraged by his play did not equate to satisfaction for Petrović—his driven nature saw to that—and immediately, when one goal was met another opportunity became his pursuit. But there were also reminders that his opportunities would only reach a certain point. Goyak remembers an April game in Seattle that had particularly eaten away at Petrović. The Blazers put Petrović in the game in the second half and he got hot quickly, his 14 points helping Portland to a twelve-point lead. But his removal from the game coincided with a 20–3 Seattle scoring run, enough to force overtime. What stung Petrović was that Seattle came roaring back behind the play of two rookies of their own, Jim Farmer and Dana Barros. Farmer finished with 26 points and the Sonics eventually won in the extra session, with Petrović watching from the sidelines. Goyak spoke with Petrović about the situation in the hours after the game; Petrović was emotionally down, feeling that even when he was playing well there would always be a limit to his playing time.

To understand how Petrović was wired was also to come to terms with his sensitivity. He was immensely proud and armed with a strong sense of self-confidence, but he also believed passionately in the order of work. Putting in the time and effort, Petrović insisted, would lead to professional rewards. "In these situations he was always tough," Stojko Vranković, his closest friend and teammate from the national team, said. "If you practice hard, if you force yourself to be better and better, *I'm going to get those minutes*. He never lost confidence because he always tried to find a way out—the best solution."

The fluctuating and unguaranteed opportunity meant Portland was largely a very difficult time for him personally. Petrović spent copious amounts of time on the telephone, often in the hours after games, calling all corners of the world. There were daily calls to his family in Zagreb. Or Vranković in Thessaloniki, Greece; or Vlade Divac in Los Angeles; or Dino Radja in Rome, Italy; or Goyak in Portland, or others scattered throughout *his* universe, the basketball universe. They would be at once his comfort and sounding board. "I can do it, I can do it," Radja remembers hearing Petrović say to him from Portland. "I can play."

Remarkably, amidst the instability, Petrović's confidence remained stable and stubborn.

He was acutely aware of the hierarchy in Portland, respected it, and respected the greatness of Drexler and the talents of Porter.

And yet he also felt that there were more minutes that he could fill. "He certainly knew how good Clyde [Drexler] and Terry [Porter] were," said Brad Greenberg. What Petrović had difficulty accepting, Greenberg remembered, was that Danny Young was playing more minutes than he was. Young certainly filled Adelman's desire for a back-up to Porter, capably ran the team, and was more suited to that role than Petrović. But for Young to play more minutes was difficult to accept. "That drove him crazy," Greenberg said.

There were a great many teams in the league, many of them bad with little chemistry and little direction, that were in a position to offer Petrović more minutes and more opportunity. But Portland was a good team and quality franchise with exceptional talent. At their stage of development they didn't require an infusion among their core, but rather role players in order for the team to take the next step, players with an ability to provide one key element that the top teams pursue as a missing piece. Petrović provided shooting off the bench. That, for the time being, was to be his role.

The Blazers finished the 1990 season with a franchise-record 59 wins. There were many within the organization who felt that it was the addition of Buck Williams, a rugged power forward, who pushed the team beyond expectations. He was acquired from New Jersey prior to the season, and aside from providing selfless intangibles and a physical presence it had been thought that this example was his greatest influence. Drexler famously was a poor practice player, but it was noted from within that the arrival of Williams lit a fire under Portland's best player, and though statistically it wasn't Drexler's best season, it had been his most influential. With Williams and a better version of Drexler, Portland had within it the ability to play various tempos.

The team won twenty-nine of thirty-seven during a stretch from January to March, vaulting them to second in the Western Conference, their play suggesting they had become a contender in a brief period of time. Petrović was a contributor during this period, his minutes regular but limited to the low teens.

Dražen provided a major spark in the second game of Portland's opening-round playoff series with a talented and potentially dangerous Dallas Mavericks, scoring 12 points in the second quarter. But it was his gyrations and celebrations post-basket that brought the Portland Coliseum to life. It had been a season-long trend for Petrović; it was evident even early in the season that between him and the crowd there was a unique relationship. Perhaps only Drexler or Jerome Kersey, with their athleticism and dunking ability, could match Petrović's influence on the home folks. The excitement was usually generated by a distance shot, after which Petrović would turn to them and celebrate, as if in Šibenik or Zagreb.

The *Columbian*'s Al Crombie noticed this and thought Petrović similar to Billy Ray Bates, a meteoric Blazer with whom the crowd had become enamored in the early eighties due to his innocence and unharnessed talent. An uncommonly devoted fan base such as Portland's was naturally susceptible to falling for a player like Petrović, whose game, dating back to Europe, was always to involve the crowd. "Dražen had a childlike quality of really being genuine," said Goyak. "I think everyone saw an unusual childlike enthusiasm that was very infectious. When a team would rally and take the lead, that's spontaneous and enthusiastic. There is a special aura in youth that lasts before the game becomes a job, and Dražen had that."

Petrović finished with 14 points in the win, and the Blazers completed a three-game sweep of the Mavericks before moving on to face San Antonio in the Western Semi-Finals. The Spurs, like Portland, were a drastically improved team in 1990, invigorated by the arrival of rookie center, David Robinson. The teams traded home wins through the first four games, and the critical fifth game in Portland went to overtime. Drexler fouled out in the first extra session and Adelman decided to go with Petrović. It was, to that point, his most meaningful NBA minutes. In the final minute of the second overtime, with the Blazers holding a one-point lead, the ball had found its way into Petrović's hands. With the shot clock winding down, he pump-faked a three-pointer, split two San Antonio defenders, and launched a jumper from seventeen feet. His fist-pump to the crowd told the story. Petrović's basket pushed the Blazers to a 134–131 lead, giving them enough room to outlast a stubborn Spurs team.

Petrović finished with 11 points in twenty-nine minutes, his third double-figure game off the bench for the series. His contributions were coming in meaningful games, outlining his progress since the season's start.

He scored 8 points in twenty-eight minutes in the sixth game (Drexler was plagued by foul trouble), which San Antonio won easily, setting the stage for the deciding match in Portland. It was a great game, favored Portland trying to hold off a Spurs team that had gained in confidence as the series wore on, there being a genuine belief after the near-miss in the fifth game that they could prevail on the road.

There was a critical sequence near the end of regulation for San Antonio with its two-point lead, when both Rod Strickland and Robinson missed from short range, which led to a gutsy dive and outlet pass by Porter, and a dunk for Kersey. That four-point swing tied a game that would eventually persevere to overtime. Strickland once again was a central figure in the play that finally finished off San Antonio. He incorrectly anticipated a cut by teammate Sean Elliott, threw the ball over his head to no one, and watched as Kersey saved the ball with a full-court pass to Drexler. In the end, Portland outlasted San Antonio, 108–105, winning the series four games to three.

Petrović played little in the seventh game. Adelman went heavily with his starters, with only Kevin Duckworth, suffering from a broken hand, playing fewer than forty-six minutes. It left little for Petrović, who scored 5 points in seven minutes. The hero was indisputably Porter, with 36 points and nine assists. Even with Drexler holding the mantle as the team's best player, Porter seemed to rise most for the bigger and more important games. In the final two home games against San Antonio he scored a staggering 74 points.

For the first time since the title year of 1977, Portland advanced to the Western Conference Finals. Waiting for them was not the Lakers, who had appeared there every year but once since 1979, but instead a talented and explosive Phoenix Suns team. Phoenix had set aside Los Angeles with relative ease, needing just five games to advance. It was a fortunate happenstance for Portland, the result handing them home-court advantage. They needed it, too, winning the opening two games against the Suns by one and two points respectively. Petrović was most aggressive in the opener, scoring all 11 of his points in the second quarter.

Phoenix, like San Antonio, proved a difficult team to beat. Portland needed a shot by Duckworth with seventeen seconds to go to win the opener, and then overcame a twenty-two point deficit in the second game to win behind a Porter bucket with fourteen seconds left. Phoenix then went home and won two in routs. Portland held a 3–2 advantage when the teams moved to Phoenix for the sixth game. Petrović began the fourth quarter on the floor and ignited his team. With the Suns up five, he broke free for a three-pointer at the top of the key, and on the next possession received the outlet pass, dribbled the floor and pulled up for another long jumper. In what would be a Petrović trademark that survived his jump from Europe to the NBA, he instantly turned to the official, seeking confirmation that it was a three-pointer. "No, Dražen," CBS's Dick Stockton announced during the game, "it's a two."

It was a confident, ballsy shot, especially in a crucial road game. Three possessions later, off a Duckworth block, he leaked out for the contested lay-up. Petrović scored 7 points in two minutes, and Portland had pulled back to even.

The starters would take it from there. Portland held on to win by three, the ball landing appropriately in the arms of Williams as time expired; instantly, he was mobbed by his teammates, among them Petrović. He was to be the first European player to appear in the NBA Finals.

Portland met the defending champion Detroit Pistons for the title. Detroit was a confident team, an odd elitist group that had muscled its way into the league's upper echelon, succeeding Boston as the Eastern Conference power and joining the Lakers at the top as the eighties concluded. Detroit won the 1989 championship, and yet the Pistons were hardly a national treasure. They had established a rugged, dirty identity, but what lay beneath was an exceptionally competitive and deep two-way team, very sure of themselves and their capabilities. Led by Isiah Thomas and coach Chuck Daly, they entered the finals with Portland as favorite.

Ultimately, it was their depth that propelled Detroit to another title. Thomas saved them in the opener, taking over late to secure the win before Portland stole the second game in overtime. It had been sixteen years since Detroit last won in Portland, but they waltzed into game three with confidence and left with a fifteen-point win. The circulating statistic by the media about a win-drought in Portland had been foolish, as the hardened, determined Pistons were a terrific road team that embraced entering a loud building and leaving it deafeningly quiet.

Game four proved to be a microcosm of the series. The Blazers started strong, but Detroit's bench turned the game on its head, and in the end they would outscore Portland's reserves by eighteen (it was twenty-three in the third game).

"It," Adelman said of the second quarter run by Detroit's bench to reporters, "was the turning point of the game."

Game five saw Portland lead by seven with just two minutes remaining, but Detroit stormed back. A 14-footer by Vinnie Johnson with less than a second on the clock proved to be the winner, 92–90. The Pistons were once again world champions. At the other end of the floor, Petrović sat and watched from the bench. It was a place from which he didn't move. By that point in the series Adelman had opted not to use him, instead going with Danny Young as his third guard against Detroit's alignment of Johnson, Thomas, and Joe Dumars.

When he did see minutes, it proved to be a difficult and unproductive series for Petrović. There was a brief moment of daylight in the second game, Portland's only win, when he hit for four field goals and 8 points in thirteen minutes. But otherwise, the series was a struggle. He found it troubling establishing himself defensively against Detroit's tough guards, and as a result he met with foul trouble: three fouls in four minutes in game one, two fouls in the second game, and three fouls in eight scoreless minutes in the third game. Consequently, it hindered his effectiveness.

By the fifth game he was strictly a spectator, a harrowing finish to a rookie season of both frustration and encouraging development.

Detroit was the better team and, more importantly, the *deeper* one, and Portland came away from the Finals with an honest evaluation of what was needed to take another step toward the title. What resulted was the off-season acquisition of a proven veteran to bolster their bench. The problem was, Danny Ainge played the shooting guard position. For Petrović, heartbreak was coming. But eventually, a new direction would emerge that drastically altered his life and career.

Dražen, aged two months, with five-year-old brother Aleksander in 1964.

The Petrović family celebrating Dražen's fifth birthday, October 1969.

Dražen surrounded by classmates during his final year of high school in Šibenik.

Photos courtesy of the Petrović family.

Held aloft by the home crowd moments after securing the 1983 Yugoslav League Title.

A heated battle between Dražen and Aleksandar (left) during the infancy of their professional careers.

Celebrating outside the Šibenik Town Hall. It was later taken from Šibenka in controversial fashion.

Enjoying life at his downtown apartment in Zagreb, mid-eighties.

It was his flashy style with Cibona of Zagreb where Petrović earned the nickname, "The Mozart of Basketball."

Arvydas Sabonis brought out the very best in Dražen. Here, they are matched in the final of the 1986 European Cup at Budapest, just two months before both were taken by the Portand Trail Blazers in the NBA Draft.

Launching a jump-shot over Vlade Divac of Partizan Belgrade. The two would spearhead the national team glory of the late eighties and early nineties, only to later see their friendship become a casualty of the war in Yugoslavia.

Photos courtesy of the Dražen Petrović Memorial Center

Photo courtesy of the Dražen Petrović Memorial Center

It was his ability to involve the fans in the game that made Dražen among the marquee athletes in all of Europe in the eighties.

At Cibona, Dražen became one of the elite players in Europe, and forced the Yugoslav Basketball Federation to break a long-standing rule on athletes who couldn't leave before the age of twenty-eight.

Photo courtesy of the Portland Trail Blazers.

At the introductory press conference with Blazers president Harry Glickman, after freeing himself from Real Madrid in the fall of 1989.

Photo courtesy of the Petrović family.

During his time with Portland, Dražen was buoyed by the constant support of loved ones (from left), Biserka, Jole, and then-girlfriend Renata Cajić.

As a rookie, Dražen was able to make the most of limited opportunities: 7.6 points in 12.6 minutes per game.

With best friend from the Croatian national team, Stojko Vranković, enjoying a jovial moment in 1992.

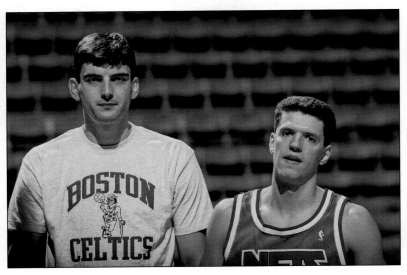

Dražen and Stojko before a Nets–Celtics game at the Boston Garden in the spring of 1991.

In New Jersey, Dražen came of age. He averaged 20.6 points during the 1991–92 season, and upped it to 24.3 in the team's playoff series against the Cleveland Cavaliers.

In his two full seasons in New Jersey, Dražen averaged 21.4 points per game, and was named to the 1993 All-NBA third team.

Photos courtesy of Steve Lipofsky, BasketballPhoto.com.

Dražen Petrović, 1964–1993.

Twelve

I WANT TO BE TRADED, 1990–91

Portland, Oregon, USA

Several weeks after losing to the Detroit Pistons in the NBA Finals, Dražen Petrović was back in Portland to participate on its summer league team. It would be a valuable experience, an opportunity to pause and learn after having missed the prior training camp. There were certainly many lessons and realities to be taken from that first season, things that would be applied to the work of the summer. The Portland staff requested that he remain in town and play in one of the competitions they entered at Salt Lake City. Anxious to improve, Petrović gladly complied. The coaches in passing told Petrović that one of their goals was for him to diversify offensively, to take a look at him at times as the point guard, the European Petrović in a diluted, controlled sense.

Brad Greenberg was tasked with putting the summer team together. The potential always was that it be an erratic squad, as the mix of talent was distributed between players with some league experience, genuine talents looking to take the next step, and then the aspirants, borderline league talent desperate for an opportunity. There was no extended period of practice before competition, and it ensured that the product had the potential for sloppiness. In mid-July 1990, Greenberg took a call from Mike Krzyzewski, who was coaching the United States team that was to participate first in that summer's Goodwill Games in Seattle before the world championships in Argentina. Krzyzewski was interested in getting his group a taste of game action as they moved toward Seattle, and asked Greenberg if it were possible to scrimmage the Portland team. Greenberg agreed. The United States team was immensely talented, headlined by serious collegiate names, such players as Georgetown's Alonzo Mourning, Georgia Tech's Kenny Anderson, and Billy Owens of Syracuse, each potential lottery picks. The game was not close, and in the end the United States overwhelmed a scratchy Portland team, winning the scrimmage by 30 points.

Petrović was forced to play exclusively the point guard position that day due to the team's lack of depth. He did not have a particularly good performance. The following day, Petrović, clutching a copy of that day's *Oregonian* newspaper, tracked down Greenberg. It contained a recap of the game and made reference to Petrović's poor showing at the point guard position.

"You see this?" Petrović said, pointing to the paper. Greenberg nodded.

"I will tell you something, Brad," Petrović continued. "In Argentina [at the world championships], we will play against this team, and we will beat them. No problem. I will score 30 points, and we will win."

Greenberg smiled. *This is a guy who knows what he can do.* What was impressive, Greenberg thought, was that despite the bad game and the worse review, Petrović remained confident—

vengeful even—in his ability should he meet the United States later that summer.[17]

There was some value in staying for the summer and working for Petrović, but his future in Portland became cloudier when the team acquired guard Danny Ainge. Ainge had been unhappy in Sacramento, and Portland was interested in him for a period of months after the Finals before prying him from the Kings at a small cost: little-used Byron Irvin and two draft picks, a deal which was most favorable. Portland had been disappointed in the performance of their reserves in the Finals against Detroit—over five games Detroit received on average 25 points from their bench to Portland's nine—and targeted Ainge as a primary solution.[18]

There was much logic in obtaining Ainge. He was proven and dependable, a name that was associated with winning and experience, elements that organizations gravitated toward, especially ones on the cusp of contending for a title. He had for the first seven years of his career been a guard with the Celtics, a valuable contributor on those great Bird-led championship teams with envious combinations of chemistry and total talent.

One of Ainge's charms was that he was effective both as a point and shooting guard. He possessed a terrific outside shot and toughness, in addition to being a high-quality complementary player alongside great players. The ability to coexist with elite-

17 Yugoslavia indeed met the United States in Argentina that August in a semi-final, winning by eight. Petrović, who overcame an illness that plagued him for a large portion of the tournament, scored 31 points. The Yugoslavs then won the final against the Soviet Union to claim the world title.

18 They also had targeted Milwaukee's Ricky Pierce, a terrific scorer off the bench who for years had been the league's gold standard reserve, but the Bucks showed disinterest in Portland's offers, making acquiring Ainge the singular focus.

level players was something not always properly appreciated in the NBA, and Ainge's skill set seemed particularly complementary when with Boston's vaunted frontline. At a time when Boston seemed to be pitted annually in the postseason against such teams as Philadelphia, Los Angeles, or Milwaukee, he was seen as an irritant and complainer, a source of disdain by opposing fans. It was in direct contrast to the esteem in which his teammates held him, for they loved his sense of humor and confidence, his dependability and fearless approach to taking important shots. Ainge had been the first to go as the Celtics took the first steps in transition from the glorious eighties, traded to Sacramento midway through the 1988–89 season, and though his numbers were greatly improved as their featured player, his shooting percentage went down, as the Kings were a poorly built team.

At age thirty-one, Ainge was much better suited as a complementary player. In Portland he could serve as a quality back-up to both Drexler and Porter, at times to even play alongside them. His skills as both shot maker and ball handler were essentially what the Blazers had hoped Petrović would bring when he arrived a year earlier, but he rarely was employed as a point guard, and those skills had not quickly developed against NBA-level defensive pressure. Portland explored the option of moving Petrović in the wake of getting Ainge; there had been interest from teams, mostly in the Eastern Conference, including New Jersey, Boston, and Washington, as well as a gunning Denver team, which held high opinions of Petrović as a shooter and offensive player. Portland realized that with the addition of Ainge there was something of a logjam at the guard positions (Drexler and Porter as the starting guards, Ainge and Danny Young their respective back-ups), and it was at that point the idea of moving Petrović was raised. "A lot of people saw him as being one of the best shooters in the league," said Bucky Buckwalter. "Everybody knew how much he loved the game, how much time he put in through practice, what a great team player, the need to win, wanting to contribute. So there was a lot of interest. To get a small forward that was a great shooter; that was the only way I'd be willing to give up on the guy."

There was a brief discussion with Washington about a swap for Bernard King, but the talks never progressed and the deal passed.[19]

So Petrović remained in Portland, and in the preseason he competed for minutes with Ainge. In time the two grew to be quite fond of each other and became friendly, despite the fact they were battling for the same spot in the rotation. The bonding occurred over shooting games after practice, and once done Petrović would invariably move from the court to the weight room; it was there that Ainge witnessed his uncommon devotion to the game. There was on one occasion during training camp, between the first and second practice sessions, when Ainge joined Petrović at Dražen's apartment. Ainge took a short nap on the couch, and shortly thereafter woke to find Petrović pedaling furiously on a stationary bike, even though there was a second practice fast approaching. "I never in my life saw anyone who wanted to succeed in the NBA more than Dražen," Ainge later told Sam Smith of the *Chicago Tribune*.

Adelman came to the conclusion at some point in the exhibition season that he did not feel comfortable playing both Ainge and Petrović at the same time, fearful of the exploitation that the opposition could have on them defensively. Playing Ainge

19 The Bullets had been a persistent inquirer about Petrović, dating back to his rookie year. General Manager Bob Ferry once called and offered his leading scorer, Jeff Malone, for Petrović and the rights to an absent Arvydas Sabonis, which Portland rejected.

and Petrović together, Adelman felt, would take something away from Ainge. As the better of the two defensively, Ainge would be expected to spend more energy on a better offensive player and then have to handle the ball at the other end—as opposed to playing off it. These were the subtle infractions that coaches agonized over, often envisioned as potentially providing the difference in a basketball game, and Adelman ultimately decided against playing them together.

When the season began, Adelman's preference for playing Ainge proved to be a valid one, as Ainge played the reserve guard role at a level significantly above the expectations Portland had for him. In the first month of the 1990–91 season, Ainge averaged 14 points on 58 percent shooting from the field, remarkable for a player who shot primarily from the outside. His play in the beginning of the season seemed to mirror that of the Blazers, who jumped out of the blocks. The Portland team that began the 1990–91 season had the feel of a team on the verge of something special. They carried with them a confidence borne from the overwhelming success of the previous season, proof that they were not an aspirant, but in fact a legitimate contender. They passed early season tests against the Lakers, Pistons, and Bulls, teams that were thought to be the only true contenders for a championship. It was the manner with which they were defeating teams, frequently recording high scoring totals with a large point differential.

Portland was, at least offensively, a team with no discernible weaknesses. They were led by the brilliance of Drexler, but balanced beautifully with depth. Porter was now an elite-level point guard. Buck Williams and Kevin Duckworth were a formidable four-five combination. There was the athleticism and energy of Jerome Kersey and Cliff Robinson. And, now, they had added Ainge's experience and outside shooting. Alongside the obvious chemistry was also tangible evidence: the Blazers won their first eleven, nineteen of their first twenty, and twenty-seven of thirty. These were streaks capable of igniting talk of historic seasons, and sat cozily alongside the previous best starts in league history. In the image of its best player, Drexler, it was a team of confidence but not of arrogance. They were not a team that delighted in the act of captioning their performance to the opponent but rather were a likeable group, athletic and skilled, and very fun to watch, particularly at the offensive end of the floor.

Petrović was a bystander to this, close to the reflection that beamed off the quick start. He was very much a team member with his practice habits and commitment, but at the same time was an outsider in the sense of being a contributor to the winning. November came and went, and he appeared in just five contests. In the end that total of appearances would move no further than eighteen games in his second season in Portland. Though as a rookie there were periods of frustration over minutes, there was a minor, gradual increase as the season played out. There was at least the assurance that with his arrival at the arena he would appear in the game. In his second season, there was no such assurance. The arrival of Ainge ended that, and in fact pushed Petrović not to the fourth spot on the guard rotation but to fifth. To Adelman he was neither a suitable first back-up for point guard or shooting guard, leaving him to a spectator role.

Petrović played just nine minutes in a thirty-one point home win over the Clippers on November 11, his first appearance of the season, as Portland moved to five straight wins without a defeat. Portland led by twenty-nine at the end of the third quarter, and yet it wasn't until three minutes passed in the fourth that Adelman called for Petrović. After the game, Petrović placed a call to his agent, Warren LeGarie. That night the agent listened to a desperate young man, the two discussing the situation long into the night. LeGarie played the role of positive confidant, promising that better days were ahead, surely in a new city with a new team. Petrović was at that point in the depths of his lowest moment as a professional, each call to a family member or friend coming in a despondent tone. The following morning he went to discuss the situation in the office of Geoff Petrie, a former standout in the franchise's early life who was in his first season as the vice-president of basketball operations. Petrović was direct in the meeting, informing Petrie that in order for him to receive the opportunity he felt he deserved he would need to leave Portland—that he would like to be traded.

Petrović had reached a point of desperation. Petrie sensed this, and told Petrović that he felt it was a request that had been fueled by his emotions. Petrie explained to Petrović that the team would be the one who would decide when and if a trade would be made, while adding that, behind Drexler and Ainge, Petrović was a valued commodity. In the case of an injury or absence, Petrie said, his services would suddenly be required and that *there* would be his opportunity. That his services would be left to chance didn't appeal to Petrović.

The day after Dražen's meeting with Petrie, the Blazers hosted a bad Denver team and beat them easily by 26 points, with Petrović playing only the game's final two minutes. When the team gathered for practice the following morning, Petrović decided to make public what he had discussed with Petrie. "I want to be traded," Petrović told Dwight Jaynes, the team's beat writer for the *Oregonian*. "I'm the twelfth man on the roster and I don't deserve that. I'm not being treated fairly. I tried to be patient, but it's not working. I am ready to go. I don't want to put pressure on Rick. He has already settled on a rotation. I'm not saying I'm better than Clyde [Drexler], Terry [Porter] or Danny Ainge. I just want to be traded. I don't want to stay here, because I'm not getting a chance."

Petrović also had mentioned to Jaynes that if his request was not met within fifteen days, which would take him to the final day of November, then he would leave Portland and the United States and go back to Yugoslavia to revive his career. There was very little logic in that particular ultimatum, for the rules at the time dictated he could not sign or play with a European team while under contract with Portland. If nothing else, the comments spoke of his intense desperation, even his helplessness; a return to Europe was in essence a signal of failure in some form, with the ghosts of Georgi Glouchkov and Fernando Martin hovering somewhere close behind. Petrović had never wanted to be Glouchkov or Martin, he had wanted to be the first success story, the first to break through and change the attitudes held towards Europeans.

It was not the public trade request that angered the Blazers organization but the threat of leaving for Yugoslavia. Jaynes, as he was journalistically entitled, sought a response from Petrie, and it was obvious he had not been pleased. "To me, it's patently unfair on his part to say that." Adelman, too, had not been happy with Petrović's public comments and was pointed in his remarks. "Let's be realistic. Here's a guy who averaged seven points a game last year. This is not an All-Star player," he told Jaynes. "We have a lot of guys playing ahead of him who are very good players. Who's to say that won't happen to him somewhere else, too? I think he's getting some very bad advice."

The advice Adelman was referring to was LeGarie's, whom many within the Blazers organization felt was behind Petrović's decision to first go to Petrie and then go public with his desire to be traded. In that first year, Petrović had shown LeGarie that he understood his situation, but there were times when playing only eight to ten minutes per game had been difficult for him. What LeGarie noticed, however, in that first year was Petrović's resolve even in the face of the uncertainty. LeGarie had been in basketball for a long time. He had been around a great many young players and had seen some of them develop the idea that their efforts were being wasted and that their continued output would never change the circumstances. In time their resolve would slowly erode, and, LeGarie noticed, gradually their dedication and enthusiasm would suffer, too. Ultimately, they would slowly release the grip on their dreams before giving up. But Petrović was different in that regard, LeGarie soon realized in that first year. Practice would finish and most of the players would file out, but Petrović would stay, isolate himself as he always had, and shoot for an hour or sometimes longer. Portland's assistant coach John Wetzel remembers many times leaving his office in the minutes after the morning shootaround that the team held on game days, and seeing Petrović alone in the gym. "Dražen, you have to go home, we have a game tonight," Wetzel would yell out on the floor.

What the coaching staff did not realize was that Petrović would often leave the Blazers' practice facility and then later in the afternoon go to a gym on the city's waterfront that he liked to frequent. For hours he would shoot on his own. "Three hundred today," he would say to LeGarie on the phone before going out.

"What, three hundred shots?" LeGarie would answer.

"Nope, three hundred makes."

"A lot of guys would have held a pity party," LeGarie said later about Petrović's limited minutes. "And all Dražen did was hold a sweat party. He used his work ethic to see him through what clearly was a difficult time."

By the second season, LeGarie saw the writing on the wall and became determined to shield Petrović from the fallout, to protect him from the breakdown that had befallen other young players who had given up. There were several people inside the Blazers' front office whom LeGarie would over time use as a sounding board to tout his client, endorsing him for a greater opportunity and more consistent playing time. There was never any conversation of that type with Adelman, whom LeGarie became disappointed in over his lack of communication with Petrović on matters relating to his playing time. "You expect people to at least give him thirty seconds of conversation, for encouragement, keeping working, we'll try to find more minutes for you—none of that conversation came," LeGarie remembered. "That's where I felt I needed to fight for Dražen in order for him to still stay inspired and to fight for himself."

A situation that at first seemed confined to Petrović, and both Adelman and Petrie, began to run deeper when LeGarie took his feelings to the newspapers. "One of the major problems is," LeGarie explained to John Hillyer of the *San Francisco Examiner*, "Rick has never been able to tell Dražen to his face, 'Hey, I really don't like you.' Or to the owners themselves, 'Hey, I really don't believe in the kid.'" Adelman, like everyone in the Blazers organization, saw the comments. He was writing a book with Jaynes that year, a diary-style account of his rising team, and it was on that platform that he had decided to directly address LeGarie and his involvement with the Petrović situation. "The one thing I resented more than anything was that his agent, Warren LeGarie, told Dražen to make the statement, thinking he could force us to trade him or play him," Adelman wrote. "He was saying things about our team and about me, saying I was lying. He said I didn't like Dražen, and it was totally untrue."

"I wonder if I could have used more diplomatic ways of doing things," LeGarie would say later. "And you always look back and think of things you could have done that were more accommodating, but ultimately at that point I became as emotional as probably Dražen, which can be good, but also still be not always in the best taste. You still have to be the level head. I also knew at that moment the only way that Portland was going to be motivated to do something was if they felt they had more to lose if they did not make the trade as opposed to making it and gaining something in the process. It was a difficult time. It probably affected my—it did—affect my relationship with Rick for many years."

The day after Petrović publicly told Jaynes of his desire to be traded he was fined $500 by the club. Then, at the team's next practice, he met with Adelman for a significant amount of time, player and coach airing their feelings to one another, with Petrović telling Adelman that when he doesn't play he doesn't feel part of the team. Everything was out and open. Petrović would stay and continue to work, the forty-eight hour rumbling not penetrating the team's forceful on-court start.

Petrović's status in the Portland rotation essentially remained unchanged from December into January, with what scant minutes he received during meaningless situations, games in which the result had been decided a quarter—or in some instances two quarters—earlier by the powerful Blazers. He appeared in eighteen games in that second season in Portland, only one—a five-point loss in Milwaukee—of which was decided by ten points or fewer, and some ten games ending with margins of greater than twenty points. Petrović was in a rotational rut, stuck behind Drexler and Ainge, and by some extension Porter, the three of them having near-infinite playing time that season. The balance and dependability of Portland's backcourt left Adelman with no reason to entertain the idea of mixing his guard rotation, not with the wins coming with such frequency and the team playing so well.

The Blazers in turn were fielding interest in Petrović, in one form or another, since Ainge's arrival months earlier. In January 1991 they finally found a deal that suited them. The team managed to work a trade with New Jersey involving a third participant, Denver, which saw them gain Walter Davis, a thirty-six-year-old forward and former All-Star. He was exactly the type of player Buckwalter and Portland had vowed as an acceptable trade for Petrović, and Davis's numbers had looked especially seductive in Denver's exaggerated offense. Portland was happy to get Davis, for there was no denying his professional chops, especially when he had been so readily sought after by other title-chasers, including Chicago.

On the day that the deal seemed a very real possibility, Adelman took Petrović aside before a home game with Phoenix, informing him of the tentative three-team agreement reached, but cautioning him that nothing was final. "Don't assume that it's over," Adelman told Petrović in an attempt to keep him mentally ready for the contest, one in which he would not play.

When the game ended and the players went to the locker room, Petrović immediately began to pack his belongings. He had been traded, Petrović announced to his teammates. There was in that room mixed emotions for Petrović, as well as a few tears. He said good-bye to the players and the reporters. Though happy for his freedom, he had come to Portland with much promise, which had been left only for interpretation. Portland first discovered him in the magic of the infancy of the Cibona era, when there was more hair and less maturity and the high point totals. They had then drafted him, established and maintained a long-distance relationship, and felt confident that he could make the leap. They reinforced that belief by going to great lengths in order to free him from Spain and secure his services. Petrović had made friends and become to the fans one of their true favorites.

Ultimately, however, it was all superseded by the self-confidence of the young man, his insistence on searching for a light and a way out, the opportunity for which he had worked all his life.

Thirteen

SECOND LIFE, 1991

East Rutherford, New Jersey, USA

There was genuine intrigue on the part of the staff of the New Jersey Nets after the arrival of Dražen Petrović. Willis Reed, the team's president of basketball operations who was so persistent in his calls to Portland showing interest in Petrović, told reporters after the trade that his new shooting guard had the tools and potential to be a very good offensive player in the league. Above that, Reed was aware that Petrović had a strong desire to be successful, and that sort of motivation appealed to the Knicks legend. "He really wants to be the first great European player to be a great NBA player," Reed told John Jackson of the *Record*. It was a bold move by Reed to surrender a first-round pick for an unproven, yet well-paid ($1.2 million in 1991) European player, but he saw something in Petrović and thought that with his ability to shoot there would be a place for him in New Jersey.

The team's head coach, Bill Fitch, had in a lot of ways more knowledge of Petrović than he ordinarily would for an incoming player. The two shared Warren LeGarie as an agent, and that led to Fitch listening many nights on the phone to LeGarie, discussing different players, including Petrović, and their characteristics. Petrović was highly recommended both as a player and a person by LeGarie in the weeks leading up to the trade, but LeGarie had begun to wonder just exactly how much stock Fitch was taking in the repeated touting of his own client. "I had a lot of confidence in Warren when it came to describing the worth of a person's value other than basketball," Fitch said. "And he was very high on Dražen as a person."

Fitch had, from his conversations with LeGarie, taken some time to look into Petrović's situation in Portland. He noticed that, in a limited amount of playing time, especially as a rookie, Petrović had shown tremendous potential as a shooter. Petrović shot 46 percent from three-point range in that first year, despite averaging only twelve minutes per game. That, Fitch thought, was not an easy thing to do. "The one thing that he was doing in Portland when he got some time, was shooting," Fitch said. "He's just playing with the wrong team."

For years, beginning in his days coaching Houston and continuing in New Jersey, Fitch received league statistical reports from a man named Roger Newell, the son of the great teacher Pete Newell, and brother of Fitch's lead Nets assistant, Tom. Beginning the prior season, Fitch noticed Petrović's name showing up in the statistical reports, portraying his offensive ability very favorably. Newell's reports, which were respected league-wide (the first two clients to subscribe to his service were Jerry Colangelo in Phoenix and Jerry West in Los Angeles), were based on productivity. The requirements were to play a minimum of ten minutes per game, and what Newell called his "hidden productivity" would be derived from minutes played, shots taken, and shots made. The end result would be a plus or minus figure that, based on minutes played, could tell which players were good at creating offense on their own, with what range or diversity, and with what proficiency.

In his year-and-a-half in Portland, Petrović had regularly been a top-ten player in the league on two of Newell's in-season offensive reports—offensive productivity and three-point efficiency—and Fitch had remembered that after acquiring him. It left him confident that Petrović could provide a boost to the team's outside shooting, an area that had been sorely lacking.

Petrović arrived in New Jersey having played very little in the season's first three months, and so those early weeks were difficult, especially with Fitch. The veteran coach had developed a reputation in his time in the league as a very hard man, but with that hardness could turn teams that were floundering into successful ones. He had done so with expansion Cleveland in the early seventies, with Boston in the late seventies (a team that seldom needed rescuing to that point and would eventually win the title in 1980–81) and then Houston, a talented but emotional team that he took to the Finals after upending the Lakers in 1986.

There was attached to the Fitch-hardness narrative a well-known Marine background. His father was a drill instructor, and as an only child Fitch was raised with discipline and toughness. His voice when angry could reach a deep, piercing level, enough to put fear into most men, and it only added to his reputation as a demanding coach. His training camps were legendary for their degree of difficulty. When Fitch took the Nets job in 1989, Bob Ryan of the *Boston Globe* wrote that his new players would quickly find three things: what pain was, what the phrase *sucking wind* meant, and that they may soon have a strong distaste for basketball. But, Ryan was quick to point out, there was a very good chance under Fitch that they would become fifty percent better basketball players. Fitch spent a season out of coaching after he left Houston, and he was sought after by the expansion teams seeking a builder. But he had been down that path before in Cleveland, and held out for another position, eventually beating out Doug Collins and Mike Fratello for the New Jersey position.

The Nets' position was not a particularly envious one. Historically in the NBA they were a snake-bitten franchise, a contrast to their glorious ABA existence, when they had won two titles. The leader of those title teams was Julius Erving, but the Nets sold him to Philadelphia upon their jumping of leagues, and with it seemed to follow a trail of unfortunate happenstances. In the eighties, there would be the occasional glimmer of hope, but it was usually squashed quickly. There were seven coaches in that decade alone before Fitch signed on, six playoff appearances and just one venture into the second round. There was an All-Star guard removed from the league for drug use, in Michael Ray Richardson. There was also one of the league's top coaches, Larry Brown, asked by ownership to resign six games before the end of the 1983 regular season after it was revealed that Brown was entertaining the idea of moving to coach at the University of Kansas. The irony was that Brown had been leading the best Nets team of the decade, one that captured forty-nine wins. "Every time we did well and we would start to climb the ladder, something bad happened," said Herb Turetzky, the Nets' official scorer, who had been with the team since its birth as the New Jersey Americans of the ABA.

The Nets' attempts at building a new era began in 1988 when the team hired Reed, then an assistant coach in Sacramento, as its head coach midway through the season. Reed initially wanted to take over the team at the end of that season but ownership pushed for him to take over immediately, and that had not served him well, with the team stumbling at both the half-season and then his only full season of 1989. The team then moved Reed upstairs to a managerial role before hiring Fitch. Fitch had coached in the league for eighteen seasons by the time he got to New Jersey prior to 1989–90; he had seen bad teams and had coached some in Cleveland, and he was confident that he could turn around the team's fortunes, even if historically it seemed against some sort of natural order.

After Fitch's first season, one that ended with just seventeen wins, they landed the first pick in the college draft and with it the right to take Derrick Coleman, a power forward from Syracuse. Coleman was perhaps most suited to lead the Nets: he was talented and loaded with potential, but was thought to be erratic and a resistor against authority. It was as if, when talking about Coleman, there were within him separate entities: the basketball player and then the personality, entities indeed that appeared incompatible and far apart in nature. He was, at his best, almost a beautiful player, not a banger or plodder. He could, at 6-foot-10, take the ball off the board and bring it up, handle it with flash and grace. Offensively, he was a very good back-to-the-basket player, but he could also face the basket, shoot from distance, or create off the dribble. Above all, coaches and teammates would marvel at the mind he had for the game, and it was perhaps that—the *He knows better*—that infuriated them when he inevitably deviated, caused trouble, or was difficult to deal with. Coleman would comfortably win the award as the league's top rookie, even if the team wasn't a great deal better than before he arrived.

Coleman had joined a team that was not cohesive but was instead composed of odd parts. They were led by Reggie Theus, like Coleman a player whose talent was never to come under question, but it was his motives, often branded individualistic, that seemed to taint the game and reputation around the league. There was the small forward, Chris Morris, a former lottery pick and athlete rivaled by few league-wide, but the consensus was that he was a poor decision-maker on the floor and prone to bouts of erraticism. Mookie Blaylock was, like Morris, a lottery pick from the late eighties who had also struggled with consistency, even when it was obvious that the point guard was very talented on both ends of the floor. Sam Bowie was acquired from Portland, but when the center wasn't fighting his constant health issues he was pitted against the disappointment that came with being the second overall selection of the 1984 draft.

The team was in bad shape when they traded for Petrović in the late winter of 1991, just a game and a half out of last place in the Eastern Conference. They had little in the way of hopeful aspirations, another season spiraling downward.

His first few weeks in New Jersey, even with regular playing opportunities, were difficult for Petrović. He arrived in good physical condition, but with his limited and sporadic minutes in Portland, he had been left in poor game shape. In practice Fitch was hard on him, first about his conditioning, and then about his individual defense. Tom Newell, one of Fitch's assistant coaches, looked at the situation and thought, *Bill is trying to break him.* "Bill was a former marine, so he had a mentality as a coach where he wanted to challenge your manhood to breaking point," Newell said. "And he didn't want Draz to think that just because you were being given an opportunity to play, that it was all going to be given to him. Bill saw the talent and he knew he could make him into a tremendous basketball player, if Draz would let him."

Near the end of that half-season in New Jersey, Petrović picked up the phone in his apartment after one particularly difficult practice and called Newell. In those first few weeks Petrović had been slow bonding with his new teammates. He had, however, become close with the two assistant coaches, Newell and Rick Carlisle. His situation with Fitch, being in a new city, and the developing unrest in Croatia (the tiny republic was attempting to secede from Yugoslavia) were combining to cause Petrović emotional difficulties. On this particular day he sought out Newell. When Newell entered Petrović's condominium, he immediately noticed two things: Petrović's television was blaring one of the round-the-clock news channels (Petrović anxiously waited for anything related to his homeland), and there were a number of boxes stacked near the door, indicating that Petrović was packing his belongings. *This doesn't look good*, Newell thought.

The two sat down on the couch and began chatting. Petrović, Newell quickly found, was at a crossroads, with his career not evolving in the NBA and thoughts creeping in about whether or not remaining in America would be in his best interests. Petrović told Newell that the car he was given as part of being named European Player of the Year several seasons earlier had been stolen from the home of his parents. The crime greatly upset them and gave Petrović the feeling that perhaps his family was now in some measure of danger.[20]

Petrović told Newell that he was unsure whether he wanted to continue in the NBA and that he had been soured by the first two seasons. They spoke about the initial struggle for acceptance and opportunity in Portland. Now, in New Jersey, Petrović spoke about how his first real opportunity had been made difficult because of how he had perceived Fitch's early treatment of him. Petrović thought about returning to Europe—Europe would

---

20 The stolen car became something of folklore. Stories surfaced that the vehicle may have been stolen by Serbians, or perhaps even Croatian freedom fighters who then turned the car into cash for weapons.

eternally be there to accept him—and felt Fitch did not respect him as a player. Petrović was clearly sensitive about the situation and Newell tried to calm him, explaining to him that Fitch and the coaches were quite excited about him, and that the first few months would be the hardest and most testing. Coming out the other side of that difficult beginning, Newell insisted, would pay major dividends. Newell then asked Petrović to reconsider his feelings about possibly going back to Europe, and to join him and the team's other assistant, Rick Carlisle, for dinner at a nearby restaurant.

The three arrived at the empty restaurant in the early evening, before the dinner crowd. Petrović began airing his grievances with the two coaches: about Fitch, fitting in with his teammates, the problems at home, and the danger that his and many families faced. Waking up each morning meant that there was always the possibility something may have happened back home to his loved ones that could potentially be devastating and everlasting. Petrović became quite emotional, which surprised Newell. Before him was a player whom he already knew to be most determined, someone who saw success in the NBA as his destiny, yet who had hit a low emotional point.

When Petrović began talking about Fitch, Newell told him about what his father, Pete, had once said to him about coaches and communication. "If a coach doesn't teach and encourage and communicate with you, Dražen, it means he doesn't care," Newell told him. "You don't ever want that, you don't ever want to be in a situation like that where the coach doesn't care." Carlisle spoke to Petrović about the tremendous opportunity that he had. "Stay with it, Draz. Get bigger, get stronger, keep working, and you'll see that this will be a tremendous change," he told him.

The coaches explained to Petrović that the Nets' roster as constructed would not be intact the following season. Theus, the talented but individualistic lead guard, would most likely not be with the team and that would open the door for Petrović, they told him. "Sleep on it, Draz, don't make any decisions based on emotion."

Newell arrived at practice the next morning and felt that such a serious discussion should at least be passed on to Fitch. When he popped his head into Fitch's office he quickly realized that the coach already knew all about it. Petrović had called LeGarie and then LeGarie had called Fitch, and the light of day made things more palatable. Fitch was at ease with the situation. He spoke with Newell about the process, that he was pleased to have Petrović in New Jersey. "Dražen," Fitch said later, "was our project." That he had been acquired by a team that was to make a direct investment in his progress was fortunate for Petrović.[21]

It was during this period of Petrović's life that his relationship with Renata Cajić ended. The two began dating in 1986, while Petrović was with Cibona, and it was Cajić who supported Petrović's demanding approach in pursuing his dreams. She watched as he took his career to Madrid, and then to Portland, and while juggling her own studies in Zagreb she emerged as a wonderful balance in his life. After five years, she wanted more. Cajić made it clear to Petrović that she wanted the relationship to move toward marriage, but Petrović, with his career—his *dream*—at a crossroads, his focus was very much fixed elsewhere.

"I told her that at the moment my whole life is basketball," Petrović said to Vasilis Skountis in June of 1993. "She didn't like that answer and we broke up. Basketball is not simply my occupation or my hobby, it's my life."

---

21 The organization even found him an apartment in Hackensack, New Jersey, in a building he shared with Fitch and teammates.

Cajić moved back to Croatia to continue her life. For now, Petrović's life was in New Jersey.

Over the final half of the 1990–91 season in New Jersey, Petrović showed that with a legitimate opportunity he could be a very serviceable offensive player. He turned out to be just as the staff had expected when he arrived from Portland: a player who could, with his ability to shoot from distance, accumulate points rapidly. He scored in double figures off the bench in twenty-three of his first twenty-six games, and averaged 16 points per game in his first full month, before tailing off slightly to finish the season. They were very good numbers for a reserve, and he was getting his points at an excellent shooting percentage, right at 50 percent.

Petrović's play reinforced a point that he had made after signing with Portland and during his time there: that with enough minutes he could easily find a shooting rhythm and be a valuable offensive contributor.

Petrović played in that half-season with very little inhibition, which made him not unlike a lot of his teammates, especially when the games had no lasting value and a shot at the playoffs had long since passed. It was a situation that suited Petrović at that point in his career: an ideal spot to audition. Fitch would insert him late in the first quarter with the sole responsibility of providing offense. He was adept at moving without the ball, the coaches quickly realized, and worked very hard to get open. Petrović had by this point in his career omitted a great deal of the ball handling from his game, a stark contrast from his days in Europe, but it underscored his ability to adjust and redefine.

One notable characteristic Petrović had adjusted in his game was the reduced height with which he jumped when shooting. When with Cibona and, later, Real Madrid, most of the offense he generated was off the dribble; often the momentum would carry from the dribble into his shot, elevating him to a point before the release. In Petrović's early NBA life a great deal of his jump shooting came off screens, and with the defender trailing he would turn his body and square to the basket, raising his toes just enough off the floor to release quickly. The reduced elevation time in turn helped him get this shot off quickly against the more athletic defenders.

Petrović played forty-three games for the Nets at the end of the 1991 season, for an average of 12 points per game on 50 percent shooting from the field. There were some moments to savor. He had a fine debut performance at home against the Lakers that included 14 points and a beautiful behind-the-back pass with his left hand to Coleman for a dunk. In February he hit for three straight 20-point games, topped by a career-high 27 points at Washington. And for a man with a mind for numbers, perhaps the one that meant the most to him was his average of twenty minutes of playing time per game. Fitch found a place for him every night, and it was giving him the chance to develop on a team that would struggle, with just twenty-six wins.

There was, however, the promise of change. Though it seemed unlikely, the Nets would be a team headed for the postseason just one year later. And the man who would lead them there was a European, one who would overcome the desperate situation in his homeland to attain the stardom he had long promised himself he would reach.

Fourteen

EMERGENCE AND ACCEPTANCE, LATE 1991

East Rutherford, New Jersey, USA

The Nets coaching staff was very encouraged by Petrović's half-season in New Jersey after his acquisition, especially with his ability to score and shoot an excellent percentage in reserve minutes. As the season finished, Bill Fitch and his staff discussed Petrović at length and decided that it would be important for him to stay for the summer of 1991 to work further on his game, and, more importantly, on his body.

The man enlisted to help Petrović was Rich Dalatri, the team's strength and conditioning coach. Dalatri had a football background but had been with the Nets for several seasons when Petrović arrived. The two formed a ready bond due to their mutual appetite for hard work. Petrović quickly felt a connection for Dalatri because of his commitment and approach; the dedication and hard work was as natural for him as it was for Dalatri, and that in the beginning was a strong bonding point. Dalatri remembered well the first conversation he had with Petrović. It occurred in, of all places, a hotel gym room in Miami on the morning after Petrović's debut with New Jersey. The team had just finished a shootaround session in preparation for their game that night, and upon returning to the hotel Dalatri went to work out, only to enter the room and find Petrović pedaling furiously on a stationary bike, covered in sweat.

"What are you doing?" Dalatri asked Petrović.

"I ride the bike every day for an hour, sometimes two," Petrović answered.

Dalatri smiled before walking away to begin his own workout. *Does he know we have a game tonight?* he thought.

In addition to Dalatri's conditioning duties, he was by title an assistant coach, and there was among his responsibilities a strong basketball component that went beyond fitness. His position behind the bench, where he sat for games, proved an ideal vantage point for observation, and as a result his programs would emanate from watching the players in-game, their athletic and fundamental strengths and weaknesses exposed night after night. Though his conditioning demands were immensely difficult, they were also appealing to players because they were based strictly on basketball, the aim always to motivate and not be monotonous.

In time he got to know Petrović's approach to not only his game but to his body, and it left Dalatri highly impressed. It was, Dalatri thought, the type of devotion to his livelihood that was absolute and most unusual, far beyond that of the average professional athlete. However, Dalatri felt that Petrović needed to advance his workouts. The origins of many of Petrović's methods were in Zagreb while playing for Cibona, when he worked with Dragan Milanovic. While they served him well, they had only served him to a point. Dalatri sat down with Petrović after the 1991 season concluded and offered a new approach. The constant bike use, the distance running, the monotony, and repetition of those activities, was all wrong. "You're training the wrong muscle fibers, Dražen," he said. "The workouts must resemble the sport you are training for." Riding great distances was great for bike riders, Dalatri explained, but not necessarily for basketball players. "You cannot train slow to become fast," Dalatri told him. "You must train fast to become fast."

Dalatri watched Petrović closely and with his athletic characteristics felt it was necessary to add explosiveness, which was of great importance at the shooting guard position. The extra strength would have obvious benefits at both ends of the floor.

Perhaps most importantly, Dalatri believed in Petrović.

"With the right training," Dalatri said to Petrović, "I can't imagine how good you can be."

After spending six weeks in Zagreb at the end of the season. Petrović returned to New Jersey for workouts and summer league play, the idea that he could be a featured player with the Nets providing the motivation. He was pleased to learn that Reggie Theus was in negotiations with an Italian team. It was a development that had not bothered the Nets, and they happily freed Theus from the final year of his contract. Petrović was confident about replacing Theus in a meaningful way, not as a playmaker but as a scorer on whom New Jersey could rely. "I want to replace Reggie," Petrović told the *Bergen Record*'s John Jackson over the summer. "I know what he did last year—leadership, taking the last shot. I think I can do that."

Petrović continued to embrace the brand of work Dalatri offered. He had never worked on upper body lifts much, nor with any great deal of enthusiasm, in Europe or Portland, as he was a subscriber to the theory that it could potentially damage his prized jump shot. He was not in the minority in believing that, but through time and patience his feelings changed. Dalatri felt that because of Petrović's very low body fat, his ravenous approach to exercise, and his abundance of fast-twitch muscles, the combination would make for rapid improvement in a brief period of time; a hard summer could make all the difference for Petrović.

A typical off-season day began with an hour of jump-shooting drills, followed by two hours of conditioning and lifting. The workouts were painful: upper body and lower body work; sweat and soreness; even sometimes tears, with Petrović working at every Dalatri suggestion. "If I came in one day and made up the most ridiculous, far-fetched, death-defying type of workout he would've done it to the best of his ability," Dalatri said. "That's how much confidence he had in what he was doing." After two hours they would head back to the court, where Petrović would shoot for another hour. It was while rebounding for Petrović's shooting that Dalatri would get *his* rest, a chance to be still, the simple matter of standing beneath the goal and catching the ball as it repeatedly came through the net. Once all was finished, it had resulted in five hours of work.

As Dalatri expected, Petrović's body began changing even early in the summer, the definition in his arms and especially his legs visible as the work continued to pile up. The results were terrific, but Petrović remained fixed on the goal of proving himself as an NBA player. "I don't want to say that I knew it, but I did know," Dalatri said. "I knew if he put his mind to it, with the way he worked from that first day on, I knew he would be able to really evolve into something special."

Even in the new workouts, Petrović remained regimented and calculating. He always counted his made shots, something that had started in his early teens. He always started at the same time each day. With that as a backdrop, Dalatri was surprised but accommodating one day when Petrović asked to rearrange the schedule for that particular week. "Dražen, you could use the break, take an extra day or so," he said.

"No," Petrović had answered, "we will still work out Thursday. But can we go early?"

Petrović wanted an earlier workout on Thursday, to then have Friday and the weekend off, only to return Monday as normal. He did not mention his plans to Dalatri, and Dalatri did not ask. When Monday rolled around a very different Petrović arrived, weary and fatigued, unusually lethargic. Dalatri snickered, assuming Petrović had an especially social weekend.

Things resumed to normal the following day, and as September finished and training camp began in October, Dalatri would on occasion think back to that Monday workout and remain curious. One morning at the APA trucking plaza, where the Nets practiced, Dalatri and Petrović were waiting to get on the floor before practice and watched as a pack of truckers puffed and panted their way through a spirited pick-up game. One trucker in particular, carrying some weight, was gasping for air, and Dalatri suggested to Petrović that the trucker looked exactly like Petrović during that Monday workout. "He looks like you, Draz," Dalatri joked, the two laughing.

After the joke passed, Petrović then turned to Dalatri. "There's something I didn't tell you."

"What is it?"

"I went home that weekend," Petrović told him, straight-faced.

"What?" Dalatri had said. "Home—as in *Croatia*?"

Petrović nodded. "I went home to see my parents and brother, to make sure everything was okay."

Petrović had gone home because he was concerned, a concern that had been felt by all Croats since the early spring of 1991, as the small republic sought independence from Yugoslavia. Dalatri was aware through Petrović of the situation in Croatia and the two had spoken about it on occasion, but he was left surprised by Petrović's gutsy decision to venture there, even for only a week-end, at a time when safety was not assured.

Croatia's attempt at separation itself had been most painful; the predominantly Serbian-led Yugoslav army responded by mak-ing its way into Croatia as the summer continued, the mission in part to establish fresh, broader borders. Croatia was vastly under-manned and ill-equipped for defense. Life became more precar-ious and dangerous as time went on, innocent lives being lost with frequency. "Our war for independence," Zoran Čutura, a Croatian and former teammate of Petrović's with Cibona, would later say. "For Serbs it will always be *civil* war."

For Petrović, for Stojko Vranković of the Celtics, and their Croatian friends on the East Coast, life was secure in the United States. But what came with security and distance was a mortal fear that each phone call from home or viewing of the television news would bring a life-altering reality.

Those close to Petrović noticed often when in his apartment that the television would be turned to CNN, for they provided the most frequent updates on the state in Croatia, and there it would play on a loop. Vranković's routine was slightly different: in Boston he could access with a shortwave radio a thirty-minute Croatian news program each night at seven. The program would go through each of the prominent towns, including Vranković's Zadar and Petrović's Šibenik, at that point in time often bring-ing more bad news than good. Vranković distinctly remembers the night that he tuned in to hear that Vukovar in the coun-try's east had been attacked by Serbian forces. It left him utterly shocked. There was a young reporter, Siniša Glavašević, whose voice Vranković would often hear each night on the radio. Gla-vašević's voice was one Vranković came to rely on as he was away from his family and friends, pursuing his dreams. Then one night the bulletin was missing Glavašević's familiar input: he had been killed in Vukovar. It left Vranković deeply shaken.

Petrović and Vranković would phone home to family and friends each day, the scenes described to them, sometimes of things that had been seen by simply peeking out the front window. There was always desperation in the tone of their voices. Petrović and Vranković shared a mutual friend, Mario Miocic, a Croat living in New York, and Miocic's family had their own stories to tell. They were forced to uproot their home in Zadar for the safety of Germany, where Miocic's father was employed. The risk had become just too great, the Miocic family decided, and they abandoned their home. "I couldn't believe it, that human beings in the twenty-first century could even do this," Miocic said of the Yugoslav army and their advances into Croatia. "Devastating the people, their futures, their businesses, everything. It was crazy."

Petrović and Vranković and Miocic would speak to each other about the plight of their Croatia every day, swapping stories that were relayed from their respective families. From that came a realization that they should at least try to contribute to the awareness in America. The three readily attended a Croatian gathering outside the United Nations building in New York City in August 1991. The group was joined by Goran Ivanisevic, the great Croatian tennis player who was in town for the U.S. Open. They had gone there with the specific purpose of helping spread awareness of just exactly what was occurring in Croatia and that it warranted the attention of Americans. "The good thing about us athletes, we had a chance to speak about the situation because people in the USA didn't know what was going on," Vranković said. "People thought it was civil war, but it's really war. People are attacked. They attacked our country. They tried to destroy cities. The people are dying over there. We tried to help as much as we could in that time."

They felt that, with the right outside help, perhaps conditions could be improved, perhaps the fighting could stop and life could resume without fear.

Petrović's trip home had been brought about by the events of that summer, and it harbored some difficult realities. Instead of enjoying a long weekend with his parents and brother, Petrović and his family spent two days in the basement of the family residence, a safety measure they had been advised to follow. When Petrović returned to New Jersey, his close friend Miocic saw that the experience had been somewhat traumatic. Petrović returned a somber man. "I didn't know what to do, Mario," Miocic remembered Petrović telling him.

Miocic came to be an important presence in Petrović's life during this period. He had migrated to the United States in 1986. He quickly fell for the City of New York, with its culture and diversity, its strong Croatian community. After Petrović was traded to New Jersey, it was Vranković who encouraged Petrović to reach out to Miocic. "He lives in New York, Dražen," Vranković told him. "He's a great guy, you will like him." Miocic was nervous before meeting Petrović. Their hometowns were fifty miles apart, and in Zadar there was an unusually strong bond between the community and its basketball team. That, of course, rendered any opponent an enemy. Miocic remembers a teenage Petrović sweeping through town while playing with Šibenka, with a bob of hair, at once rambunctious and artful on the floor. Miocic had come to dislike Petrović, who always seemed to play well against Zadar. When Zadar got the best of Petrović in the 1986 Yugoslav league finals while he was with Cibona, it was a moment that was to be eternally treasured.

The two men first met for a meal, and it was there Miocic decided to tell Petrović of their apparent history together. It proved to be the icebreaker. Miocic spoke of the great emotion it engendered in him watching Petrović go against his beloved Zadar. Petrović smiled sheepishly. Petrović then spoke of the challenges of playing Zadar. At the Jazine, the old arena, fans would shake the basket while he was attempting a free throw. Petrović remembered sprinting to the locker room after a win in order to minimize the verbal abuse directed at him and his brother, Aleksandar. "It was a great challenge to play there," he told Miocic, "that's why it was my favorite arena to play in." The two men laughed as they swapped stories of their homeland and of the sport they loved.

Miocic decided that night that the Petrović he had watched from afar, on-court, was very different from the man with whom he was enjoying dinner. Petrović was a young man who liked to laugh, who wanted to care. He could talk endlessly about the sport that consumed his life and about the country that raised him. "Dražen liked to be around the people who talked twenty-four/seven sport," Miocic remembered. "He liked to be around the people who talked it twenty-four hours, basketball, particularly, and other sports in Croatia."

Soon Petrović and Miocic became inseparable. Petrović quickly gave Miocic the moniker of *Kume*, "Godfather" in the Croatian language. Miocic was given his own seat at Nets' home games, where he became a fixture, on a first-name-basis with the arena employees. After home games the two would venture to Houlihan's, the restaurant that housed all New Jersey players after games, and share a booth.

They would rely on each other as 1991 played out, two young men living in a strange new world, their old world appearing to be falling apart thousands of miles away.

It was a difficult opening month of the 1991–92 season for the New Jersey Nets. As of the first week of November they were without the signature of lottery pick Kenny Anderson. Much was made of the Anderson selection, and the local reporters motioned on several occasions that the fascination and subsequent selection of Anderson came not from Willis Reed or Bill Fitch, but from co-owner Joe Taub. Taub had been a majority owner of the Nets in the late seventies and early eighties, and in the weeks leading to the draft he had re-purchased a stake in the team. As the story went, Reed and Fitch reportedly were both favoring the selection of Billy Owens, a versatile small forward from Syracuse, but Taub pushed hard for Anderson. It had been only an hour before the draft that the team settled on the player they would take with the second overall pick.

Anderson was a phenomenal college guard, creative and pro-lific offensively, and with the ball in his hands he was a dynamic presence on the break. Though he averaged 26 points per game as a sophomore at Georgia Tech, the Nets sought Anderson as a natural playmaker, someone who would first be looking to pass to Derrick Coleman, to Petrović, to Chris Morris. With Reggie Theus gone, and Anderson unsigned, it presented a unique dilemma. "Right now," Fitch told the writers, "we're last year's team without a first-round draft pick and its leading scorer."

Anderson eventually came at a steep price, with the team restructuring four contracts and releasing two players, a move that angered Fitch.

November was a hard month. The team won just three games, and Coleman missed most of it with, first, an injured back and then a sprained ankle. What came with the typical Nets agony was mounting speculation that Fitch would be gone. One national paper insisted that he would be fired when the team returned from a road trip to Texas in late November. Another said that college coach Rick Pitino would be handed not just the coaching position, but the title of general manager and even a part stake in the franchise. Then came a television report that Mike Fratello was among the team's preferred candidates; Reed had earlier been his assistant in Atlanta. And when Doug Collins was in town in December to do the team's only nationally televised game with the Turner Network (one in which they would be embarrassed at home by New York), he met with Taub, only to inform him he was not interested.

Shortly after Coleman returned to the line-up there was a home game with the Lakers, and it wasn't until the third quarter that Fitch put him in the game. "You call that coaching?" Coleman was quoted as saying in the *Record*. It had not painted Fitch well. Finally, there were rumors that Jim Valvano had been approached to leave his lucrative TV mantle to coach the Nets. But ultimately, that also that dissolved.

Strangely, such disharmony served as a backdrop to the on-court product turning for the better, a result that perhaps above all others defined the heartbeat of this dysfunctional group. What was extracted was a *win streak*. Petrović was a major contributor to the four-game streak, which included a 32-point performance at Charlotte, when he missed just three shots from the field. Through two months of the season he had been very good, his average sitting at just under 21 points per game while shooting 53 percent from the field. His influence on the group was a positive one, and he could, with a shot or play, bring the Meadowlands to life. Even in a building that might on some nights be only half full he could animate the attendees, and he began consistently to play with a level of confidence that was once familiar to his fans in Europe.

The turning point for Petrović came in late November with Coleman out, when he submitted back-to-back 30-point games on the road against Houston and San Antonio. He was given the responsibility of carrying the offensive load in the absence of the team's best player, and responded emphatically, which laid the foundation for a hot December. His shot was particularly on-point, benefiting greatly from the additional strength in his legs and the increased speed with which he released. Fitch used Petrović primarily off the ball as a catch-and-shoot player, and he was quickly becoming one of the league's elite. He could catch the ball and, with a quick hitch of the knees, generate enough strength to raise the ball quickly from his waist, always square and centered, the results following. "He was smart, he could see early on that his success in the NBA was going to be number one because of his shooting ability," Rick Carlisle said. "And number two his ability to move without the ball to create shots. As a catch-and-shoot player, up and down, he was one of the best I have seen."

Though the recipient of strong backing from the coaching staff during his sudden emergence, Petrović came to believe that perhaps his exploits were not fully welcomed by his teammates. There were instances when Petrović strongly felt that, after a hot start, the ball would slowly stop finding its way to him. Emotional and competitive by nature, this frustrated Petrović and was something he took personally. "There are still players that have not accepted I am the key player," Petrović told *FIBA* magazine. "And it will take time for those problems to be solved." In the hours after games, Petrović and Dalatri would discuss his performance and the game patterns, and it was then that Dalatri could see the pain it was causing Petrović. Dalatri thought simply that it was a result of the team's overall immaturity, the classic characteristics of a team perilously teetering on imploding and where individual agendas would quickly emerge. "This often happens on bad teams. There is no chemistry between players," Dalatri said. "It was probably just a me-first attitude that individuals have when they never understand a team concept. If we win, it does not matter who scores. If we win we all win, we all have our individual roles, and that is what constructs winning at any level. Dražen was willing to do anything to be good. He was willing to make any sacrifice, the others were not."

There was an incident shortly after Petrović was acquired by New Jersey that had an everlasting effect on him. Two of his teammates, Reggie Theus and Derrick Gervin, poked fun at his decision to stay on the floor and work long after practice had finished. "Sometimes I would stay late after practice and shoot and some of the players would complain about it," Petrović revealed to Mike Freeman of the *New York Times*. "It was always, 'Why are you working so hard?' I was confused. I thought, 'Am I wrong?'"

"It put pressure on them to maybe do something extra that they were not willing to do," Dalatri said. "So instead of them raising their level of professionalism, they would try to lower his."

Petrović was generally well liked by his teammates, even if between them very little was shared, professionally or culturally. In Portland he did not have difficulty fitting in. It was a veteran, professional, and businesslike group, and they respected his approach and work ethic even if away from the floor he had not developed a particularly close relationship with any of them. In New Jersey the demographic was different, younger, and for Petrović it wasn't as easy a fit. In spite of the obvious gap, he was not immune to the ribbing that occurred on teams. In the course of the long season he was an ideal candidate for the good-natured kibitzing, jokes that could last for an entire campaign. They would kid Petrović for his unique fashion sense (one teammate later took him to an upmarket Philadelphia tailor for a wardrobe overhaul); for his haircut (a sharp military-style crew-cut); for a sharp accent that rivalled Arnold Schwarzenegger's; and even on occasion his body odor.

Petrović was accepting of the ribbing, and certainly capable of returning serve, but there was always a distance between him and the others.

"Dražen was liked by all, but was not one of them," Dalatri said.

One of the issues in New Jersey was that of territory, which made them no different than other professional teams. What *was* different was that one of the players trying to carve out a piece of stardom was European. It made for a fascinating test case. Petrović needed to prove himself, first to his teammates before anything else, and that process in itself was trying. Harvey Araton, the *New York Times* writer who was among the most insightful and thoughtful of the basketball scribes, remembered a fascinating conversation he once had with Derrick Coleman about Petrović. Coleman explained to Araton the process of having to overcome his first impressions of Petrović: Petrović's arrival in New Jersey, the unusual haircut, the mechanical movements on the floor, almost of another era planted in the modern game. But Coleman was quick to add that he overcame that judgment of Petrović in time, since beneath the appearance was a very good player, perhaps one capable of one day becoming an All-Star.

Breaking down the perceptions held about European players served as a motivator for Petrović, and before it could be spread league-wide he needed to establish it on his own team. "The Europeans at that time, they weren't thought of as good a players as the NBA players," Chris Dudley, the team's reserve center and one of Petrović's friends said. "I do think the reputation was:

a good player offensively, a good shooter, but can't play defense and not tough enough. Dražen fairly or unfairly fit that mold a little when he first came in the league. I give him so much credit because he worked on it. He was driven. He worked extremely hard to become a better player."

What Petrović truly coveted was stardom in the NBA. Though he would not publicly tout it, his goal was to be the first European to be a star in the United States. To do so in 1992, when the scrutiny toward Europeans and their need to prove themselves was never greater, was a trying, difficult exercise. The league itself was changing in a fundamental sense with the addition of more European players, but it had left the top of the league, the cast of stars and the galaxy in which they resided, largely unchanged. Šarūnas Marciulionus and Vlade Divac were very talented and were good NBA players, but neither was considered his team's best, or even second-best, player. There was Detlef Schrempf, the German forward, who after initially struggling in Dallas became a very good player for Indiana. But he had been in some way considered a product of the American system, having gone to high school and college in the United States, placing him in his own sort of category when discussing the European players.

That left Petrović. He was cultivated in Europe, pre-packaged when he signed with Portland, and by the time he became a 20-point scorer for the Nets he was by some definition the first player of a strictly European basketball background to experience a level of stardom in the NBA. "What we saw with Dražen was the first sign of a kind of push back," said Araton, who felt that Petrović's determination was in part driven by a perceived notion that European players were entitled to only including Petrović in a secondary role. "I do think whatever he felt about those biases were strong, and I think they were based on a certain reality that was emerging. Dražen was the first one to put up with that. The others dealt with less of it because they were role players. I think Dražen was the first guy to carry himself like a star. It was his body language on the floor. He carried himself physically like a star, he had a certain swagger. There was no question about it, the way he walked, talked. I think he thought it was the proper path to play out for him."

His emergence would come to be a defining moment, an indicator of the direction his sport was heading—that of true globalization. With the second half of the 1991–92 season to play out, Petrović was bravely at the forefront of a Nets team facing an uncertain future. Behind his elevated play, it would turn out to be one of unexpected success.

Fifteen

COMING OF AGE, SPRING 1992

East Rutherford, New Jersey, USA

The Nets won eight of nine games during a stretch in January, at times playing a brand of ball that defied their level of personnel and turbulent early season. But then they fell again. There was an eight-game losing streak into February, the team giving no inclination as to which direction it could go next, the potential always that it would end up in a place that was not ideal. They were five games out of a playoff spot in the Eastern Conference with two months to play. Even in the periods of inconsistency, they were still within reach, and thus there was reason for hope.

In late February, there was a game with Indiana that took on extra importance because of the standings. The Pacers were a game-and-a-half ahead of New Jersey in the race for a playoff spot; the Nets viewed it as a game they had to win. That morning at the shootaround Tom Newell, Bill Fitch's lead assistant and defensive specialist, went over with Petrović the assignment of guarding Reggie Miller, Indiana's top shooting guard. Since Petrović had arrived in New Jersey, his duels with Miller provided fascinating theatre. As offensive players they were quite similar: hard workers off the ball, good at getting space from the opponent, and superb shooters with an ability to get their shots off quickly and with great accuracy. But perhaps above all else, each was a competitor of the highest order, which usually fueled a mutual mouthing off, Miller in English, Petrović in something Miller knew only as a language other than English. Miller came to dislike Petrović, irked by both his ability as an offensive player and his fearlessness as a trash talker. In time it appeared Miller was most disturbed by the similarities between them. "Maybe it was because I was jealous of the way he shot the ball," Miller would later write in his autobiography. "Quickest release in the game. One shooter to the other, I envied his ability."

Because Miller was indefatigable as an offensive player and the Pacers' offense was structured to cater to his constant move-ment, the assignment of guarding him was always emphasized by the Nets in game preparations. Miller was the type of offen-sive player who could move as easily in the fourth quarter as he did in the first. An opponent could not afford even a single possession for Miller to be left open; a string of distance shots could be especially demoralizing. Rick Carlisle, New Jersey's other assistant, went over the film with Petrović, indicating that he was to chase Miller through every screen. Under no circum-stances was Petrović to switch defensively as a result of being screened off. Out on the practice floor, Newell showed Petrović how to guard him.

"When Reggie comes through the lane, Draz," Newell began, "you've got to dance with him." Newell started pitta-patting his feet, a technique that would allow Petrović to commit to which-ever route Miller chose. "Put a hand in the lane and usher him through," Newell continued, "just like you're in a slow dance." A *slow dance*, Newell said, sure that Petrović would understand his concept. "You've got to dance with that motherfucker now, Draz, just dance with that motherfucker."

The game was tight throughout, and Petrović unlocked a tie on a jumper with thirty seconds to go. His 19 points ultimately helped New Jersey win by four. More importantly, he defended Miller better than the coaching staff had expected, holding him to just one point as he missed all eight of his field goal attempts in twenty-eight minutes. Newell and Carlisle were at once shocked and delighted.

Can you believe Draz? they said to each other as they walked the corridor to the locker room, stat sheet in hand. Together they shared genuine shock that such a maligned defensive player had held Miller so well. When they entered the locker room, there was Petrović sitting at his locker stall, beaming. He derived a great deal of satisfaction in having a measure of success against Miller. A loud voice caught the attention of both Newell and Carlisle as they entered the locker room.

"Dance motherfucker, dance!"

It was Petrović. The room erupted in laughter. It was, to those in the inner sanctum, a seminal Petrović moment, one that was not to be forgotten.[22]

Petrović gained more confidence as the season wore on. It was, thought Carlisle, all these little milestones along the way—success against a certain player, against a certain team—that reinforced to Petrović his long-held feeling that he could be a top player in the league. It served as further motivation. Petrović always had a healthy sort of greed when approaching his career; he could gain satisfaction from something, but only fleetingly,

22 Even in the years that followed, whenever Newell and Carlisle would leave each other phone messages, they would invariably end with *Dance motherfucker, dance!* before hanging up.

because there was the next hurdle or next goal. In his bloodlines, Carlisle had a stint with the eighties Celtics, a team that from afar Petrović admired, and the two would talk about those teams and about Larry Bird in particular, a player for whom both had a particular fondness. Petrović would lighten those conversations by insisting that he remembered Carlisle's eternal contribution to those great Boston teams. He would mimic the waving of a towel, as Carlisle and other Celtics reserves had done during the mid-eighties, while Bird and Kevin McHale and Robert Parish acted out their glory.

"I remember you, I remember you," Petrović would say to Carlisle, waving an imaginary towel above his head.

There was a game against Boston in March of 1992 that Carlisle remembered as particularly important to Petrović, when the success seemed to carry a little more weight. The Celtics still had Bird, McHale, and Parish, assuring that they were still *the* Celtics, and were to be feared (they would go on to win the Atlantic Division in what proved to be Bird's final season). They jumped on the Nets, especially to open the third quarter, leading by nineteen before Petrović got hot. It seemed that with each passing shot his release got quicker. Petrović had an amazing ability to catch the ball and turn his body to the basket to begin the shot. He had a great sense of balance that would allow him to square his body in an instant and manufacture a high-percentage shot. There was one basket in particular during his personal streak where he ran from below the basket out to the corner, in front of Boston's bench, and when he took the pass he in one motion turned his body over his right shoulder, cocking the ball and shooting instantaneously. The ball fell through the net as he landed on the Celtics coaches.

He would attempt twenty-six shots from the field against Boston, making seventeen, a remarkable percentage in an evening that featured mostly outside shooting. His 39 points was a career high as the Nets came storming back to win by two, 110–108. "That," remembered Carlisle, "was another thing that just sent his confidence soaring."

With his dramatic improvement in New Jersey during the 1991–92 season, Petrović gradually rebuilt his game, including the *verbal* game. It was a true indication of his comfort level and confidence. There was always something in Petrović's game that was irritating to an opponent, dating back to his early professional career in Europe. He could body them, sneak in a small elbow after the whistle, or whisper in their ear—the feeling of irritation by the defender was always heightened when Petrović scored on them. He had distinct bravado, and no matter the native language in the country he was playing in, he was an especially skilled talker.

In his early NBA career there were moments of confrontation for Petrović, but without the performance to reinforce it.[23] As his play reached a higher level, what accompanied it was the in-game verbal barbs. The night after the Celtics win, the Nets played the Knicks in New York. On the game's first possession, Petrović was separated from Gerald Wilkins before a shot was taken. Wilkins had run straight to Petrović when the Nets claimed possession, and Petrović began hitting Wilkins's arm off his waist. Wilkins finally turned to Petrović after the whistle, raised his right index finger and began to fire expletives. It was to set the tone for the evening. Later, Petrović hit a jump-shot in front of the New York bench, posing with his shooting hand up and staring down guard John Starks before jogging back down the floor. He scored 22 points in the overtime win.

---

23 He took a punch in the jaw from Utah's Blue Edwards in a 1990 summer league match after a game-long talking session, and it shook Petrović quite badly.

Later in the month, when Boston visited New Jersey, Petrović landed a bigger hit. With Bird lunging out at him on the perimeter, Petrović had pump-faked before stepping back and hoisting a long three-pointer. Instead of retreating on defense, Petrović ran a step behind Bird, barking in his ear. It was a startling moment. The act having occurred at close proximity to the Celtic bench, a good deal of the Boston players found it humorous, some even seeking an explanation from their own resident Croat, Stojko Vranković, who simply responded silently, shrugging his shoulders with palms raised upward. "A milestone in Nets history," Bill Pennington of the *Record* wrote.

Petrović was brilliant in March, averaging 22 points per game on nearly fifty percent shooting from three-point range. As the season wore on he had in fact gotten better and stronger, a sure indication of his fitness and renewed body. The Nets' television analyst, Spencer Ross, noticed that Petrović's conditioning distanced him from his contemporaries as the season wore on. "If you watched him early in the season, he was quick, but not the fastest," Ross said. "He would have to get the shot off, but not from the dribble. He'd need a pick, come off and curl, he could move without the ball. Come March or April, his game would change. Dražen, because of his conditioning, wasn't faster—they were slower. Late in the season he was able to get his shot off the dribble by himself because he still had much more left in the tank."

Petrović was the steadying force amidst the Nets' insistence on being inconsistent. "He gives us life and he gives us a shot at victory," Fitch told *The New York Times*. The Nets were eleven games below .500 around Christmastime before winning twelve of fifteen. They followed that run with a losing streak in February. The Nets then won eight of ten before plateauing through March, as the race to the playoffs heated up with Atlanta (minus Dominique Wilkins, lost for the season with a torn Achilles) and Philadelphia (and their famously unhappy star Charles Barkley) floundering. New Jersey then won seven of eleven to move into the eighth spot in the Eastern Conference in the first week of April, and stayed there for the remainder of the regular season.

There was, as with any success in New Jersey, something to linger and then taint the situation. Fitch asked Derrick Coleman to re-enter the fourth quarter of a game against the Heat in Miami. The bull-headed forward refused. "I'm not going back in for you," he was heard to say, according to a report by the *Record*'s John Jackson. The two had apparently exchanged words at halftime; Coleman was disappointed about being taken out with six minutes remaining and the result still in doubt. Two days later, at home against Indiana, the Nets trailed the Pacers by four with twenty-five seconds remaining when Fitch asked Chris Morris to re-enter. "Mo . . ." he repeated four times, looking around, before spotting him and yelling, "Morris!" His voice pierced through the huddle down to where Morris was sitting, isolated from the team. Fitch got up from kneeling and walked down to Morris. "You want to play the rest of the season?" Fitch asked him. Morris remained unresponsive. "You don't want to go? You don't want to play?" The words hung in the air. Morris finally said no. Fitch walked away in disgust.

The Nets beat Orlando in their final game of the season and with that earned a playoff spot, seventh in the East, something that essentially served as a backdrop to the drama that surrounded Fitch and the actions of his two young forwards. Though Fitch had survived the tumult of the early unstable job security and the owners' enthusiastic pursuit for a replacement, he had steered the Nets in a better direction. And yet, they never truly bought into him, his strong personality and demanding nature. The results came—historically, with Fitch they always had—but in this generation there was a different and changing acceptance of the methods he employed. His relationship with some of his players was compromised; a difficult mix of old-fashioned general leading the young, talented resistors to his authoritarianism.

Petrović was the only player on the team who played and started in every game. He averaged a team-best 20.6 points per game (seventeenth in the league), while shooting over fifty percent from the field. He was the NBA's second-best in three-point percentage, and broke the franchise's record for three-pointers made in a season. Later, he would finish second in voting for the Most Improved Player award.

Petrović came into the campaign largely an unknown quantity, but put together the type of season that exceeded the expectations of those within the organization, whose faith in him was unwavering from the beginning. The Nets' coaching staff was ecstatic with his progress. They had been especially delighted that he'd held his own as a shooting guard in the Eastern Conference, which saw him face a variety of talented players, including Michael Jordan, Joe Dumars, Miller, Hersey Hawkins, Alvin Robertson, and Reggie Lewis, all of whom had been named All-Stars at times over the previous three seasons. But above all else, Petrović proved that his individual transformation and stylistic overhaul—from flashy playmaker in Europe to spot-up shooter in the NBA—was the correct one. In short order, he became among the best at his position.

The Nets drew Cleveland in the first round of the playoffs. The Cavs were a balanced opponent, steered by an experienced core that didn't appear susceptible to the types of drama the Nets seemed unable to avoid. Led by Mark Price and Brad Daugherty, and guided by coach Lenny Wilkens, only the Bulls won more games in the 1991–92 season. Tucked away in Cleveland, they had built a very good team that, when healthy, was damaging during the regular season, but which had fallen short in the playoffs due to a combination of injuries and the existence of Chicago's Michael Jordan. They entered the 1992 postseason with genuine hopes of upending the Bulls, and certainly saw the Nets as just a stepping stone toward the Eastern Conference title.

Game one was very well played. Contested on a Thursday evening, it was not nationally televised and thus confined to the local markets. Petrović was very excited to participate in his first playoff game as a Net, and he jumped out of the gate with a lot of offensive aggression. Steve Popper, who covered the Nets for the *Asbury Park Press*, theorized that Petrović's hot start was due to his feelings about a story that had appeared in the *Record* two days earlier. In previewing the playoff series, one reporter referenced Petrović's brief playoff history in Portland in 1990. It spoke of his struggles, especially in the Finals against Detroit, and how it was the catalyst for both the acquisition of Danny Ainge and Petrović's eventual departure. Many around the NBA, it was written, were interested to see how Petrović would respond once again under the postseason spotlight. "I remember he bristled at that and being very anxious to prove himself," Popper said.

Petrović the competitor used the article as a slight, and turned it into a challenge of his game and capabilities. Popper remembers the sight of Petrović pulling for his shot early in the contest, pumping his fists while trying to quiet the Richfield Coliseum. "I think that was what he was about—proving people wrong," Popper said. "And whatever doubt people had of him, he was up to it."

The Cavs opted to assign Steve Kerr to guard Petrović, a player at least three inches shorter, yet who was starting alongside the diminutive Price in the backcourt. Petrović used the match-up to his advantage, scoring 24 points in the first half with many of his looks unimpeded. He was, Harvey Araton of the *Times* wrote, playing like "a Croatian Jerry West." New Jersey took encouragement in that its two best players—Petrović and Derrick Coleman—were holding their own. Coleman was pitted against Cleveland's enormous frontline (Daugherty, Larry Nance, and John Williams each stood over 6-foot-10) and had met the challenge. During Petrović's hot first half it was Coleman who controlled the rebounding and even playmaking; in the third quarter he began looking for his shot, scoring 12 points while pulling New Jersey to within four. Coleman had a unique ability to contribute in a variety of ways at a high level, and would eventually finish the game just one assist short of a triple double, to go with his 21 points and 11 rebounds.

What made the game so pleasing to watch was the individual brilliance that sparkled from it, the Cavaliers countering Petrović and Coleman with the performances of its own two best players. Daugherty finished with 40 points, 16 rebounds, and nine assists, and Price had 35 points to go with 10 assists. The Nets took that hit and yet played a stubborn game, staying within striking distance late in the fourth quarter. Petrović scored 14 points in the fourth, and his off-balance hit over two Cleveland defenders with ninety seconds remaining gave the Nets a one-point lead at 111–110. But the Cavs remained stable in the final minute, at home and more experienced, capitalizing on several New Jersey errors before pulling away for a seven-point win, 120–113. The score was not indicative of the tightness of the contest.

For Petrović it was a major offensive effort in his New Jersey playoff debut—40 points on thirty-one shots. He gave Cleveland a legitimate fright, forcing them to use three different players defensively in an attempt to slow him. His point total was enough to break the Nets' individual record for a playoff game for their time in the NBA, beating out a performance by another shooting guard, John Williamson, who had scored 38 in 1978 against Philadelphia. After the game, Petrović allowed himself to be happy with the output, but ultimately was more fixated on a three-pointer he had missed in the game's final minute. "If that one goes, I think we win," he told reporters.

The Nets appeared to be a different team in the second game. Though Petrović scored 23 points, intensity-wise New Jersey did not resemble the team that almost stole the opener. The final was 118–96, in favor of the Cavs. A team that had been terribly inconsistent all season was now perilously close to elimination.

The series moved to New Jersey, and on the evening before the third game Petrović called his friend Mario Miocic. The two often capitalized on an off-night by venturing into New York City to their favorite Italian restaurant. However, on this night, Petrović was not thinking about socializing. "I want to call the team," he told Miocic.

"For what?" Miocic answered, somewhat concerned.

"Tomorrow's game is at 7:30," Petrović explained. "I want to go to the arena and practice tonight at the same time."

"Are you crazy?" Miocic answered. "Come over to New York, we'll go get some dinner."

"No," Petrović said. "I have to be ready for tomorrow."

With the building's other tenants, the New Jersey Devils of the NHL, in New York playing a postseason game, Petrović managed to gain access to an empty Meadowlands arena. There he stayed for several hours, jump shot after jump shot, acting out success before the time had arrived. "It's who he was," Miocic said later.

Twenty-four hours later, in what was New Jersey's first home playoff game in six years, that same building had a significantly greater occupancy. It was not full of people, but instead full of *life*, the building resonating in a way that it infrequently had that season. The Nets responded and rode the wave for a good portion of the first half before the Cavs forged ahead, quieting the building as the good teams did, leading by ten with seven minutes to go. All season long New Jersey portrayed the image of a fragile team that could summon good basketball at odd times. With their season on the line, in the fourth quarter they somehow found life. Petrović, who to that point in game three had not experienced the same success he did in Cleveland, led them. He used a double down-screen to break free for the mid-range shot, then scored a layup off a steal. He demanded that the crowd join him, waving his arms and yelling; the momentum began to shift.

With New Jersey down by four and less than five minutes to go, Petrović became tangled with John Battle. A reserve guard who had been something of an antidote for Petrović, Battle was the only Cavalier to have success defensively to that point. He threw a punch at Petrović as the two ran down the floor, and was promptly ejected. With the tension rising, Mookie Blaylock found Petrović on the next possession at the top of the key. With Kerr chasing, he turned and fired. The crowd erupted when he made it. *Badabing!* yelled both Spencer Ross and Bill Raftery, broadcasting the game for SportsChannel New Jersey. The game was not yet secure. With New Jersey ahead, 104–103, and one minute to play, Fitch ran the same play that freed Petrović earlier.

He once again caught, squared himself, and fired. "Petro for three . . ." yelled Ross. *"Got it!"* The Meadowlands erupted.

Ross had developed the battle cry for Petrović as the season played out. He had a voice made for broadcasting, deep, strong, and succinct, unmistaken. He was tutored early in his career by the great Marty Glickman, the original voice of the Knicks, and the first basketball broadcaster to be at once presenter and identity. Glickman had a fondness for Ross, and made a special point to offer him advice along the way. One thing that never left Ross was that Glickman offered a subtle point regarding the difference between radio and television play-by-play. "When you're doing TV, why tell them the shot is good?" Glickman reasoned to Ross. "They saw it. They know the shot was good." Yet when Petrović arrived, Ross found himself stretched to his descriptive best, calling his distance shots with an enthusiasm that exceeded most who found themselves in the half-filled arena. There began an anticipation when Petrović would launch from distance. *Petro for three*—pause for emphasis when the shot goes through—*Got it!* "I would get chills through me when I said it," Ross said, his call quickly becoming synonymous with Petrović's trademark shot.

The shot gave New Jersey a four-point lead. Petrović turned to run back down the floor, throwing his hands up in the air and looking skyward. Then his hands returned to his head before throwing them in the air once more. It was a moment of unique, pure jubilation. Few athletes—certainly in Nets' history—had captured the locals in such a way. The team's scorekeeper, Herb Turetzky, a man who had been with the franchise since its inception, would later think back to that shot and the crowd's reaction and decide that Petrović was the most popular player in team history.[24]

---

24 It also proved to be the defining moment of Petrović's time in New Jersey, the one that seemed to best encapsulate him. The highlight film clip was often shown when looking back at his time with the Nets.

The Nets eventually held on to win by five, 109–104, behind Petrović's 20 points. The series stood at 2–1.

There was renewed optimism for the fourth game, with hopes to push the Cavs to a fifth game back in Cleveland. The Nets jumped out and took a fourteen-point lead after the first quarter but in time the Cavs were able to slowly reel them back in, pulling to within eight by the half and then six at the end of the third. Then New Jersey imploded. For the better part of the season Petrović appeared immune to the frailties of the team, pushing through amidst his own personal mission for success. But in game four he did not play well. Cleveland started Craig Ehlo for the first time in the series, and he proved to be an effective defender, forcing Petrović to miss eight of his fourteen shot attempts while limiting him to just 14 points. Ehlo was able to crowd Petrović as he caught the ball, getting close enough to him to ensure that all his distance attempts were challenged.

As the game wore on, Petrović struggled, and frustration took hold; the fourth quarter began and the lead slipped away. Twice Chris Morris yelled at Petrović to increase his effort on the defensive end, and twice Petrović yelled back. The team huddled for a time-out late in the game, and once again the two exchanged words. The season hung by a thread, the two young men succumbing to the emotions of the moment. They were separated. With seventy seconds remaining and the Nets down by only five, after one last exchange Petrović turned and sat down at the end of the bench. He effectively removed himself, not only from the game but from the season. The move was most uncharacteristic of him. "They'd spent the year fighting the coach," wrote Mike Celizic of the *Record*, "and they ended it fighting each other."

Cleveland finished off New Jersey in their own building by nine, 98–89. The Nets' season was over. As the final seconds ticked away, the home crowd stood and applauded a team that had endured a confusing, yet ultimately successful, season.

Nothing came of the incident with Morris. It ended as soon as the game did. Morris spoke to reporters after the game and told them that perhaps Petrović was frustrated about not getting more touches. "And I was just trying to motivate him to play some better defense, that's all," he said. Petrović was less succinct in his appraisal: "It's all part of basketball."

It was a difficult way to end a season of achievement for Petrović, but certainly not an apt way to define it.

The bad taste from Portland was left behind; Petrović now stood among the elite shooting guards in basketball. And what awaited in the summer of 1992 was a continued opportunity to improve. There was the chance to suit up for the Croatian national team, to lead the country he loved at the Barcelona Olympics, and a date with the greatest basketball team ever assembled.

Sixteen

LEAVING THE PAST BEHIND,

1983–91, Yugoslavia; 1992, Croatia

With Croatia's push for independence in 1991, it set in motion the possibility that the country could send a men's basketball team to the Barcelona Olympics. In December 1991 they took minor steps toward getting to the Olympics by first seeking admission to FIBA, basketball's governing body. Within a month they were approved, just in time for the country to gain its independence in the middle of January 1992. It was an immense undertaking, the effort of sending a team to the Olympics. Mihovil Nakić, a recently retired player and former teammate of Petrović's, remembers well the exhaustive days and months leading up to the summer of 1992. With the Croatian basketball federation recently formed, a seemingly endless list of responsibilities and errands fell on the plate of Nakić and two others. One of the countries that many believed to be a real threat to claim an Olympic medal had a grand total of three employees. "We had to do all possible work in order for things to get done around the national team," Nakić said.

Sending a team to Barcelona was a tremendous boost for the country. The Olympic basketball tournament had been highly anticipated for three years, dating to the 1989 ruling that allowed the participation of professionals. The United States team was announced in the interim, the names—Jordan, Bird, Magic, Barkley—quickly afforded a type of stardom beyond that of the typical Olympian. They became demigods even before Barcelona, their presence ensuring victory and thus stripping the competition of any opportunity for a chance upset. Yet for the wider audience that seemed okay, for what would be woven into a lopsided contest was an exhibition of the highest athletic order. The Dream Team was a collective the likes of which would likely never be repeated.

For Croatia, winning an athletic contest seemed secondary to the act of simply being there and competing. It was a tremendous opportunity to bring joy to the country in the face of incredible darkness, and it was Petrović and Stojko Vranković who best embodied that approach. They were unmistakably the team's leaders. It was not something that needed appointment, but, rather, was evident in that they were the team's most experienced and respected players. Both men were immensely pleased that Croatia was able to submit a team to the major tournaments, for although they had long been servants of the Yugoslav national team, by 1991 they mutually decided to no longer represent them. With the tension mounting, and with Croatia openly considering seceding from Yugoslavia, Petrović and Vranković decided together not to play in the 1991 European championships. It was not a basketball decision. They removed themselves from the picture in a respectful manner, both citing a need to spend a portion of the summer in the United States as their NBA careers reached important junctures. Below the surface, though, they anticipated the trouble that was awaiting Croatia and decided against representing Yugoslavia.

It was a decision that Vranković later conceded was related to the war, though it was not publicly noted at the time. That Yugoslavia continued on and won the 1991 Eurobasket (Vlade Divac, Toni Kukoč, and Dino Radja all played) certainly eased the situation, but it would soon prove to be the last time that Yugoslavia competed with players from both Croatia and Serbia.

As 1991 continued, and as the situation in Croatia became more precarious, fast approaching a point of no return, both Petrović and Vranković gradually became more outspoken about the situation in their homeland. The prospect that they would ever again appear in a basketball contest representing Yugoslavia was not something that diminished with time—it was a decision considered final. To Petrović, to Vranković, to the many Croatian athletes who had once represented Yugoslavia, what was occurring in Croatia was impossible to overlook. To appear in a major competition for Yugoslavia from that point forward would be a form of betrayal. "He was not a zealot for the Croatian cause," Nick Goyak said of Petrović. "Now, that doesn't mean he wasn't supportive and proud and all of that. But he was not an inflammatory nationalist at all. That just wasn't his make-up. But he was hurt by what was going on. He had family and friends that were being attacked when the war started."

In the last week of October 1991, an article appeared in *The New York Times* about the political unrest in Europe and how it was affecting the basketball landscape. It was then that Petrović told a reporter he would not play again for Yugoslavia. "If it is a Croatian team, I will play, but only if it's a Croatian team," he said. "I will not play for Yugoslavia unless it is for Croatia."

Vranković held the same position. "I'm sure that I will never again play for the Yugoslavian national team. If Croatia sends a national team to Barcelona, I will play and so will all the guys from Croatia," he said. Of all the players who were affected by the breakup of the national team, Vlade Divac seemed most disappointed that such a prolific, cohesive team was no longer whole. "I just hope the government says to the Croatians, 'OK, guys, this is the last game you play for Yugoslavia,'" Divac told *The New York Times,* somewhat hopefully. "That way, we'll go together to play in the Olympics and it will be a chance for us to show how we can play against NBA players."

In light of what was happening outside the confines of a basketball court, it seemed a far-fetched idea.

Though clearly a secondary issue when compared with the delicate circumstances woven into the war in Croatia, the sport of basketball was losing a tremendously gifted collective. The Yugoslav national team of the late eighties and early nineties was one that blended beautifully, a splendid mix of movement and creativity and—ultimately—of winning. In addition to the 1991 Eurobasket, Yugoslavia won the 1990 world championships and the 1989 Eurobasket, this after competing for the gold medal at the Seoul Olympics in 1988. In international basketball, it was a group that threatened to hold the remaining countries at bay in non-Olympic competition for a good while, with all of its leading players in their early- or mid-twenties. Petrović was the face of that particular group, their most noticeable player and certainly most flamboyant. To see him no longer part of the Yugoslav team, to see him back away because of the obvious problems occurring away from the court, was a reflection of his feelings and loyalties.

Before 1991, Petrović had never missed an opportunity to play for Yugoslavia, having served a national team of some description each year between 1980 and 1990. He broke into the senior national team for international competition in 1983, in the afterglow of his breakout club season with Šibenka.²⁵ Even while in descent from its glorious era, the national team still had names then, notably Kresimir Cosic and Dragan Kićanović, remnants from the prodigious seventies. The national team was chosen by the Yugoslav Basketball Federation and its longtime president, Boris Kristančič. He spearheaded an assembled group of coaches and other officials, and the annual deliberation sessions were often heated and contested, the state of the game and its players hashed and re-hashed. It was in one of these meetings that teenager Dražen Petrović was first selected as a national team member.

That Petrović's first taste of the national team came when Cosic and Kićanović were making their final appearances was a matter for posterity, one generation passing as the leader of another arrived. Both Cosic (nineteen) and Kićanović (twenty) were destined early for the national team just as Petrović was, and what resulted was an Olympic gold, two world championships, and three European championships in the Cosic era. It was a period of dominance. There were a great many people in Europe who considered Cosic to be the best European player ever, a reputation he continued to hold even after Petrović and then Arvydas Sabonis rose in the eighties.²⁶ Cosic was a tall, rangy player at 6-foot-11, who combined unusual instinctive abilities with a game seemingly void of weaknesses. He was an all-American at Brigham Young in the early seventies before being drafted in back-to-back years, by Portland in 1972, and then the Lakers in 1973. It was

25 Petrović had toured American colleges with the national team as early as November 1981, just after his seventeenth birthday.

26 Part of the initial attraction with Sabonis was that he reminded people of Cosic, which in European basketball was the greatest form of flattery.

his conquering of the American collegiate system that added to the reverence, even if his personality was not suited to worship by others.

By 1983, Cosic's best was gone. He was nearing thirty-five years of age, and his plight seemed to mirror that of the national team. It was a team selected with more than a touch of sentimentality, some of the *names* no longer capable of rising to the challenge of the bigger tournaments. Both Janez Drvaric and Faruk Kulenović were assistant coaches on that national team, and they noticed that there were signs in the camp prior to the European championships that it was not a balanced team, one dangerously close to falling away, some of the older players lacking in motivation. The Yugoslav federation and the team's head coach, Josip Gjergja, believed the group was capable of one final push at a major tournament, and that proved to be poor judgment.

Petrović showed up at the national team camp enthusiastic about taking his place even among the big names. Drvaric came away very impressed by how hard the kid was willing to work, how hard he attacked those workouts, not shying away from competing against the likes of Kićanović and Zoran Slavnić, who were established at the guard position. When the Eurobasket began, though, Petrović rarely played in the early games, and it was only when Kićanović went down injured did he get an opportunity. Gjergja opted to start Petrović in the final two games and he played well, scoring a combined 45 points, but it had been lost amidst the curtain call of the falling stars and the team's obvious need to rebuild.

Mirko Novosel led the national team at the Los Angeles Olympics in 1984, and they played well enough to earn the bronze, but by 1985 Cosic had taken over as coach. The Eurobasket ended badly that year, with the Yugoslavs finishing seventh despite Petrović being the tournament's leading scorer. The program needed to be rebuilt if it was to move forward. By the 1986 world championships in Spain there was a sense that the transition was in full swing, as Divac debuted at age eighteen; then, for the 1987 Eurobasket, Cosic opted to send Kukoč (eighteen), Radja (twenty), and Žarko Paspalj (twenty-one) to their first major senior competition. Petrović was twenty-two years of age at the time, and yet there were five members of the team younger than he was. Additionally, just two other players—Aleksandar Petrović and Ratko Radovanović—remained from the 1984 Olympic squad, a sure sign that the overhaul was near completion.

Because the Yugoslavs failed to win either the 1986 world championships or the 1987 Eurobasket, tournaments they had entered with great expectations and yet finished third on both occasions, many felt that Cosic failed the national team as a head coach. Just five days after the 1987 Eurobasket finished, Cosic decided that he no longer wanted to coach the national team, and resigned. Though Yugoslavia had not won a major tournament under Cosic, he demanded of the federation that they infuse youth into the national team. In the end it was his insistence that kick-started the rebuild, with a younger, more exciting generation coming through. "Absurdly, he was never publicly recognized for that," Zoran Čutura said of Cosic. Though Cosic had shortcomings as a coach—planning and discipline, most notably—it was his vision for the very good players coming through that cleared the path for eventual success.

Dušan Ivković took over as head coach prior to the 1988 Seoul Games and immediately handed the keys to the younger players, who made their way to the gold medal game before falling to the Soviets. The Yugoslavs controlled the early part of the game but then faded, and in the aftermath there was a real sense that something special had been within their grasp, even if it was just their first true emergence as a group, an arrival perhaps a year early.

Then in 1989 everything seemed to click and make sense. At the Eurobasket in Zagreb, a team with great potential instantaneously delivered, destroying its opponents. It was the best tournament of Petrović's international career. He averaged 30 points on a staggering 69 percent from the field, anchoring both the team's running game and half-court improvisation. After scoring 35 points against Greece and then 33 against Bulgaria to open the tournament, Petrović was rested for the first half of the team's next game against France. The Frenchmen promptly took a seven-point lead at halftime. Ivković inserted Petrović for the second half, he scored 30 points, and Yugoslavia won by 17. By force of will, he was dominating the tournament.

What worked beautifully with Petrović's explosive offense was the cohesion of his teammates. Divac operated out of the high post and it was his vision with the ball, his ability to see the man moving over his shoulder and willingness to dump the ball to the cutter, that seemed to invigorate the team as much as Petrović's offensive strikes. Watching Petrović and Divac work together was something to be appreciated, the two seemingly working to a shared beat. One of the true beauties of the team was that Petrović was able to score in the high twenties and low thirties, as he did for the less successful national teams of the mid-eighties, but this team didn't rely exclusively on that. Part of the success was due to the balance provided by players such as Divac and Kukoč, players who were just as influential apart from any scoring contributions. The team was molded equally from Petrović's confidence and Divac's unselfishness; a team with no distinct offensive weakness. They could be unrelenting as a running team, their size enabling them to secure rebounds, and then with Radja, Kukoč, and Paspalj, each over 6-foot-9, able to fill a wing and run. In the half-court they played on instinct: cutting, hand-offs, strong jump-shooting—a team that spent two years together appeared to have been a unit for much longer.

Yugoslavia won its first four games with ease, the closest margin being 17 points. It was widely expected that they would meet the Soviets in the final, and yet Greece appeared. The Greeks had hosted and won the 1987 Eurobasket, and were capable of denting the European powers within forty spirited minutes. They had their own Petrović, a player named Nikos Galis, an aggressive, inventive offensive player who stood just six-feet tall. He had this wonderful ability to release the ball on his jump shot from deep behind his head to elude a taller defender, even falling away, and because of the unusual release point it was a shot almost exclusive to him. He could work against a defender from the top.[27] He could in one game be capable of 30- and 40-point efforts, and in a semi-final or final at a major tournament he could solely be the difference between winning and losing. Galis led the Greeks to the final in Zagreb with a win over the Soviets, a team at full strength with Sabonis and Šarūnas Marčiulionis, scoring 45 of his team's 81 points. Greece's one-point win was nothing if not an upset.

In side-stepping the Soviets, the final with Greece was almost celebratory for Yugoslavia. The game carried, from the very beginning, an odd predetermined tone. The Yugoslavs ran and scored and then celebrated, and it was aesthetically a basketball exhibition not generally known in Europe. Every Greek miss turned into a fast-break opportunity. Players winked at each other after made shots. At times the Yugoslav players appeared haphazard, their riskier approach having little consequence when the score got out of hand. Petrović had 18 points at the half with his team

---

27 The Yugoslavs liked to use the height of Paspalj with Kukoč against him to little avail.

up by nineteen, and then there was one quick strike, a devastating offensive run when the lead ballooned to 76–47 after ten minutes in the second half. In the end, Yugoslavia won by twenty-one. Petrović scored 28 points, missed just three shots from the field, and passed for 12 assists. A team so young had become so fluent, its play suggesting that basketball would have a new power for the nineties, at least in non-Olympic competition.

The next year, Yugoslavia went to the world championships in Argentina and won seven of eight games, including the final against a Sabonis-less Soviet team.

There was an incident in the moments after the win against the Soviets that did not initially seem major, but in time would prove to be highly controversial. In the final moments of the deciding game with victory assured, Petrović whipped a pass to Kukoč, whose miss was put in by Franjo Arapović as the buzzer sounded. They had ended the game in their own unique style. Petrović turned to Divac with a broad smile, and they embraced. They then turned and walked to Kukoč, arms raised. As the three men celebrated, photographers and fans trickled out onto the floor. One man directly approached the three players near the top of the key, holding with two hands an early Croatian flag, an independent flag, waving it and appearing to look at and speak to Divac. What happened in the immediate seconds afterward is unknown, as the cameras for the European network carrying the game left the scene and focused on the crowd, but when it panned back down towards the court Divac was by now under the basket. He was flanked by the flag-carrying man, pointing to the stands before grabbing a Yugoslavian flag from elsewhere and proceeding to take it to his teammates. The man who initially was carrying the Croatian flag followed Divac back onto the floor, appearing to be trying to take something from him, but Divac nudged him away and continued on to his teammates. By that time the court was inundated, the team itself submerged among a sea of celebrators.

Though at the time the incident itself largely slipped through the cracks when pitted against the high of victory, as tension between Serbia and Croatia escalated over the coming years it *became* a moment. Soon 1990 turned to 1991, and Yugoslavia was increasingly fractured, Serbia aggressively moving on Croatia. What ran parallel to the country's deterioration was Divac's relationship with his Croatian-born teammates from the national team. Where once phone conversations occurred between teammates and friends, Petrović in Portland and Divac in Los Angeles, two young men living out their dreams and sharing it with each other—those conversations stopped completely. Ties were severed. Divac came to believe that the friendship suffered in part as a result of the flag moment in 1990, though it had not. "The situation with the flag incident happened way before Dražen's and Vlade's friendship ended," Vranković said.

Those closest to Petrović at the time insist that it was not the incident with Divac and the flag that caused their relationship to suffer. Instead the difficult situation at home, with Serbian forces entering Croatia, made it tough for the friendship to continue. "One of the things that troubled Dražen was the fact that the Serbs attacked his hometown of Šibenik, which again was a coastal city far from the areas where there's conflicts between Serbs and Croats," said Goyak. "In the inland, east and southeast of Zagreb, there's quite a bit of mix of populations and resentments. But Šibenik is a Croatian Dalmatian town, and it's historical. To have that city attacked was just repulsive to Dražen and others."

"In that time, to the players, they didn't get right into it. The war hadn't really started. At that time, I remember watching that game and talking to Dražen. It was made more of a deal in Croatia than it was elsewhere, that flag incident. That wasn't the key thing. I noticed that he stopped talking, or stopped seeking or calling out to Vlade. That was apparent. I'm very confident that it wasn't the flag incident."

What became a private falling out would in time attract the attention of reporters, and in March 1992, the *Associated Press* asked Petrović about his relationship with Divac. "We're still friends, but we don't talk like we used to. It's because of the war. It's bad for everybody, and it's real tough to be focused on your job here when you're thinking about your family and friends and everything that's going on over there."

It was a breakdown that went unresolved. Petrović and Divac continued to play against each other in the NBA as life back in Croatia continued to deteriorate, but the relationship was never the same. They would cross paths in the pregame of contests between New Jersey and Los Angeles, perhaps lock eyes if only for a brief moment, but the conversations were never of any real depth or substance as they had been in the past.

The magic of the Yugoslav national team, like the friendship of Petrović and Divac, was no longer tangible, confined instead, eternally, to memory.

Seventeen

PRIDE OF THE CROATIANS,
SUMMER 1992

Zaragoza, Croatia; Barcelona, Spain

In the early summer of 1992, the Croatian national men's basketball team gathered at Slovenske Konjice in the northern region of Slovenia. They were there to prepare first for the European Olympic qualifying tournament in Zaragoza, Spain, and then the Barcelona Games, which were to begin in late July. Even with a relatively clean slate and the freshness of being the first representative team from Croatia, there was familiarity within the playing group. Yugoslavia's recent great teams, with the exception of Vlade Divac and Žarko Paspalj, had been made up mostly of Croatians, with Petrović, Toni Kukoč, Dino Radja, and Stojko Vranković. The familiarity was important, because the team was hastily put together in time for a handful of exhibition games, and then for the qualifying tournament.

During the team's preparation, what loomed above each individual was the impact of the war back home. It was a constant in their lives, the promise that each day could bring something painful and everlasting. The players talked about it constantly among each other, wondering when the war could possibly end. They would talk of friends and family who were witnessing the brutality, so close was the action. Practice would end and the players usually headed straight back to their hotels and to the telephone, always in search of the assurance that loved ones were safe and out of harm's way as another day passed.

It was a delicate subject, war, especially when bundled together with sports and other activities that in comparison seemed inappropriate. The possibility of a game being lost was heavily outmatched by the possibility of lives being lost. The players seemed determined to have their efforts bring attention to what was happening back home. "It was an unbelievable moment for us to represent our country," Dino Radja said. "We really wanted to show everybody that there is another country that is suffering and going through these problems." For the team the war was a driving force and endless motivator. "You are representing your country," Petar Skansi, the team's head coach, drilled into his players. "This is your opportunity to show everyone who Croatia is and what we are going through."

Petrović embraced the opportunity to lead Croatia. He was the most identifiable of the Croats, an athlete whose patriotism appeared in his play and intensity. Highly emotional and aggressive on the floor, his play carried a distinct synchronization with the pride with which he represented his country. Early in the preparations he became the team's tone-setter. There was an esteem felt for him by his peers that went beyond the normal player hierarchy, one he had earned even before his successes in New Jersey, for his standards as an individual international player in the eighties had been unmatched. While many of those in the group had been born in the late sixties, Petrović was always a step or two ahead in his career progression. "I think he definitely made my path over there a bit easier than it would be otherwise," Radja said.

Radja had been drafted by Boston in 1989 and his initial attempt to join them was blocked, but the desire to go to the NBA remained strong after he watched Petrović make the leap. When Petrović first struggled for an opportunity in Portland, however, it forced Radja to consider his own situation, and it made him nervous. The thought that Petrović could have trouble led naturally to the assumption by Radja and others that *they too* would suffer the same fate. *Sports Illustrated*'s Alexander Wolff remembers speaking with Toni Kukoč, whose rights were held by Chicago, around the time of Petrović's problems in Portland. "He shared with me his anxiety," Wolff said. "It was a huge source of insecurity that Dražen had not done well initially, a complete mystery to him—against the order of the universe."

Radja admired Petrović most for his work ethic. Invariably, when Radja would show up for national team practice there would be Petrović, before him, already working out. There were constant reminders to Radja and the others that Petrović's devotion forced the others to evaluate their own efforts. There was a practice session during the first Croatian team training camp that had ended what Petrović perceived as too early. He promptly went to the team's physician, Dr. Ivan Fattorini, and asked if indeed Skansi had ended practice, as if a mere two hours was incomprehensible. Fattorini went to Skansi, who confirmed, yes, practice was over for the day. With that, Petrović hurriedly left the gymnasium and made the short walk to the hotel, where he rented a bicycle. Fattorini remembers the sight of the other players lying exhausted in the sun on the grass outside the gymnasium shortly after practice when Petrović furiously pedaled past on the bike. He ended up leaving the Slovenske Konjice town center and riding to nearby Konjiska Mountain, before riding back into the town—a sixteen-mile roundtrip. The next day, when practice finished, Petrović once again rented the bicycle, but was joined by two teammates. The day after, Fattorini noted, there were five players. On the fourth day of practice, a new team-wide activity was born. They had received Petrović's message.

The Croatian team played well enough in Zaragoza to qualify for Barcelona, placing second overall to Lithuania. But they had been rusty at times, off-beat, a characteristic that in recent years was unseen in Yugoslavian teams. The goal, however, was reached and their sights were now set firmly on Barcelona.

Unbeknownst to Petrović, his play in Zaragoza was being closely monitored by an upcoming opponent. USA Basketball had sent Brendan Suhr, an assistant coach on Chuck Daly's Detroit teams, to Spain to scout the best European teams. Suhr had recently followed Daly to New Jersey (Bill Fitch resigned at season's end amidst the late-season turmoil), and the qualifying tournament presented a unique opportunity to see Petrović play in person. Even though the Americans were preordained as Olympic gold medalists, Daly refused to be unprepared or uninformed. The European teams, though they lacked comparable depth to the Americans, were the possessors of talented players—Petrović, Arvydas Sabonis, Detlef Schrempf of Germany—capable of putting a dent in any defense.

Daly and Suhr were aware of Petrović and his offensive capabilities from coaching against him in his early NBA career, and yet Suhr found that the version of Petrović on the Croatian national team was a very different player from the New Jersey version. In a Croatian uniform he was the primary ball handler; the offense funneled through him, but not singularly as a mover without the ball. Instead he was a playmaker, the ball in his hands, a redux to the eighties in the old Yugoslav league where creativity and improvisation had given birth to *Mozart*. But it was a simplified, more efficient Mozart who was in Zaragoza. His confidence was reinforced from his breakout season with the Nets; his body was reshaped from an off-season of work. His body was distinctively different when going against the other European guards, and as a result he was able to do as he pleased on the offensive end.

At a time of dissolving countries and disheartening wars it had been presumed to be Lithuania and Croatia—remnants of the former international basketball powers, the Soviet Union and Yugoslavia—who were the best of the non-Dream Teamers, of the awaiting defeatists. It was a tournament highlight when the two teams met late in the competition. In defeat, Petrović was relentless, submitting a complete offensive performance. He penetrated and attacked, taking seventeen free throws on his way to 30 points. Suhr watched Petrović intently, quietly marveling at the surprising diversity of his offensive game, a game with far more depth than merely catching and shooting jumpers.

What Suhr noticed about Petrović at the European qualifying tournament, and in the season before with New Jersey from afar, was his mentality. "Why he was so good was, I think he was a true believer," he said. From the stands, Suhr watched Petrović play with an overflowing sense of confidence and assurance. When the Lithuania game ended he dashed back to his hotel to call Daly, who was in Portland coaching the Dream Team at the Tournament of the Americas.

"We have got ourselves a player, coach," Suhr said to Daly.

"What do you mean?" Daly answered.

"Dražen"—Suhr began—"he's the best player in Europe. He's right there with Marčiulionis, he's better than Kukoč. This guy can flat out play."

"I've seen this guy play," Daly said, cautiously optimistic. "I already know."

"Chuck, we have seen him, but we haven't seen him in *Europe*," Suhr continued. "When he's in Europe he's so confident. He can do everything. He can handle the ball more. He can play pick and roll. He's a complete player—the best outside the United States."

With Daly coaching first in Barcelona and then the upcoming season in New Jersey, Petrović targeted the Summer Games as a proving ground to his new coach. It was a challenge that he embraced.

Croatia won its first group game in Barcelona against Brazil, and then faced the Americans. In the weeks leading up to the contest, some of the Croatian players came to Petrović wanting to know about the United States, about what do to and how to play against them—*them* representing the demigods. "Just go out and play normal," Petrović said. The pre-installed aura was one of the everlasting traits of the Dream Team, even opponents snapping pictures from the bench during games or sidling up to particular stars during dead-balls, hoping that someone, somewhere would photograph them alongside their heroes. In the lead-up to the Games, Petrović tried to put his finger on the mortality, on just how close a team could get to the Americans. He spoke with Harvey Araton of *The New York Times* at length, in private, about the capabilities of his Croatian team and how far they could push the Americans. He estimated that with all things playing out to expectations—full strength against full strength—the Croatians could keep the game close for a half. "Dražen was in many respects a basketball visionary," said Araton, who enjoyed the thoughtful and detailed way that Petrović viewed the expanding basketball globe. "He could see the possibilities."

The group game vs. the Dream Team will historically not be remembered for Petrović's involvement, but for that of his teammate, Toni Kukoč. There was elegance to Kukoč's game. With the ball in his hands he was very creative, often appearing to find more gratification in distributing the ball to others than scoring, a characteristic that earned for him the nickname, *The Waiter*.[28] He was a splendid offensive player, his passing skills complemented by an ability to score in a variety of ways. Because of his height and slender frame, it was easy to view Kukoč as someone who lacked physicality, but he combated it with his unique evasiveness and length.

Kukoč was very publicly wooed by Bulls general manager Jerry Krause after being drafted in 1990, and followed up not only with constant affection but also a handsome contract offer. Consequently, that annoyed some of the established yet underpaid players, none more than Scottie Pippen. Pippen himself was an elegant player, albeit a vastly more diverse one than Kukoč. He was a rising star in the league, already an All-Star, and worse, a poorly paid one at that. Krause's affinity for Kukoč left Pippen feeling disrespected, and the unique opportunity to play Croatia on the Olympic stage had given him the opportunity to embarrass not just Kukoč but Krause as well. In addition, for the Dream Team there already was a hunger for them to be challenged, so a matchup with a touted Croatian team was something to hold their focus, if only for a short while.

Pippen used the Dream Team's first offensive possession to attack Kukoč, his teammates acting as accomplices, clearing out so that Pippen could approach from the top on the lonely Kukoč. It was the type of vengeful approach and opportunistic challenge

---

28 Like Petrović's *Mozart*, that moniker added to Kukoč's pre-NBA mythology.

that Michael Jordan was used to scrounging up, but Pippen seemed to have inherited that mantle for this game—the possessor of some potent athletic venom. Less than three minutes into the game Kukoč turned the ball over, leading to a Jordan dunk at the other end, and Skansi removed him from the game in order to emotionally restore him. But when Kukoč returned a short while later he was obviously reticent; he was passing quickly, leaving his feet, and at times fading completely out of play. Kukoč's natural inclination always was to pass, but it seemed that sense was heightened by Pippen's and Jordan's approach, making him deferential and counterproductive. There was a moment late in the first half that seemed to crystalize it all. Kukoč penetrated the lane and left his feet, but Jordan, as if coming from nowhere, snatched the ball out of his hands. It led to a Pippen transition score on the other end and Kukoč didn't even summon up the energy to cross mid-court. Steve Jones, broadcasting the game for an American Olympic cable network, thought that Pippen and Jordan were trying to "squeeze his heart" in order to get him to play with them. "Kukoč hasn't shown that he wants to dig down and compete," Jones said during the telecast.

Petrović seemed more readily enthusiastic about this type of high-tension competition. Staging his own sort of mini-battle with Jordan in the first half, he scored 17 points. It seemed at times that he was overly aggressive, constantly attacking Jordan with varying degrees of results. But it appeared that his intent was more about showing his teammates that there was only one way to approach the Dream Team, one that didn't involve hesitation. Mike Celizic of the *Record* was in Barcelona, covering the game. He couldn't help but notice Jordan bumping Petrović in the first half, talking in his ear. From having closely followed Petrović's on-court character evolving with the Nets, Celizic knew a potential tale when he saw it. Later he asked Petrović about the exchange. "You can't score," is what Jordan repeatedly told Petrović, according to his version of events. It was a remark to which Petrović finally stopped, looked Jordan in the eye, and replied, "You don't intimidate me. I score my points."

Celizic ensured that the story made its way into print.

When the Americans held a twenty-three point lead late in the half, Petrović produced his defining moment as a member of the Croatian national team. He hit a three-pointer from the right side. Jordan took the ball out of the net and launched a quick baseball pass to the other end of the floor. Petrović anticipated it, and intercepted the pass. He immediately dribbled to the same spot, and pulled up over Larry Bird for another trey. His form was perfect on that second shot; six points in less than ten seconds. He then turned to the crowd and pumped his fist with clenched teeth as he ran down the floor, defiant and brave. Ultimately, it was the only gasp the Croatians could muster. When Petrović picked up his fourth foul early in the second half he begged Skansi to leave him in the game. However, what resulted was altered aggression. He wouldn't score in the second half until two minutes remained, finishing with 19 points. By the time Kukoč found any semblance of rhythm, the sting had long left the game. The Dream Team, at once entertainers and bloodthirsty, handily won 103–70. "I did this because I can't put Jerry Krause out on the court," Pippen said afterward.

As the teams left the court Daly made a beeline for Petrović. The two chatted as they left the floor, smiling as they walked. It was their first interaction since Daly had been named New Jersey's coach some two months earlier. Daly, already thinking ahead, told Petrović that he needed to rest after Barcelona. That he needed to enter the 1992–93 NBA season fresh.

Celizic went to Daly after the game for an appraisal of Petrović. "I love his intensity," Daly said. "We scouted him in the European [qualifying] championships and I've seen him here. We've seen things we didn't know he could do. He can beat people off the dribble. He can run the pick and roll. I like what I see."

Moments later, Celizic went to see Petrović, informing him of Daly's words. Petrović, as Celizic wrote later, beamed with pride.

The loss did not devastate the Croatians. The result was widely anticipated even before the Games began, casting an unusual competitive environment over the tournament. The loss did not cause deviation from the final goal, which was to meet the United States in the gold medal game. Croatia beat Spain, Germany, and Angola (while Petrović rested) to finish second in its group behind the United States, and then overcame Australia in the quarter-finals. One hurdle remained—the semi-finals—with Croatia to meet the Commonwealth of Independent States, an amalgamation of one-time Soviet states. With the Dream Team waiting, it was essentially the Silver Medal Game.

In the hours before the contest the Croatian team bus sat idle near the Olympic village, preparing to move toward the arena for the afternoon game, when with little warning the door swung open. Onto the bus climbed Antun "Tonci" Vrdoljak, the president of Croatia's newly formed Olympic Committee. Vrdoljak was a colorful and charismatic character. He had made a late entrance into politics after a lengthy acting and film-making career, and superseded the favored Mirko Novosel seemingly from nowhere in the race to become head of Croatia's Olympic Committee. He was a major force for the national team in the lead-up to Barcelona, pushing and pushing the government to put funds into the basketball program even as the country suffered. The basketball team, Vrdoljak argued, had a very real chance at winning a medal, which would be a tremendous boost for the stricken country.

Vrdoljak had a very short speech prepared for the team when he stood before them in the aisle. "You better win this game," he told them. And with that, he turned and stepped off the bus. *You don't have to tell me*, Radja thought to himself on the bus in the moments after Vrdoljak's words. The players did not consider it an ultimatum, and Vrdoljak perhaps better than anyone had read the thoughts of his players. The pressure was long built-in. "It was probably the most important game of my career," Radja said.

Croatia, perhaps weighed down by the enormity of the contest, came out flat in the semi-final, falling behind by nine after just five minutes. Petrović was guarded by Igors Miglinieks, a rugged, unglamorous player who decided to be physical in his approach to the matchup. He helped the CIS take a ten-point lead into halftime by not allowing Petrović to find any sort of flow and controlling the game's pace. At one point during a particularly poor stretch for Croatia, Petrović gazed up into the stands, spotting Vrdoljak. *We are in trouble*, Petrović thought to himself.

Early in the second half Petrović became irritated by Miglinieks's physicality and general presence, and the two exchanged shoves on Croatia's first offensive possession. Shortly after, Petrović drew a technical foul after drawing a charge on Miglinieks and then trying to yank the ball from his hands. He was trying to force his way into the game by way of intensity and tension. Later, facing Miglinieks at the top, he ripped the ball through and hit a pull-up three-pointer going left. Trotting down the floor, he began chatting in Miglinieks' ear. "I was talking in English," Petrović said later. "I don't know if they understood."

He then hit three more field goals over the next four minutes, giving him 10 points to open the half. He was dragging Croatia back. After briefly taking the lead, Croatia once again surrendered control to the CIS, who went back up eight with just under six minutes to go. Petrović had tried to lift Croatia, but he had no help from Kukoč, who to that point had made just one field goal and was being out-muscled in his duel with Alexander Volkov, a player with NBA experience.

It was Volkov who late in the game began forcing the action, getting to the free throw line again and again. But instead of reinforcing his team's advantage, Volkov struggled at the line, missing the front end of four one-and-ones, his team ending up with empty possessions as Croatia scrapped back.

Down four with just under forty seconds to go, Kukoč fired a three-pointer and converted. It was a gutsy shot, quite improbable, the type that could erase the prior thirty-nine minutes of disappointment. Volkov once again missed from the foul line with twenty-four seconds to go, and Croatia secured the defensive rebound. Even though Croatia boasted the offensive talents of Kukoč and Radja there was no mistaking in whose hands the ball was to end up. Petrović broke free to receive the pass, and he bulled his way through three CIS defenders, drawing a foul with nine seconds to go. Petrović made the first, tying the score. He made the second and jumped in the air, throwing both fists up, even as the play moved on past him.

The CIS advanced the ball, and after a broken play the ball squirted out of bounds. Volkov tried for one last time to finish it, but his fall-away jumper from the baseline was short. Croatia had stolen the game. The result earned them a trip to the gold medal game and a guaranteed medal. Volkov's final shot attempt fell short, Miglinieks contested the rebound and was knocked to the ground as time expired. Petrović came to him, stood over him, and blasted the game's final words in his face. "I just told him we won the game," he told reporters afterward.

The emotion of the win brought about a collective exhale and tremendous relief for the Croatians. Petrović climbed into the first rows and took a Croatian flag, before returning to the floor and his teammates. There, the team embraced.

What streamed down Dražen Petrović's face that afternoon were tears of joy, as the group clutched the flag. For a country that had endured exceptional hardship, it was a moment of pure emotion.

On the night before the gold medal game, Petrović came to Vranković in the Olympic village to discuss the matchup with the United States. "We have a good chance to beat this team," Petrović said.

Vranković managed to maintain a straight face, despite the proclamation of his best friend.

"Okay, Dražen," he said, his voice deep and without a hint of emotion. "Let's go to sleep and be ready for tomorrow."

Vranković was not the only one to whom Petrović floated the idea. Aleksandar Petrović, serving as the team's assistant coach, remembered Petrović telling other players, too. The elder Petrović thought that a game with a predetermined outcome just didn't sit well with his younger brother, even one that was to come against the sport's greatest collection of talent.

Even though it was a gold medal game, the United States' level of intensity was not at the same level as it had been for the group game against Croatia. That one had resided at a level all its own. They were excellent when it came to beginning games, the Dream Team. Aware of what a destructive start could do to teams, they would unleash one quick strike to begin a game and then coast. They quickly jumped out by ten, but the Croatians remained persistent. Croatia made a run midway through the opening half, pulling close behind Petrović's 10 points. Then Croatia forced a turnover and broke to the other end, with Kukoč finding center Franjo Arapović roaring down the lane for the dunk plus a foul. Croatia led 25–23. An appropriate reaction would have been for someone to take a photograph of the scoreboard before the United States raced the ball back up the floor. Vranković was on the bench when Croatia led, and Petrović turned to him and pointed excitedly. "What did I tell you!?" Petrović yelled. Vranković remained stoic. *We still have thirty minutes to play*, he thought to himself.

The moment quickly passed. Charles Barkley hit a three-pointer on the Dream Team's next possession and carried out a result that had been foregone since 1989. The final score was 117–85. For the Americans, it represented their "closest" margin of victory.

Croatia had put up a better performance than in the prior meeting, and it was a satisfying finish to come up with a silver medal so soon after the dissolving of Yugoslavia. Petrović scored 24 points in the final against the Dream Team, making him the game's leading scorer. He finished the tournament second behind Brazil's Oscar Schmidt in points. More importantly, he proudly exhibited his own unique Croatian spirit on the floor, and played some of the best basketball of his life.

It was the beginning of his best stretch of play. For what awaited Petrović post-Barcelona was a campaign that saw him become one of the fifteen best players in the world.

It also, tragically, would prove to be his last.

Eighteen

STAR GUARD, 1992–93

East Rutherford, New Jersey, USA

New Jersey reached the playoffs for the first time in six years, in 1992, and yet their season did not end harmoniously. In the week after the Nets were eliminated by the Cleveland Cavaliers, there were reports seeping out of the organization that Bill Fitch's days were numbered. Seeing the writing on the wall, Fitch resigned with a year remaining on his contract. It was obvious that the relationship between the coach and his top players had deteriorated as the season wore on, and that concerned ownership. The late-season problems, especially those that had occurred in games, helped seal Fitch's ending. "Bill is from the old school," minority owner Bernie Mann told *The New York Times*. "But 1992 is a lot different from 1982."

In the days after Fitch's departure, Nets general manager Willis Reed placed a call to Detroit Pistons assistant coach Brendan Suhr, the lead assistant to Chuck Daly in Detroit. With Reed there was something of a history between him and Suhr, as the two had been assistant coaches in Atlanta under Mike Fratello in the mid-eighties. Reed took a strong interest in Daly's recent departure from Detroit just weeks earlier, and placed a call to his friend. "Is there any chance Chuck would consider coming to New Jersey?" Reed asked Suhr. The conversation set in motion the process of landing the heralded coach.

Daly eventually accepted the job from Reed. The motivation for Daly to take the Nets job came not from the closeness to New York City nor the lucrative money offer, but as a result of the basketball opportunities that were promised. Reed sold hard to Daly the opportunity to build something special in New Jersey, coaching Derrick Coleman, Dražen Petrović, and Kenny Anderson. He sold the talent and the *future*. It was a future that didn't exist in Detroit, at least not with the aging cast who were no longer capable of competing in the upper echelon, a situation in need of rebuilding. Something had already started building in New Jersey, Reed told Daly. All it needed was someone of his stature to push it further.

Daly at that point was without peer among NBA coaches in terms of respect. He had proved to be the ideal choice to coach a United States Olympic Team comprising professionals that summer in Barcelona. Throughout his relatively short professional coaching career he had always given the impression that he understood the league offered little in the way of guarantees. It was an approach likely borne from his own very deliberate, late-blooming path to the NBA that easily might have been detoured. Daly's resume included high school head coach, college assistant, college head coach, and professional assistant, before finally becoming a professional head coach at fifty-two, his dues paid in full even if at that level he had been unproven. Despite later success in Detroit he held onto that uneasy, uncertain feeling. Often in games he sat among his assistants, elbows on knees, tongue tucked and firmly pressing against his lower lip. He gave off an overwhelming impression of stress in spite of the score, which was usually in his favor. It belied his hair and expensive suits, elements that received more acclaim as time wore on and served as a cute sidebar to his greatness as a coach.

He had, with the help of Jack McCloskey, rebuilt the identity of those Detroit teams in a methodical and gradual way. He took them from being a very offensive-minded team (that holds the NBA record for most points in one game—186—at Denver during the 1983–84 season) to one that was defense-driven. Those teams were tough, hard, less glamorous and less liked, but infinitely more successful. Daly's leading man through that transition was Isiah Thomas, the decade's preeminent traditional point guard, a player whose personality demanded a certain amount of entitlement and ownership within the group. Daly was able to grant that to Thomas, and to his other veterans, without surrendering any of the leadership or decision making. Daly had a very keen sense—a heightened sense among his contemporaries—that coaching was less about the coach himself, that any measure of success started and ended with the players. The team earned the moniker of "Bad Boys," and yet even while at the controls Daly was never cast in a negative light like his key players. He was, instead, lauded for his ability to first raise them, mold them, and then maintain them as NBA elitists.

Detroit took their lumps and used that to become great. Daly's teams were incredibly strong-willed, with the ability to battle back from what appeared to be debilitating losses (1987 Eastern Conference Finals to Boston, 1988 NBA Finals to Los Angeles) by beating those same teams in the following seasons. It spoke of Daly's resolve and ability to convince his Detroit teams that they belonged with the Celtics and Lakers in the hard-to-penetrate NBA echelon of the eighties.

Reed watched over the years and was left impressed with Daly's ability to maintain control over a group that, viewed from the outside, had a reputation for being tough minded and harsh. Reed hoped that Daly could do the same in New Jersey, albeit with a younger, immature group, one that had spurned Fitch's attempts at authority and direction. Daly had on his side very recent success that the younger players would be aware of; it was an element that Fitch, some eleven years removed from his title as a coach, couldn't muster with men in their early twenties. It seemed a natural fit to place Daly with this group. Coleman was from Detroit, where Daly had made his name. Anderson was a point guard with high potential, and at that time the idol of all point guards was Thomas, who was tied to Daly through their successful working relationship. Petrović was most studious when it came to basketball and those associated with the game, so someone of Daly's stature was someone to whom he was quickly drawn.

Petrović arrived in training camp fatigued from the summer. He took several weeks off in the wake of Barcelona and his commitments with the national team and consequently played very poorly in the preseason. "He was having a horrible time, and I was kind of thinking that it was because he had played a lot of basketball in the summer," assistant coach Rick Carlisle said. It was important to Petrović that he continue to make an impression on Daly, even after Barcelona. Upon joining New Jersey, and in speaking to his coaches, it was obvious that Daly had established a deep respect for Petrović. Daly told Carlisle that his goal had been to coach through the entire Olympic tournament without calling a time-out. "He told me the closest he came to calling a time-out was against Croatia, when Petrović got going," Carlisle recalled of his conversations with Daly in the preseason. "And he was *this close* but he didn't do it. But he gained a healthy respect for Dražen's game. Not only his game and ability, but his will and the fact that he really believed—Chuck could tell—that Dražen really believed he could win the game, really trying to compete to win the game. Whereas ninety-nine percent of the guys were in awe."

The presence of Daly promised that Petrović would be more diverse and have more freedom as an offensive player. In the early going, as Daly was still becoming acquainted with Petrović, a good deal of the instruction came from the lone hold-over coach from Bill Fitch's time, Carlisle. He and Dražen had become close in the year-and-a-half Petrović had been in New Jersey. One of the wrinkles of the relationship was that Carlisle had taken the time to get to know key Croatian phrases, ones that he would yell to Petrović during the course of a game. "I enjoyed that kind of stuff," Carlisle said. "And it just helped create a little bit more of a bond between he and I." Anything from demanding tougher on-ball defense ("*Igraj obranu*") to getting his toes off the three-point line when shooting from distance ("*Nagazio si liniju*"), Carlisle and Petrović had their own private line of communication within the team. The phrase Carlisle used most frequently with Petrović, the one most welcomed, was *Pujac tricu*—shoot the three. Early in that season, with New Jersey trailing late in the fourth quarter of a game, Carlisle approached Petrović in the huddle. "When we are down, what do you do?" he asked.

"Pujac tricu," Petrović responded.

The 1992–93 Nets opened their season in a way very different from that of the prior year. There were distinct expectations from this team, not just because of Daly's arrival, but with the talented nucleus of Petrović, Derrick Coleman, and Kenny Anderson. Each was expected to raise the level of his game. The logical deduction was that if a dysfunctional team could manage a playoff appearance the previous year, then with that same talent and a renowned coach they could push even further. It was a team that, when compared to previous editions, was infinitely more stable; there would be no suggestion of coaching changes in the season's opening months, there would be less bickering between players and coaches or between players and players. Daly simply would not allow it. In only the second game of the season, at Miami, Petrović and Kenny Anderson exchanged words during a time-out. It came after Petrović felt that he had stopped getting the ball after taking two straight shots. When the team convened in the locker room after the game, Daly spoke to the group sternly, telling them that those types of incidents would not be tolerated. He stamped his authority on them quickly.

Daly's most notable adjustment was thrusting Anderson into the starting line-up. It was a confident decision by Daly, who had seen the value in handing the keys of the team to a twenty-two-year-old, even if it surely meant there would be a steep learning curve. Anderson's rookie season had been inconclusive, as his playing time under Fitch was spotty. Daly made a point after taking over that the point guard would be Anderson, not Mookie Blaylock. Anderson was tremendously gifted, with a long reach and an incredible driving ability. He was uniquely capable of finding cracks in the defense, twisting and contorting, to either find an open teammate amid a sea of people or finish the play himself. The new coaching staff had quickly fallen for him.

Paul Silas, a former NBA veteran and one of the team's assistant coaches, told reporters that within Anderson was both the quickness of Lenny Wilkens and the offensive game of Tiny Archibald, both of whom were superb point guards from Silas's playing days. It was an especially high compliment for a young player who was still proving himself. Four days before the opening of the regular season, the Nets traded the previous season's starter, Mookie Blaylock, to Atlanta. It was an enormous stake of faith in Anderson's ability to thrive under Daly. He quickly acclimated himself to the dynamic of Petrović and Coleman, and the three young men became the foundation of a developing team.

The challenge for Daly was that each of his three young stars was at a different level of development, both in maturity and performance. Petrović was trying to prove that his previous season was not a fluke, and that he belonged among the league's best shooting guards. Coleman had shown flashes of greatness, especially in the playoffs, but was not yet taken seriously among the best of the power forwards—not with the baggage from his relationship with Fitch and the perceptions about his personality and consistency. And Anderson was, everyone agreed, an exceptional talent but mostly unproven as a professional.

So it was a trio with significant potential, which in New Jersey was an especially cautious predicament: in Nets history even the sure things found a way to become tainted and underwhelming.

Talent-wise it was a triumvirate of beautifully blended functions, post and perimeter and shooting and creativity, and they were among the main reasons that Daly took the job. Even beyond the obvious history of the franchise and its problems, Daly could see the possibilities and be confident that he could pull them together coherently. Beyond that, Daly believed in his ability to create a professional environment, one that especially Coleman and Anderson needed at that point in their careers.

The new Nets staggered out of the gate at 4–7, and their play mirrored that of Petrović's, who also struggled. But things turned around when the team went for a western swing in late November, winning the final three games, first in Los Angeles against the Lakers, then in Utah and Sacramento. The Sacramento win had been a tight game, but the Nets pulled it out behind Petrović, who scored 14 of his 26 points in the fourth quarter. New Jersey returned home for a win over Atlanta, and then hosted San Antonio. The Spurs took an eighteen-point lead into the third quarter before the Nets climbed back. "We didn't want to roll over. We were having too much fun being ourselves," forward Rick Mahorn articulated to Mike Freeman of *The New York Times*.

They still trailed by five in the final minute before two Anderson free throws and then a Petrović three-pointer, first pump-faking San Antonio's Lloyd Daniels, then stepping back and calmly making the distance shot. San Antonio held a two-point lead with four seconds to go in regulation when Petrović took Sean Elliott off the dribble before plowing into the paint and into David Robinson, releasing a difficult shot from chest height. He and Robinson were in a heap in the paint, and the ball fell in. What followed was classic Petrović. After lying on the floor awaiting the result of the shot, he quickly rose to his feet, ran to the first row of fans, and pumped his fists. Then, on his way back to the huddle he made a beeline for referee Ron Garretson, barking quickly in his ear over the missed foul call before continuing on. The Nets managed to hang on in overtime behind Petrović's 34 points and a masterpiece by Anderson: 31 points and 17 assists.

The Nets won in Miami the next night behind Petrović's 29 points, and he was named the NBA's Player of the Week. He averaged just under 28 points per game in the team's undefeated week, and the Nets had ripped off a streak of six straight wins, largely without Coleman. The NBA award was a satisfying one to Petrović, who under Daly was continuing his development. It was Petrović whose number was called down the stretch in the Spurs game, with the team going to him while down by two, and with just four seconds to play. Daly told reporters that he was not afraid to go to Petrović in pressure situations, that the type of players who are best in those times are the ones who have the most confidence in themselves.[29]

Petrović averaged 24 points per game on 53 percent shooting in the month of December as the Nets rebounded from their slow start, and into January he continued his strong play. The team was among the top five in the conference since the calendar turn of the new year, and it was evident that with Daly as coach, Petrović and Coleman maintaining their high level of performance, and Anderson continuing to develop, it was a team with great capabilities.

Near the end of the month, New Jersey hosted a fine Houston team. The game initially appeared to be nothing unusual, with the Nets leading and Petrović scoring 19 points through three quarters. But in the fourth quarter Petrović found something extra within himself. He made eight field goals in the quarter alone. The Nets continuously called his number, isolating Petrović on one side of the floor with Coleman. There seemed to be rising interest from the crowd with each passing shot, increased anticipation. After Petrović tied his regular-season high of 39 points, and with the lead safe, he began peeking at the bench out of the corner of his eye at every opportunity, as if hoping not to be taken out by Daly. Late in the fourth, he found a seam in the paint and hit an awkward leaning shot over Robert Horry for point number 41. As he jogged back down the floor once again, his eyes were

---

29 Later in December, in a game at Milwaukee, Daly again went to Petrović, who hit a last-second field goal to beat the Bucks.

fixed on the bench. On the team's final possession he was spotted up in the corner, and after taking a pass from Rafael Addison he squared up, his legs balanced, body straight—the perfect shot with the perfect result. The crowd erupted. He walked over to Coleman, and the two hugged. Forty-four points with just six missed field goals in twenty-three attempts, a win, and a standing ovation.

Afterwards, the Nets' head of scorekeeping, Herb Turetzky, made his way into the crowded locker room to congratulate Petrović on his career-best game. The two had become close over time. They had first spoken not long after Petrović's 1991 arrival in New Jersey when he introduced himself to Turetzky—and then informed him of an inaccuracy in his game box score. "You had me as three for six on threes," he told Turetzky, wide-eyed, but mostly serious. "But I was three for five." In his twenty-five years to that point in professional basketball, Turetzky had seen on a rare occasion a player make a query about something that showed up on a stat sheet. He remembered one night in the Meadowlands an irate Bill Laimbeer castigating him over a missed *rebound*. But in Petrović, Turetzky soon found, there was nothing off-putting about his queries. He noticed Petrović had a unique, calculating mind, an uncanny routine of keeping his own stats in his head as he competed. He could recite these numbers as soon as the contest was finished. It was a rare quality in a professional basketball player that, in Turetzky's experience, was equaled only by former Warriors forward Rick Barry. "He knew everything he was doing," Turetzky would say of Barry. "Very similar to Draz."

Early in Petrović's tenure in New Jersey it became something of an expected visitation. Thirty minutes or so after a game would finish, Turetzky, a gentle, sweet man, loved within the organization, would find himself smiling as he listened to a conversation initiated by Petrović. The player would be kindly pointing out a missed number here or there that had showed up on his line. From that began a friendship. Even Turetzky's son, David, at the time a ball boy with the Nets, found himself part of Petrović's routine. In the hours before games, the youngster would play a key figure in Petrović's famous pregame shooting session, tossing the ball back to his idol on the otherwise empty floor. "Draz realized that David could get him the ball to the same spot," Turetzky remembered later. "And he appreciated that."[30]

Petrović was happy to see Turetzky after the Rockets game. He reached into his bag and gave Turetzky his size twelve Nikes to keep. Turetzky was taken aback. "Would you mind signing these for me, Draz?" he asked. Petrović looked at him quizzically.

"You scored 44 points against a great team," Turetzky added, justifying his request.

Petrović smiled.

"Forty-four isn't much," he said. "I once scored one-hundred points and much more in Europe."

Petrović was playing well enough to where 44 points against a very good team was pleasing, and yet only served as a motivation to do more. Internal satisfaction was fleeting in Petrović's career; it was always a secondary accomplishment, for the priority

---

30 It was one of Petrović's lasting traits that he would touch those within the organization who generally would not have a close relationship with the players, people such as Turetzky or broadcaster Spencer Ross. These men, in the years afterward, would continue to hold those friendships close to their hearts.

would always shift to the next hurdle. By the first week of February he was the league's ninth leading scorer at 23.4 points per game, which placed him fourth in the Eastern Conference. Only Michael Jordan, Dominique Wilkins, and Orlando's rookie center, Shaquille O'Neal, were ahead of him.[31] As a team the Nets were ideally placed to send a representative to that season's All-Star Game in Salt Lake City, Utah. Both Petrović and Coleman were playing well enough to be considered. "I deserve to be there, like Derrick," Petrović told Mike Celizic of the *Record*.

Petrović was insistent that he was a better player than in the previous year, much more devoted to the overall game and not just a shooter and scorer. Daly challenged him early in the season to be a competent defender, and there were nights when he had been quite effective at that end of the floor. He entered the season even stronger, and was less willing to give up a spot on the floor. "It was very clear that Chuck had gotten to Dražen's head how important defense was," said John Brennan, the Nets' beat man for the *Record*. "Not every player would want to do that, especially big scorers. He had that panache and style, and he could've maybe figured that 'I don't want to do the work.' But he was learning, and he became a much better defensive player during that season."

The offense had continued strong. Petrović was an enhanced version of the player who finished the 1991–92 season: his body had continued to build up, and he was a more controlled, balanced offensive player. Petrović was scoring off catches and quick-fires at the same rate, but under Daly he had opportunities to square himself to the basket, handle the ball, force a switch on the wing, and be defended by a bigger man. Daly loved to go

31 New Jersey, coincidentally, was perfectly calibrated with Petrović: they were the owners of the league's ninth-best record and the East's fourth.

to Petrović and Coleman on one side of the floor, and make the defense choose (to switch was to concede defeat), and Petrović found a comfort area in that side pick and roll. Stylistically, his offensive game tempered dramatically since he had first come into the league. There was more fluidity, fewer wasted dribbles or motion in his offense now, his body and game fully complementary. It was as much a testament to his ability to learn as it was to his work ethic, as he had found within his body and limitations the ideal game, one tailored to his unique capabilities.

With a second straight season at an elite level, Petrović desperately wanted to be named an All-Star.

After a poor showing via the fan vote (Petrović finished just eighth among Eastern Conference guards), his only hope at being named an All-Star resided with the coaches. Voting was usually a popularity contest, so to be selected by the coaches carried its own authenticity. However, when the reserves were announced in the weeks leading up to the midseason contest, they did not include Petrović. Nor did they include Coleman, nor any member of the fourth-place Nets. When considering the performance of each individual, coupled with the success of the team, it was unusual that the Nets would not be sending a representative.

Being overlooked was a tremendous disappointment for Petrović. It caused him to scrutinize, perhaps overly so, the reasons for his exclusion. He looked at the Eastern Conference selections and noticed that three players from Cleveland (Mark Price, Brad Daugherty, and Larry Nance) were named, and he told reporters that there was imbalance there. "Cleveland has three guys, New Jersey has no one. I think that is not correct," he told the *Record*. Brennan was around Petrović in the days after the announcement, and came to theorize that part of Petrović's disappointment came from the player's stern belief of some natural order that should have carried out into being selected. He had put in the hard work, been professional, and done all the right things. Brennan felt that Petrović saw that as something that should have been reciprocated in the selection.

Away from the reporters, Petrović came to believe that perhaps the fact he was European kept him from being selected. It was something that he did not speak of publicly, but it was a notion that he had passed on to his former teammate, Danny Ainge, when the Nets visited Phoenix in March. Ainge relayed the story to Harvey Araton of *The New York Times*. "He felt that his nationality had something to do with it [missing selection]" Ainge told Araton. "I think so, too. He really wanted to prove that someone who grew up playing in Europe could make it big in the NBA."

It was a thought that had emerged from great emotion and disappointment. There was a great struggle in Petrović to be accepted, not just among his teammates but by the league as a whole. He targeted the All-Star Game as being the ultimate acceptance, for it placed him, even as a European, among the league's best. What was interesting about Petrović's perceived reason for omission was that the coaches had selected Indiana's Detlef Schrempf, also a European. There were many similarities between Schrempf and Petrović in terms of career arc: Schrempf had initially been in Dallas, but after three-and-a-half seasons was traded to Indiana, and, like Petrović, the change brought about instant rejuvenation. He was the league's top sixth man in both 1991 and 1992. By 1993 he was among the league's most complete forwards, with averages of just under 20 points, more than nine rebounds and six assists for a team that was perennially in the East playoff picture. It had taken several years of playing at a high level to be selected, and it appeared that Petrović would be subjected to a similar course. Petrović's omission was largely a non-story outside New Jersey, but it was one that disappointed him greatly, and caused him to approach the second half of the season with even more aggression.

The timing of Petrović's omission from the league's All-Star team coincided with the increased public speculation in New Jersey over his contract. He was to be a free agent at the end of the 1993 season. As the season wore on and as Petrović continued to elevate his game, it became apparent that in order to remain in New Jersey he would need to be paid handsomely. New Jersey was willing to pay Petrović, but within limits. When he was acquired by the Nets the team had tacked on an additional year to his existing contract. In the summer of 1992, after Petrović's breakout season, his agent Warren LeGarie sent a contract proposal to the Nets. LeGarie was fielding offers from European teams that were aware of Petrović's fondness for his home continent and that had the ability to compete at least financially with what New Jersey was offering (and included mostly tax-free deals, deals with cars and houses and other attractive assets). It was important to offer lavish money, because they could not offer a comparable competitive level of play. The European offers proved to be influential in the negotiation process, driving up the price just as Petrović's stellar play was making him increasingly valuable.

One interesting aspect of Petrović's contract situation was the sharp conflict in reports that were printed in European and American papers. The European papers, most prominently in Spain, reported in the opening month of the 1992–93 season that Petrović would return to Europe in the event that a contract was not completed by the end of the playing year. Conversely,

Petrović told the *Record* in that same month that there was no rush. "I just want to concentrate on my game. If you work hard in this league, you'll get taken care of. I don't feel any pressure," he told the paper.

The first real red flag came in December in a report in *The New York Times* by Mike Freeman, who hinted that Petrović was unhappy with the slow pace of New Jersey's movements regarding his contract. That it had yet to be signed and closed was perhaps an indication that the Nets were not willing to pay him what he deserved. "At this point, the percentages are against it," LeGarie told Freeman. "I don't see him coming back, and only the Nets are to blame." It was in that story that LeGarie told Freeman the contract proposal that was sent to the team over the summer had yet to be acknowledged, a period of six months. That, it was insinuated, bothered both Petrović and LeGarie. Later that month, when Petrović was named the top European player in an award given annually by the Italian publication *La Gazzetta dello Sport*, he told them, "I joined the NBA to prove that a European can compete at such levels. I succeeded. Thus, I am looking forward to a comeback to Europe next season."

February brought about a strange new development. Petrović and LeGarie rejected an offer from the Nets, not because of the price (reportedly somewhere over $3 million per season) but because of its duration—five years. That was one year *longer* than Petrović was willing to sign for. It meant he would have been away from Croatia for a total of ten years, and there was something unsettling about that idea. "It's probably the first time that an NBA player has refused extra years," LeGarie told *The Times*. The Nets remained confident that they could secure Petrović, but when the negotiations between LeGarie and Reed suddenly became events that were being written about, being drawn out, the concern grew. "I know if you wait too long on this sort of thing [contract negotiations]," Reed told the *Record*, "it can get screwed up."

The five-year offer was made the day after the announcement of the All-Star reserves, and shortly after LeGarie made the trek to New Jersey to meet with Reed, following some time in Europe. It was believed that a deal would be hashed out over the All-Star weekend, but that meeting came and went without a deal being finalized.

New Jersey was entering dangerous waters, one in which at first they appeared to have control over the contract of its best player. Yet as time went on, that control slowly, gradually left them. What remained was uncertainty at the very time of the best playing stretch of Petrović's career.

Nineteen

"I PROVED EVERYTHING I HAD TO PROVE IN THE NBA," SPRING 1993

East Rutherford, New Jersey, USA

To close out February 1993, the Nets hosted New York. It was a big game for the New Jersey franchise, the first such major national television appearance since 1984, and no matter the state of the team there was always additional motivation when playing the Knicks. With the close proximity of the two franchises, and the inferior feeling when considering their respective media coverage and fan bases, the games were always a little more heated. Traditionally, the games at the Meadowlands were heavily populated with Knicks fans, but on this Sunday afternoon it proved different. Marv Albert called the game for NBC and commented that it was indeed the first time he could remember a pro-Net crowd for a *home* game against the Knicks, a sure sign that the Nets warranted the following by the locals. Petrović seemed to enjoy the competitive environment that came with Knicks games. Earlier in the season he was involved in a shoving match with reserve guard Rolando Blackman. "He's a trash talker with an accent," Blackman told reporters afterwards. He was then asked to elaborate on the type of chatter Petrović was spouting. "Rambo-type words, words you would find in a Rambo movie," he answered.

With the loss of Gerald Wilkins, a noted Petrović sparring partner, to Cleveland, John Starks had become New York's starting shooting guard. Starks relished getting under the skin of opponents and was first-rate at taunting. He had in the same game as the Blackman incident in December taken to repeatedly head-butting Petrović in the chest when the players were off the ball, and the two had to be separated. By the February game, Starks was fully emerged as New York's leading guard, and with his flammable competitiveness, he and Petrović seemed destined for extra-curricular activities.

Harvey Araton of *The Times* reported that early in the game Starks got up in Petrović's face and told him that he believed Petrović was involved with the group that had been involved in the bombing of the World Trade Center just two days earlier. It was a ridiculous notion, one spouted by Starks purely to rankle Petrović, to get in his head early and agitate. As Araton later wrote, it was not a subject that Petrović found humorous, especially when taking into consideration the daily events in Croatia. What impressed Araton was how Petrović responded. "I think more telling in that situation than Starks's ignorance was how Dražen responded," Araton said. "He didn't back down." Petrović began attacking Starks, running him through a series of screens, finding room to score. He had 14 points at the half, and then scored 12 in the third quarter when New Jersey was able to put a destructive run on the Knicks. He finished the game with 28 points and six assists as New Jersey won, 102–76. It was a most impressive performance in front of a national audience.

Though Starks and Petrović left their exchange on the floor, it was Starks's foul on Kenny Anderson that would have a more lasting effect on New Jersey's season. In the third quarter, Anderson retrieved a ball that squirted free. After taking the ball in transition, he faked a pass to the left and took the ball to the basket. Starks led with his body and then, on impact, brought both of his outstretched arms into Anderson. The impact caused Anderson to lose control of his body; the point of impact had been crucial, as Anderson was in mid-air and more vulnerable to falling hard. Starks caused impact at the worst possible time for Anderson, who predictably hit the floor hard. Steve Popper of the *Asbury Park Press* remembers seeing Anderson's mother rush down from her seat to the floor just seconds after the incident, angry and vocal that her son had been hit and potentially hurt. Her voice was prominent as the arena was hushed.

Anderson got up and managed to shoot the free throw, but had to leave the game immediately. The following day an x-ray showed a fractured bone at the base of the thumb, in the wrist. When a leading hand surgeon looked at it the following weekend it was determined that Anderson needed season-ending surgery. It was a major blow for the Nets. He was among the league leaders in assists at just over eight per game, but it was his compatibility with Coleman and Petrović—the dribble penetration, the attention he drew, and his ability to make a play in the paint even at a smaller size and create easy opportunities—that the team would miss. There were still twenty-seven games left when Anderson went down, a full third of the season.

The team lost its first game after the Anderson injury and then managed to win eight of its next nine, the only loss coming in the final game of a four-game western trip to Portland. There had been a resourcefulness about that Nets team that would reveal itself often through the season, a reflection of the leader and motivator in Daly. Petrović and Coleman sensed the importance of what losing Anderson meant to the team, and it was during that stretch in early- to mid-March when together they played their best basketball of the season. It was arguably the best playing performance of Petrović's career. He scored 29 points in a home win against Orlando, and then 25 two nights later against Denver. There was a moment in the Nuggets game that reflected his confidence: he stopped short on a fast break, pump-faked a Denver defender who ran by, then unnecessarily attempted a three-pointer when the lane was open to drive. After making the shot, he turned and stared at Daly and the bench, then ran back down the floor.

The highlight of the stretch came in back-to-back road games at Golden State and Phoenix. In Oakland, Petrović started sluggishly but caught fire in the third quarter. Daly sensed this and began calling plays for Petrović continuously, freeing him on the right side of the floor to attack at his choosing. Petrović responded by scoring 20 of his 28 points in the second half, turning a double-digit deficit into a double-digit win. At Phoenix it was Petrović, then Coleman, who controlled the game. It seemed an odd setting for the Nets to turn on their best performance of the season in, of all places, Phoenix, a place where the Suns had lost only twice to that point. Petrović began the game hot and helped push the Nets out in front; at one point in the third quarter the lead reached forty. Petrović told John Brennan of the *Record* that he was shocked when looking at the scoreboard. "I was thinking, 'Are we really up by forty points? Isn't this Phoenix? Is this a dream?'" The Nets eventually won, 124–93, with Petrović hitting for 29 points with six assists.

Brennan was among a handful of writers covering the game and was told by his employer in the hours before the contest that his story was not required with any urgency: there was a major snow storm back in the New Jersey area and it pushed back the deadline. Brennan looked out on the floor and thought about how disappointing it was that this most unusual Nets performance would be quickly forgotten. "Sitting courtside you kind of felt, this is typical," Brennan remembered. "It was incredible to see. But how many actually saw it because they were worrying about the storm or shoveling snow? Whether they bothered watching on TV, and by the next day the story was buried in the snow. The team couldn't seem to have the perfect game at the perfect time."

In the latter part of March the season was to change for the worse. That it did seemed to follow a natural order for the Nets, such was the snake-bitten aura that surrounded the franchise. That Petrović would succumb to an injury just as he was playing the best basketball of his NBA career seemed just a touch more cruel than the average Nets ailment, for he was one of few players the franchise had who was capable of rescuing them. The injury occurred in Washington. Petrović was chasing LaBradford Smith through a screen when Smith tripped and fell. Petrović was unable to stop in time. His knee thrust right into Smith's body and he fell to the floor. Petrović initially thought he had banged his knee on the floor, and attempted to run out the soreness, but after several trips up the floor he had to remove himself from the game. The Nets staff looked at the knee when the team returned home, and at first the diagnosis was that he had a strained ligament. With rest, the line of thinking was, he could return in a brief amount of time, certainly a report Petrović endorsed. But one week later a second scan was deemed necessary, and it revealed that an exterior cruciate ligament was torn about 35 percent. It was a crushing revelation, one that forced Petrović to the injured list and an estimated month on the sidelines. It was a critical period of the season to miss, when the already-fragile Nets looked to secure themselves as the conference's fourth seed.

Though the injury changed matters, it had not dampened Petrović's mentality. He had at the onset of the injury talked up his supposed healing power to the writers. His point of reference was the sprained ankle he had suffered in January, and how he defied the doctor's initial return date by coming back sooner and resuming his stellar play.

"Call me the Iron Man," he told the writers, boastfully.

It was one of the charming things of his personality, the bravado and belief in himself. To fill the competitive void that was left by not playing, Petrović devised a challenge to return to action sooner than the diagnosis dictated. He began showing up at the team's practice facility, the delightful APA *trucking* plaza, early in the morning, at least ninety minutes before the other players filed in for practice or workouts, in order to get in some rehabilitation with strength and conditioning coach David Pavao. Within two weeks he was doing some light running, alternating between jog and sprint work, and jump shooting. Soon he was introduced to a stimulation device that promoted blood flow and healing. It was recommended that he use it twice a day, but Petrović inquired about taking a machine home. Once he did, he was using it as many as six times a day. His methods became a laughing point among the coaches.

Petrović shortly thereafter declared he was fit to return to games. There was a conversation between him and Daly about the possibility of returning early, but the coach resisted. "I need eight or nine games to end the season to regain my form," Petrović bargained with Daly, promising a return of the flow with which he had played in March.

In the first week of April, the Nets were in Cleveland for a game with the Cavs when Daly took a call in his hotel room from Petrović. It was just thirteen days after the injury in Washington, and Daly was once again unenthusiastic about a premature re-joining of the team for his leading scorer. It was important, Daly stressed to Petrović, that he be as close to one hundred percent as possible, for the best interests of not only the team but of himself, with his contract and his bargaining position. Daly was unaware of Petrović's bigger picture and contract situation. But Petrović's bigger picture focused on wherever the next game was, and he finished the conversation by stating that he would like to fly to Cleveland and try to play that night.

"Dražen, if you come to the airport then I will have someone send you home," Daly said to him. "And if you fly here, I will fine you."

Petrović's shot at a game was denied, but he refused to sit idle. He called Spencer Ross, the Nets' television analyst. "Are the boys home?" Petrović asked, in reference to Ross' twin boys, David and Jonathan. "Can they come and rebound for me while I shoot?" They were not home, Ross told him, instead were attending a school function. The next day, Ross asked Petrović if he had gone to shoot and for how long. "Three hours," Petrović replied.

Sitting and watching was not easy for Petrović. There was a home loss to the Pistons in the latter part of his absence in which Chris Morris missed a jump shot at the end. It was an outcome that caused Petrović's mind to wander to an alternate universe, one where he was healthy, one where the ball had been in *his* hands, and where the shot had been *his*. Mike Celizic of the *Record* spent a great deal of time with Petrović during his injury for a story he was penning, and the Morris shot came up in conversation several times. Petrović told Celizic that the Pistons game had by far been the most difficult to miss, and Celizic noticed that he was still thinking about that final shot, sure that he would have made it.

As his time on the sidelines drew to a close, Petrović reiterated to the coaching staff his anxiousness to return, and with that came a moment of sorts. At the end of a practice session, the writers were let in as the players slowly deserted the court, leaving assistant Paul Silas to make the conversational rounds with the reporters. Petrović, at a nearby goal, was the only player left, shooting on his own. The small group soon noticed Petrović had started a drill where he was alternating shooting from one corner to the next: he would retrieve the ball after one shot from the corner and then sprint to the opposite corner, turn and fire from three-point distance. It was a gut-busting exercise, a Petrović favorite. "It was a ridiculous display of shooting, endurance, and work. Probably enough to put anyone through an entire practice," remembered Steve Popper.

Petrović soon found a rhythm and made over ten consecutive shots. When he reached the mid-teens, Silas and the reporters were hanging on each shot, with the *Record*'s John Brennan informing Silas of the count. "He's at seventeen in a row, coach." Silas then began captioning each make for all to hear.

Petrović hit his twentieth three-pointer in a row. In this purified environment, without defenders and crowd noise, it was a true display of his shooting prowess. Silas made plenty of noise after the twentieth make, and on the twenty-first shot Petrović missed. The small group groaned; Silas turned to the writers once more, and continued on with his conversation. Both Brennan and Popper noticed Petrović staring down Silas with his dark eyes, as if it were Silas who had blown the magic of the drill and the moment. "He glared at Silas as if he never would have missed had Paul not said anything," Brennan said. The next day, Petrović was activated.

Daly brought Petrović off the bench at first. The comeback game was in Indiana, and it had been a grand total of twenty-three days since the injury occurred. Petrović had won his own personal challenge, but had he chosen his own return date it would have been around half the estimated month he was to miss. Daly instead made the final call. The Nets played a truly bland game against the Pacers, trailing by thirty-one at the end of the third quarter before falling by nineteen. Petrović got through twenty-six minutes and missed ten of his thirteen shots for 6 points, his rhythm residing somewhere back at the trucking plaza. He was cautious in his movements during that first game back, but with five games remaining in the regular season he was confident it would be enough time to rediscover his form.

In Petrović's third game back the Nets played in Washington, the site of the injury, and he struggled in his limited minutes in the first half, missing all four of his field goal attempts. In his reduced state, he was having trouble chasing his opponent defensively, especially Rex Chapman, more than a full step behind as the player ran around endless screens. Daly took Petrović out and that upset Dražen, who complained that a shortened stint on the floor didn't allow him to find an offensive rhythm. Petrović and Daly vented words in the locker room at halftime; one man frustrated with not playing more despite playing hurt, the other at his team's seven-game losing streak.

The moment hurt Petrović. He later told Vassilis Skountis, a Greek reporter with whom he was friendly, that he felt "belittled" by the incident. He had come back early from his injury, earlier than most players would have. In his eyes his sacrifice to play hurt in the face of the seriousness of his injury, and despite his contract situation, had not been appreciated. In the second half Petrović continued to struggle, missing his next three shots and then getting into a shoving match with Washington's Harvey Grant. Oddly, the incident acted as the catalyst for a mini-turnaround: he made seven of his last nine shots, including 12 points in the fourth quarter, and New Jersey came roaring back from seventeen points down in the final six minutes to win. Afterward, both Daly and Petrović had calmed down—the win had done that—and both downplayed the halftime incident. Daly cited his love for Petrović's passion, Petrović for his own need for time to find his usual flow. It was a moment that quickly passed. The core of the problem had been Petrović's injury, his absence halting the Nets' brilliant March form. David Pavao remembers Petrović sitting alone on the bus before heading to the airport after the Bullets game, his knee tightly wrapped in ice accompanied by the frustrated look on his face, lost in thought.

Playing with a torn ligament and a brace proved to be very tough physically for Petrović. Early in games he was especially favoring it, slow to come to a full stop and then slow to start once again. As the game wore on it would loosen, but only to a degree. The core of his game since coming to the NBA had been to work off the ball, to gain room to shoot the ball, but in playing hurt that was compromised. Petrović had to work very hard off the ball to free himself from his opponent; that alone proved to be tough because of the limits to his movements. Because of his trouble getting open, there were stretches in games late in the season when he was essentially invisible. With the ball he was more methodical, less of a risk taker, getting by on his offensive instincts and what little daylight he could muster. It was a great challenge for his shooting ability. Instead of being a 20-point scorer in those final six games he averaged in the middle-teens, his shooting dipping below 50 percent, numbers he was not accustomed to when healthy.

Daly elected to start Petrović for the final three games, and he responded at a watered-down rate. He was encouraged by his play in the final game of the regular season, a nationally televised loss at Detroit. He had also felt in good enough health that afternoon to return to a semblance of his normal self emotionally, as well. In the Nets' locker room before the game, the *Record*'s John Brennan told the *Asbury Park Press*' Steve Popper that Petrović needed to make two three-pointers without a miss to reassume lead of the league's three-point percentage over Chicago's B.J. Armstrong. Brennan's calculations were based on the assumption that Armstrong would not attempt a three-pointer in the Bulls' game that afternoon in New York. Popper then went to Petrović's stall in the locker room and told him this. Petrović was immediately interested. When the team came out onto the floor, Petrović dashed over to where Popper and Brennan were sitting, confirming with Brennan that the calculations were correct.

Petrović made the first three-pointer he attempted that afternoon. As he jogged back down the floor he was pointing at Brennan and Popper. "He's pointing over to us as if to say 'What's the number now?'" Popper remembered, both writers finding hilarity in Petrović's in-game fascination with statistics. Petrović missed his next three-point attempt and with it a chance to finish first in the league, leaving the title to Armstrong.[32] In missing the percentage title he took solace in regaining his form and confidence, finishing with 19 points, feeling good enough to contribute at a normal clip in time for the playoffs.

It was a difficult finish to an otherwise successful campaign for Petrović. He increased his scoring average to 22.3 points per game on 51 percent shooting from the field and just under 45 percent from three-point range. Daly upped his minutes to

---

32 It was the second successive season that Petrović had lost out on the three-point percentage crown on the final day, doing so to Seattle's Dana Barros at the end of the 1991–92 season.

thirty-eight per game, and it required tremendous endurance for Petrović to log those minutes and be able to maintain a high shooting percentage. With back-to-back seasons averaging over 20 points per game, Petrović was now among the top handful of shooting guards in basketball.

The Nets staggered home to finish the regular season. They had on the night of Petrović's injury in Washington been sitting in fourth place in the Eastern Conference behind New York, Chicago, and Cleveland. But from that point on, they essentially were in free-fall, winning only four of their final seventeen, including just one of their last eleven. When Petrović got hurt, the team was granted an injury hardship allowance by the NBA, one that was employed infrequently and reserved for unusual circumstances. By virtue of the seriousness of his injury, Petrović was placed on the injured list even though the Nets had already filled the three allotted spots, with Anderson, Jayson Williams, and Dwayne Schintzius. Then as April opened Chris Dudley, who had been very consistent in his role as a rebounder and defender, was diagnosed with a stress fracture. The discovery was made by a foot specialist after the Nets' medical staff failed to find any reason for Dudley's foot pain in the prior fortnight. Once again they were granted an exemption by the NBA, their injured list now containing five players.

There were four especially wrenching losses at home as the season closed that seemed to symbolize the Nets' flailing fortunes. Most teams endure a buzzer-beating loss during any given season, but New Jersey had the misfortune of it happening three times in succession as their confidence waned and they became vulnerable. They were beaten by Detroit when Isiah Thomas made two free throws with four seconds to go and the Pistons won by two. Forty-eight hours later it was Danny Ferry who hit an 18-footer as time expired, for a one-point Cleveland win. In the next home game, Boston's Sherman Douglas's 15-footer with less than a second left gave the Celtics a one-point victory. And then, with the Nets battered as they hosted their home finale against Orlando, they squandered a late eight-point lead and watched as Nick Anderson scored 50 points off the bench. The Magic won by three. It was a disheartening run home, in spite of Daly's continued insistence that he had been happy with the team's effort through the tortured streak.

New Jersey played well enough in the middle part of the season to have a hope of finishing with over fifty wins. As late as the last week of March that seemed attainable, but in the end they finished with forty-three and the sixth spot in the Eastern Conference. That record secured them a date with the Cavaliers for the second straight postseason, a team that had also been streaking, but in a different direction, winning eleven of their final twelve games. Cleveland was a team that posed its own challenges. They were sound and consistent, never one to beat themselves. There was, however, some urgency to this version of the Cavaliers, with talk of perhaps breaking the team up should they once again come up short of the Finals. In the interim, they had to get by an undermanned but pesky Nets team.

The opener played out in keeping with how each team had finished the season. By halftime of game one, Cleveland was up by twenty-one. It was a lead, at home, that they simply weren't going to surrender. In the end the margin was sixteen, at 114–98, but the sting had left the game very early and the Nets were sorely outplayed.

Petrović's play was particularly difficult to accept. Physically, he seemed incapable, his knee restricting his movements and shooting rhythm. He finished with just 10 points, missed 9-of-13 shot attempts, and turned the ball over five times. What deserted him was his ability to at first create room to shoot, and then, once free, finish the shot. But there was a hesitancy in everything he did, simply a lack of trust in the knee, the residual power in his legs unable to compensate for his lack of *zip*. "I couldn't find my rhythm tonight," he told Mike Freeman of *The New York Times*.

There was a lot of pride in Petrović, especially in his self-evaluation, and he entered game two with more competitive force. He was separated from Gerald Wilkins, Cleveland's athletic shooting guard, several times, the two screaming trash at each other throughout the game. Daly repeatedly spoke to Petrović during the game to get him to focus on the bigger picture, not on his matchup with Wilkins. "I don't think he's that great," Petrović said of Wilkins to Brennan of the *Record*. "He thinks he's great, but I don't think so." The matchup seemed to invigorate him, at least on this night, resurrecting the healthier, cockier, early-season version of himself. He finished with 21 points on a more recognizable 50 percent from the field.

Petrović's performance was one of several pivotal contributions that swung the game New Jersey's way, and they won 101–99. It was later revealed that Daly had made a plea to the group on the day before the second game, demanding more. It seemed to spark something within the group. He understood they were depleted, Daly told them, but for those who were healthy they needed to play with more courage and less sorrow. He demanded desperation from them. In closing he told the group that he loved them, and spoke of the pride he had for them as they battled through this most unusual arduous stretch of freak injuries and equally freakish late-game losses. It was, team-wise, an inspiring moment that lifted them through the despair.

The player who seemed to derive the most from Daly's words was Coleman, who showed his own courage by demanding to play the full forty-eight minutes. He was relentless on the boards, finishing with fourteen, which was a splendid addition to his 27 points. In the end, Coleman was the difference between a split and a 0–2 series deficit.

Typically, in their stricken state the team was unable to sustain that momentum. New Jersey fell at home in game three by nine, with Cleveland's Brad Daugherty and Larry Nance combining for more rebounds (33) than the entire Nets team. Petrović scored 17 points, but he awoke the next day with a great deal of pain in his knee and couldn't practice. The scene at the Nets' workout that day was somber. In addition to Petrović sitting out, Coleman missed with a bad back. There was no Chris Morris, sidelined with a sore hip. Sam Bowie hurt his foot in the third game and rested. Rick Mahorn had the flu. Rumeal Robinson's thumb was sore. Dwayne Schintzius, the team's *third* center, had bronchitis. Anderson, Dudley, and Jayson Williams had all been out for weeks. Daly joked to the reporters about activating his assistant Paul Silas, and maybe even Willis Reed.

In game four the Nets summoned a remarkable effort. There was something at once startling and inspirational about their performance. Coleman was everywhere: 21 points, fourteen rebounds, nine blocks, and eight assists in forty-eight minutes. There were some within the Nets organization who felt it was the first of what they had hoped would be many such Coleman moments. He stood on the scorer's table at the end of the third quarter, with New Jersey ahead by twenty-seven, and there was a mutual embrace between the player whose reputation was oft-battered and the usually sparse but suddenly populated crowd. It made on this night for an odd marriage. Coleman played so well that the *Record*'s Mike Celizic suggested he be bronzed and installed outside the arena.

Petrović was able to leak out in the game's early going for some easy scores, and it opened up his offense. After he hit a three-pointer in the third quarter that pushed the lead to eighteen, he turned to the crowd with his arms raised, smiling. In front of the crowd, *his* crowd, it would prove to be his final moment of joy in the NBA. He finished with 19 points in thirty-five minutes.

The 96–79 victory tied the series at 2–2, and the Nets' play was so unexpected that the crowd responded in a childlike way. Daly had been most resourceful, jumbling lineups and playing whomever seemed to have a partially healthy body. Even in the aftermath he could not explain to reporters what had happened. His team flew to Cleveland for an elimination game, weary, but essentially capable of anything.

Petrović needed to produce something just to be better than in game four, but it quickly turned bad in game five. He picked up two early fouls and Daly was forced to take him out. He had struggled with foul problems, not only in the Cleveland series but also late in the regular season, the lateral movement just not there with his bad knee, making defense even more challenging.

Cleveland, at home, assumed control in the middle two quarters, even as Coleman kept the Nets close. He finished with 33 points and sixteen rebounds. It capped an incredible series for Coleman, one that was captivating enough to hint not only at his grand possibilities, but to those of the power forward position, which appeared to be further evolving, in part due to his unique skill set. He had done so against a big Cleveland frontline of Daugherty, Nance, and John Williams, each taller than 6-foot-10, and he proved to be the best player in the series. Coleman was reason enough to feel good about the team's future, going forward. Later, Daly gushed to reporters about the phenomenal series. He cited Coleman as one of the league's top five talents, dabbling with his team's potential, an always dangerous but tantalizing subject, especially with Coleman.

Petrović played little in the first half, and even in the second half with a fresh start he could not find the rhythm in his shots. His knee betrayed him first, and then his jump shot. He simply could not get the space he needed against the defensive combination of Wilkins and Craig Ehlo (Petrović attempted just six three-pointers for the entire five-game series, a statistic that best underscored his lack of space). The two held Petrović to just 2-for-8 shooting from the field through a large portion of the game. He did break free late, hitting two jumpers that dragged the Nets within eight with ninety seconds remaining, but it essentially did little more than tidy up his final line—11 points on 4-for-10 from the field. Cleveland won by ten, claiming the series 3–2, and ending New Jersey's season.

Minutes after the game ended, the doors to the Nets' locker room opened and the media entered. Petrović was usually the first target of the reporters for two reasons: he was always quickest to shower, and he was always honest with his comments. His candor with the reporters impressed John Brennan of the *Record*. There were on occasion nights, even as the team was improving, when the Nets reverted to being *the Nets*, and the players were often reluctant to talk. But Petrović, Brennan felt, was always open and honest, sometimes while the rest of the locker room was silent.

The reporters gathered around Petrović as he dressed. It quickly became obvious that his emotions—dealing with the contract and injury and frustration—finally reached a boiling point. "I'm not staying in the NBA. Maybe this is my last game for the Nets," he opened with, shocking the writers, who were forced to adjust their line of questioning from the just-completed game to

Petrović's future. Someone asked Petrović about Europe. He said he was 95 percent sure he was going back. Another asked about his contract playing out. "The Nets took their chance but they waited too long. It's about respect. I can't stand someone saying one thing and doing another. I was ready to sign last summer, in July. They came with an offer in early March. I was waiting seven months. That's too late."

What was unusual about Petrović's comments, Brennan thought, was its timing. "It was almost as if as soon as the game was over he was in off-season mode," Brennan noted. "Some players take days or weeks to get there, and he was there in minutes. As soon as the game was over he realized his American career, at least for a few years, might be over. Here we were, fifteen minutes after the game, and he was venting about it, how unfair it was—it was utterly out of character for him. Not the intensity, or the bluntness, but just the topic, using those characteristics with that topic was unexpected and startling. I would've been less surprised had it happened the next day or after."

Petrović was upset and not finished talking. He had shown patience and passiveness all season long when pressed about his contract, but it seemed that he could no longer keep his feelings in check. He continued on by openly wondering who other than Coleman and Anderson would be back in New Jersey next season. He was critical of management's past mistakes, such as trading Mookie Blaylock, not re-signing Terry Mills, and bungling Chris Dudley's negotiations. He then spoke about how he sacrificed by playing hurt, even when his contract was up in the air and his bargaining power could have been compromised by poor play. He was left hurt by two internal incidents. First, the halftime argument with Daly at Washington in mid-April. Although it had not grown beyond the initial stage, the moment still hurt him. Secondly was with Coleman, a story surfacing later that the forward yelled at Petrović to get out of the way as he struggled with his sore knee and with his movements. "Something happened between me and Coleman," Petrović would tell Vassilis Skountis just weeks later, "which bothered me even more."

In the locker room that afternoon Petrović did not appear a man at peace with his NBA life.

"I proved everything I had to prove in the NBA," were among his final words to the writers, before stopping himself, getting his things, and walking down towards the team bus and out of Richfield Coliseum.

Dražen Petrović, the league's first great European player, was never again to set foot inside an NBA arena.

Twenty

AN UNCERTAIN FUTURE, FIRST WEEK OF JUNE, 1993

Wroclaw, Poland

Some forty-eight hours after his season had ended, on the afternoon of May 11, 1993, Dražen Petrović left his apartment in Hackensack, New Jersey, for the drive to New York's Kennedy Airport. His close friend Mario Miocic offered him a ride, and that evening Petrović planned to fly home to Zagreb. In the wake of the Nets' elimination, the Monday edition of the local papers were filled with content about Petrović's postgame comments, words that scared a great many people within the organization. Chuck Daly responded by promptly meeting with Willis Reed and other New Jersey executives on that Tuesday, pleading with them to re-sign Petrović at all costs. He was too talented a player, Daly said to them, too critical a piece of the future to let walk without a fight. Team ownership had built—perhaps even earned—a reputation as a group that was reluctant to pay players, and had thus hurt their consistency in building respectable teams.

The car ride to the airport featured nothing out of the ordinary. Petrović and Miocic chatted and laughed, and began planning the next time they would meet. Miocic had not brought Petrović's playing future into the conversation while driving, nor had he done so the night before, when he and Petrović joined assistant coach Rick Carlisle for dinner. Yet the uncertainty had not stopped him from thinking of life without his friend, should Dražen go back to Europe to continue his career. When Miocic arrived at the airport, he turned off the ignition and took a deep breath. "Dražen," he began, "we see each other again here soon?"

"Probably *Kume*," Petrović said, smiling. "Probably."

It was the only time that the two spoke about the future after the Cleveland elimination, in a quick five seconds, before Petrović got out of the car and left for home for the off-season. He kept his cards close to his chest, his mind remaining open to calculate his options. In many ways, Petrović had not changed since he was a teenager. When teams in the Yugoslav league lined up for his services, the nineteen-year-old had evaluated and mulled each option in private, with constant voices in his ears. "He was special how such a young man can be serious and see plans, like an older person," Petrović's childhood friend, Neven Spahija, said. "Around him there were many people, many suggestions, many in the clubs—at the end of the day he was the guy to bring the decision and decide everything. And he never made a mistake about a decision in his career. This is the most important part of Dražen. He was much better than those around him at decisions, even those older than him."

From that point on he had conditioned himself to dealing with the outside pressures, while maintaining an inner calm and focus as his career progressed.

That Petrović even considered leaving the NBA went against the competitive spirit by which he lived. The NBA had always meant something to him, always presenting itself as special and otherworldly, especially in the beginning when the league was a faraway fantasy and not occupied by Europeans. His climb to that league was planned meticulously; he said throughout the eighties in Europe that he would go there at twenty-five, and so the work it took to get there played out accordingly. It was always *the* destination. His mother, Biserka, theorized that perhaps Dražen had visions for a short life, such was his insistence and demand for goal-setting and achievement. "I remember asking him once why he was in such a hurry, when he had accomplished everything," she said. "He told me he couldn't explain that. *When I don't work, when I stand still, I fall down.*" Petrović's life became that cycle.

It was left to Petrović's agent, Warren LeGarie, to wade through the lavish European offers that were pitted against the Nets. The offers became more frequent and enticing as the season wore on, and as word spread that there was a chance Petrović could leave. There was Real Madrid and Barcelona from the Spanish league. Benneton Treviso in Italy. Olympiacos, Aris, and Panathinaikos in Greece. These were among the wealthiest clubs in Europe, and they were willing to pay for Petrović. They could not offer comparable competition, however, and for someone who craved a competitive environment, it was an issue that was not lost on Petrović. He met with Nets broadcaster Spencer Ross late in the season in Ridgewood, near Ross' home, for dinner, and the two discussed a particularly attractive offer from Spain. "Spencer, I have a very good offer to go to Spain to play. They offered me four years, sixteen million dollars," he told Ross.

"That's amazing," Ross answered, "that's a lot more money than you're going to get in the NBA."

"That's alright," Petrović told him. "I want to play in the NBA. When I'm thirty-five I can go to Europe and score 35 points a game shooting left-handed."

"That's a direct quote," Ross said later. "I'm not embellishing."

It was among a number of subtle indications that he would not leave the NBA. Even against the difficulty in reaching an agreement for a contract, there was an emotional attachment to the Nets, who had given him his start. "I'm really tight with this organization," he told Miocic during the season. "The people here love me, they really care for me. And I owe them a lot. They gave me life in the NBA."

Petrović especially felt an affinity for Willis Reed, even as it appeared that Reed and LeGarie were in disagreement. It was Reed who took a shot on Petrović. He assured LeGarie when he traded for Petrović two years earlier that not only had he watched Petrović play and came to like his game, but, yes, he was going to play a lot in New Jersey. There was going to be an opportunity. Petrović's relationship with Reed had as its foundation that belief in him, and as they grew to know each other it developed to the point where they could kid one another in a playful way.

Late in the season following a Nets home game, Reed came walking down the hallway when he spotted Petrović and Miocic chatting outside the locker room. It had come in the weeks following a Petrović rejection of a Nets offer. "Come on Draz, we need to sit and talk," Reed said in his deep southern voice.

Petrović turned to him, smiling. "You know Willis, you have to come to me on my territory [to Croatia] with a big bag full of money—then we will talk."

"Draz, I will go. Me and my man," Reed said, pointing to Miocic, "we are going to come together to see you."

"But don't come without the big bag of money," Petrović said, laughing.

Unfortunately, Reed and LeGarie had not managed to reach that same level of affection. They last sat down to discuss Petrović's contract in the weeks leading to the playoffs. Reed had, according to newspaper reports, tried to accelerate the talks in light of the Nets' dire struggles while Petrović was out with his knee. In that meeting, Reed offered LeGarie a contract for just over $13 million for four seasons, which would pay Petrović $3.3 million annually. The offer was at once below what Petrović and LeGarie were seeking, and yet would have made him the second-highest paid shooting guard in the league, behind Michael Jordan. LeGarie was seeking $4 million per season, but Reed had looked around the league for comparisons. He looked at Reggie Miller of Indiana, at Reggie Lewis of Boston, and his offer was slightly above the annual salaries of those two players. It was even exceeding that of what the likes of Clyde Drexler, Joe Dumars, and Hersey Hawkins were making per season. It was a point that made further discussion difficult.[33]

The day after the Cleveland game the media had wanted to follow up on the Petrović outburst, and tracking down LeGarie for a soundbite was the logical step. He was open to talk. LeGarie noted to several outlets that even with Petrović's rise as one of the top shooting guards in the league there were never any complaints about his current contract, that it had always been honored. LeGarie argued that it was New Jersey—and Reed—who were making it an issue, at times distracting Petrović late in the season, especially in the playoffs, by constantly bringing it up. LeGarie also pointed out that Petrović's level of play increased from last year to the current season, and yet the Nets' offer remained unchanged. LeGarie was, much as he had done in Portland, fighting for Petrović.

---

33 The question was never about Reed wanting Petrović, for that desire was strong. Reed went as far as discussing with Chuck Daly and the coaching staff the idea of bringing Petrović's brother, Aleksandar, in as an assistant coach. The coaches had agreed to the idea.

There was a genuine threat among the interested European clubs: Panathinaikos of Greece. Two major factors weighed in their favor. Firstly, one of Panathinaikos' two allotted foreign players was Stojko Vranković, Petrović's closest friend from the Croatian national team. Second, they were coached by Željko Pavličević, who had coached Petrović at Cibona (first as an assistant, and then as head coach in 1985–86). Pavličević was told by a close mutual friend near the end of the 1993 Greek league season that Petrović was unhappy with how things were panning out in New Jersey, and in being a free agent there was a chance he would be willing to listen to outside offers. As coach, Pavličević had significant say about the team's roster. He soon went to the club's president, Paul Giannakopoulos, to alert him about the possibility of chasing Petrović. Giannakopoulos was an ambitious and creative man, susceptible to such an enticing opportunity to boost his team, and he showed immediate interest.

With that, Giannakopoulos sought to meet with Vranković about Petrović. "What do you think about Dražen?" Giannakopoulos asked. Vranković quickly realized that Giannakopoulos wasn't talking about what he thought about Petrović's basketball ability. Instead, Giannakopoulos was inquiring about the chances of getting him to Greece for the 1993–94 season. The president was aware that Vranković was very close to Petrović. He knew they would have discussed Petrović's future in one of their famous late-night phone chats. "Does he want to stay in the NBA or come back to Europe, Stojko?" he asked. "I want to know first. I don't care about money. I will pay him the best money."

Giannakopoulos made preliminary contact with LeGarie, informing him of his strong interest in Petrović. That interest was equaled only by his team's ability to offer a substantial contract, one which, unlike a standard NBA contract, would be tax-free, an enticing wrinkle. The initial offer was somewhere in the range of $2.2 million per year over the course of two or three seasons, at the time a very attractive offer. Panathinaikos appealed to Petrović with both financial reward and sentimentality.

Petrović met with Pavličević in Zagreb in May before a testimonial match that was being held for a former teammate, Andro Knego. The two spoke for an hour, and Pavličević did not tell Petrović anything that Vranković had not said already. Petrović was receptive, typically well-informed, but also non-committal.

"Look, I will come if the offer is a good offer," he said to Pavličević. "I will think very serious about it."

Panathinaikos was never far from his thoughts. In the summer of 1993, Petrović planned to play for the Croatian national team on its march to the European championships. That included playing in the qualification tournament in Wroclaw, Poland. Any convening of the national team meant reacquainting with Vranković, and that ensured Panathinaikos would never be far from Petrović's view. Seeing Vranković meant upholding their long-standing tradition of being roommates on the road, dating back to their days on the junior representative team for the former Yugoslavia.

They seemed an odd couple, Petrović and Vranković. Petrović was smaller, more driven, more emotional; Vranković was bigger, stoic. The friendship became very strong as the years wore on, stretching beyond the sport they shared. In the infancy of their friendship as junior teammates there were small moments of bonding. Vranković remembered that once, as sixteen-year-olds participating in a tournament in Germany, following a team meal the coaches instructed the young men to go straight to bed as there was an early practice the next morning. The two got to their room and closed the door, and Petrović immediately turned and looked at Vranković with a sly grin. "You know what we are going to do now?"

"Yes," Vranković answered monosyllabically, "we are going to go to sleep and get up early for practice."

"No," Petrović shot back. "We are going to practice now."

Vranković rolled his eyes at Petrović and took a deep breath. For the next forty-five minutes, Petrović led Vranković as they sprinted up and down the long hallway, working up a sweat while their teammates slept and the clock raced toward midnight. The running was followed by a series of push-ups and then sit-ups, and when Petrović felt that they had done a sufficient amount of work, they then were permitted to sleep. A decade or so later, the scene in Poland was essentially the same. The boys were now men, in their late twenties, hardened and matured by their travels and experiences, their conversations long since stripped of innocence as they talked of million-dollar offers and in what league or side of the world they would play. In Vranković's mind, Poland represented to Petrović an opportunity to quietly ponder his future, away from the backdrop of his family and agent and the NBA. No avenue appealed to him more than any other. Vranković remembers Petrović speaking enthusiastically about the idea of playing with Houston, a team he had carefully chosen as one that would be ideal for him and his strengths. "They could use me," he told Vranković. "They need a shooter like me."

The Croatian team had an off-day on the qualification tournament's fourth day, and Petrović spent a part of the afternoon in the hotel lounge with Vassilis Skountis, a Greek reporter. Skountis travelled to Wroclaw specifically to speak with Petrović for his paper, *Ta Nea*, about stories that had emanated from Athens to the effect that the offer from Panathinaikos was something more than just lucrative and was actually being considered. Petrović had been largely silent to the American media in the weeks since the season had finished, but on the other hand had been open with the European media. The *Boston Globe* obtained an interview that Petrović did with *FIBA* magazine, and the words revealed a man who was seemingly feeling burned by his recent NBA experience. Petrović spoke of being underappreciated, of resenting Chuck Daly pushing Kenny Anderson to the forefront in the season's infancy, and his disappointment over missing selection to the All-Star Game. "After everything I've done, I still haven't received the acclaim I deserve, and I am offended by that," he said.

Petrović spoke truthfully and openly, perhaps under the naïve assumption that the interview would stay safely tucked away within the European media's circulation. He had not shied away from Skountis when asked for an interview. The two were quite friendly, and had known each other for the better part of a decade, dating back to Petrović's early professional career. When in Greece for games, Petrović and Skountis would often speak.

Skountis asked Petrović about a comment by Giannako-poulos that stated the signing was imminent. "I didn't say that I've signed," Petrović said. "But the president of Panathinaikos [Giannakopoulos] is right to say what he said. Truly, we are very close. I want a third [European] championship cup more than anything. I won two while with Cibona, in 1985 and 1986, and at the moment I'm anxious to return to Europe and earn more titles. You have to understand, that I'm not playing just for the money. I prefer to win and get nothing rather than lose and get rich. I promise that Panathinaikos will become a different team."

The conversation shifted to the NBA, with Skountis asking Petrović about his 1993 season, one that Petrović called the best basketball of his life. He talked of the more rounded game that he had developed, of the increased discipline at both ends of the floor. Petrović spoke openly about what he had learned in the NBA, calling himself ignorant when he first came to Portland, expecting that he could get by just because of his ability as a shot-maker. That had not been the case, Petrović told Skountis, and with that came the acceptance that he would need to improve other areas of his game, namely defense. "I realized that without defensive playing I would have died," Petrović said. "And that is why I spent a whole summer practicing hard. Besides, defensive basketball gives a player confidence."

The Petrović interview ran in the Saturday edition of *Ta Nea* on June 5, 1993, and instantly there was a great deal of excitement that came with the article. The idea of Dražen Petrović playing for Panathinaikos for the 1993–94 club season suddenly pierced the realm of pipe dream and entered the infant stages of reality.

Croatia was predictably dominant at the Eurobasket qualifiers in Wroclaw. Of their first six games, just one was decided by fewer than 29 points. It enhanced the notion that they would have survived had Petrović either not played or played less, but even while still nursing an aching knee he insisted on being there. "He wasn't supposed to be there," his mother, Biserka, said of the qualification tournament. "But at that moment he wanted to go. He would have suffered more if he hadn't been there with his teammates."

Croatia's last game on the tournament's final night was against Slovenia, a team they had never lost to in their short history of independence. The game was at times sloppy and poorly played, the drop in intensity perhaps due to the fact that both had already qualified for Eurobasket, and thus it was a meaningless contest. The beautiful old building, Hala Ludowa, was hardly brought to life even by Petrović, who appeared a step or even a step-and-a-half slower than his usual standard, a brace strapped tightly around his still-injured left knee. It caused him to constantly bend down to adjust it during dead balls and fouls, as if he couldn't quite get used to it.

Just one week earlier, Petrović was named to the All-NBA third team, an honor that itself at least numerically was even more impressive than the All-Star berth he had publicly coveted, assuring that he was one of the fifteen best players in the world over the course of a full season, as opposed to the top twenty-four over half. Petrović receiving that honor had made his presence in Poland all the more unusual. His team was deep enough and talented enough that it would have safely qualified without him and his bum knee, but with the glare of his homeland and the war and the suffering, he embraced the opportunity to represent Croatia. On the television broadcast, it did not seem like a game that warranted his attendance or unrelenting intensity; the lack of crowd noise exposed a rather lifeless beat, nothing but sneakers squeaking and the occasional bark from a player or coach. It wasn't the type of game in which Petrović usually thrived.

Slovenia shot the ball very well from the outside, and this in turn frustrated the Croatians, their body language suggesting that they were looking forward to the several free days they had been promised after playing nine games in eleven days. Petrović himself looked worn down. There would be in this game no fist-pumps following made shots or fan interaction, and his knee slowed him to the point that he had difficulty both accelerating past his defender off the dribble and shooting from any great distance. He finished with 30 points, but was just 8-of-18 from the field and 11-of-16 at the foul line. The points resembled a fully-functioning Petrović, but the shooting percentage did not.

Slovenia ended up winning by four, 94–90.

What came with losing to a less-talented opponent, even in a game that meant nothing, was frustration, and late in the game Petrović exchanged words with Dino Radja during a time-out.

The harsh words between the two, Radja remembered, were over ball movement. "It's funny, that last game we had a fight, a stupid fight," Radja said. "You know, 'Pass me the ball, why didn't you pass me the ball?'"

It was not the first time Petrović had spoken harshly to his teammates that week. When the team arrived in Poland eight days earlier some openly expressed disappointment over the conditions of the chosen accommodations, wondering why their hotel was not of the same standard as those where the FIBA officials were staying. Petrović decided to address those teammates in front of the entire playing group, emphasizing that the team was there to play basketball, not live in luxury, especially when so many of their countrymen were back defending their homes in a battle where lives were at stake. "All teams are here and we will be here," he said. "We came to play basketball, so we will stay here."

The team followed his command and no longer complained of the accommodations.

The Croatian national team left Poland the following morning, Monday, June 7. Their plan was to fly first to Frankfurt, Germany, and then on to Zagreb. Some members of the team continued on to Split, which was closer to their homes. Petrović had been up most of the previous night, talking with Vranković about their respective futures, the loss to Slovenia eating at him. They got very little sleep that night, maybe two hours in Vranković's estimation, and when it was time the next morning to depart for the airport both were quiet and fatigued. They stood off to the side of the group, heads down, bleary-eyed, and when the bus pulled up outside the hotel its side mirror nearly clipped Petrović, who had to jump back out of the way. "What's this guy doing? Does he want to kill me or what?" he said to Vranković.

At the airport in Wroclaw, Petrović bumped into his former coach at Cibona (and Slovenia's head coach) Janez Drvaric, who was waiting for a mid-morning flight with his team to Vienna, Austria. The two chatted about the previous night's game. To Drvaric, Petrović seemed still upset about the loss, his competitiveness always on display. Radja, too, detected that Petrović was upset. The two had not spoken since their verbal exchange during the game. Radja later remembered the scene at the airport, Vranković sitting with his best friends on either side of him, neither of whom were talking. If something were said by one, then Vranković would turn and relay it to the other, and thus the silent treatment remained. "We were sitting at the same table. When I had something to tell him I would tell Stojko, and then he repeated the same thing to him [Dražen]," Radja said. "When he answered, he tells it to Stojko, and Stojko repeats to me. It's a funny thing, but that's how we used to do things." In hindsight Radja would scoff at how silly that seemed, two young men, so close, who had been through a great many battles, not speaking to each other as a result of a petty exchange of words in a meaningless qualification game.

The Croatian team then boarded a flight to Frankfurt and it was there that Petrović parted from his teammates, telling some of them that he was going to check whether his friend Klara Szalantzy was waiting outside as she had promised. "I'm going to see if she waited for me," Petrović told Vranković. "If not, I will fly back to Zagreb." Croatian coach Mirko Novosel remembers speaking to Petrović as he was walking towards the exit. Novosel had not planned on having team practice until Wednesday, two days away, and Petrović told him of his plans to drive to Munich with his friend, and be back in time for the midweek workouts. Aware that Petrović was going to use the road to find his way back to Croatia, Novosel told him something very simple. "Be careful," the coach said.

Petrović nodded, before turning and walking away. It was the last time Novosel would see him.

Twenty-One

HE BECAME ETERNAL, JUNE 7, 1993

Ingolstadt, Germany

There was a call placed to the Nets' offices one day late in the 1993 regular season, a young woman with broken English calling about Dražen Petrović. She was a big fan, the girl told the secretary in Willis Reed's office, and almost demanded a meeting. The girl boldly asked for Petrović's phone number, but the secretary refused. "We don't give out the personal phone numbers of any of our players or employees," the girl was told. It left her no other option but to leave her own number to be forwarded to Petrović, to call if he chose. Petrović was told of the inquiry and given the number, and with that he called Mario Miocic to ask about how to handle the situation. It was not uncommon for Petrović to ask Miocic for practical advice, for Miocic was four years older than Petrović and something of a protective figure in his life. "Some girl is calling for me," Petrović told him. "I don't know if she's Croatian or German."

"Who is it?" Miocic answered. Her name, Petrović told him, was Klara Szalantzy.

A day later Petrović called Miocic in the early afternoon, as he usually did on game days, asking if he would be at the game that night. "Of course, Dražen," Miocic said. "This is my religion," he joked. The two then brought up the topic of Szalantzy. Petrović called the number that was given to him, and it was answered in a hotel in New York, where Szalantzy and a friend were staying. She seemed friendly, Petrović said, and he offered Szalantzy and her friend tickets to that evening's game in New Jersey. When Miocic arrived at the Meadowlands Arena that night he was in and around his usual quarters; the Nets provided him a pass that allowed access to the locker room and the corridors. When he found Petrović, who was out on the floor shooting, the two discussed the women, with Petrović being very curious about them. He told Miocic where the girls would be sitting, and that perhaps it would be a good idea for Miocic to introduce himself first, and check their legitimacy and their intent.

After the game, Petrović and Miocic joined Szalantzy and her friend for dinner at Houlihan's restaurant, which was close to the arena and frequented by players after home games. Miocic sat there that evening and wondered about the situation. He was wary of outsiders who were seeking a sudden entrance into the world of his close friend, the star athlete. He was aware of the type of young women that often sought the company of athletes or celebrities, and carefully tried to decipher exactly the intentions of the young girls. Petrović was characteristically very comfortable with his fans, often accommodating them not only with an autograph but also a photo and a conversation, but even then there was a limit to his interaction and involvement. It was, thought Miocic, unusual of Petrović that he was so quickly enamored with Szalantzy.

Szalantzy was a beautiful young woman, just twenty-three. At the time she had a promising, two-sided career as an international basketball player and model. She and her friend had traveled to New York, and in two days would be headed back to Europe for an extended period of time. But in the end, two days turned into a week. With her friend departing, Szalantzy spent most of her time with Petrović, the two exploring the sights of the big city.

By the time Szalantzy left, she and Petrović had established a mutual attraction for each other and were on friendly terms. "It was very short [the trip]," Miocic remembered. "It was not a relationship." They remained in contact after Szalantzy departed for Europe. Petrović, with his season winding up in New Jersey, called her often, at one time sending his young friend flowers for a special occasion. He mentioned to Miocic that he planned on visiting Szalantzy in Germany sometime in the summer. That trip would be to further explore the possibility of a relationship, meet her friends and family, and find out what sort of person she was.[34]

On Monday, June 7, with Petrović touching down in Frankfurt from Wroclaw, the two had arranged to meet. Szalantzy, as promised, waited in her car at the Frankfurt airport, where she planned to drive Petrović to Munich. Once there, the two would spend the next night at a hotel. Along with Szalantzy for the trip was Hilal Edebal, a friend, herself a very good basketball player who also had dabbled in modeling. The girls were brought together by basketball, first introduced while teammates for a traveling team in Munich. Szalantzy, Hungarian, was the team's point guard. Edebal, born in Germany but an accomplished basketball player in Turkey and later in the American college system,

---

34 Nick Goyak remembers one such instance after the season finished when Petrović, at home in Zagreb, missed a flight to Germany because his mother, Biserka, did not wake him in time. It was, Petrović told Goyak while chuckling, a little devious on the part of his mother, who was wary of the queue of women who sought her famous son.

was the center. Edebal had been a member of the Turkish national team and was at one point named the Most Valuable Player of the Turkish league while playing for Galatasaray.

In the early afternoon Petrović climbed into the tiny, red Volkswagen Golf, taking a seat in the passenger side as Szalantzy drove.

Back at the departure gate the Croatian national team boarded their flight for Zagreb. Take-off was held up as the airline checked and double-checked their flight numbers; one traveler was missing, yet all of the baggage had been checked through. Petrović was the missing traveler. Aleksandar Petrović, traveling with the team as its assistant coach, stepped forward and informed airline staff that his brother had made alternate travel arrangements. With that, they took off on the flight for Zagreb, a trip of a little less than two hours. A short way into the trip there was a slight hitch, with strong turbulence as the plane made its way over Munich, Germany, so the passengers were encouraged to fasten their seatbelts until its force had been endured. It was a fine early summer day in Munich, a high of twenty-six degrees Celsius (79 degrees Fahrenheit), but a late-afternoon thunderstorm closed in on the city and its immediate neighboring towns. The downpour of rain left the autobahn slick and difficult, with a darkening sky in the background.

The Golf driven by Szalantzy had by then been on the road for some time. From Frankfurt they traveled along autobahn three, east to Nuremburg, before heading south along autobahn nine towards Munich. The car made a stop at some juncture during the trip, and once continuing Petrović, weary from having little sleep the night before, decided to nap.

Shortly before 5:20 p.m. central European time, a truck driver from the Netherlands was traveling north some fifteen miles out of Ingolstadt on the autobahn when he was forced to swerve and avoid a car that had, with the sudden downpour of rain, aquaplaned and moved toward his lane. The driver swerved his truck off the road and broke through the median barrier that separated the northbound and southbound traffic. The driver was shaken, but had quickly regained his senses when he suddenly realized that his truck was now in the middle of the three southbound lanes, covering all three. He got out of the truck and from the side of the road began waving his hands in the hope of gaining the attention of drivers who were heading toward Munich. He was trying to prevent a collision. Szalantzy's Golf approached the truck at a high rate of speed. "Going way too fast," Edebal said. "In Germany there are some speed limits, but in short places. But on the autobahn you can go as fast as a car goes." According to the accident report, Edebal said her friend was driving at 180 kilometers per hour (112 miles per hour). On the wet road, it left the car in a very vulnerable position.

Szalantzy saw the truck and clutched the steering wheel hard with both hands, hitting the brakes as the car slid left into the guardrail and back on to the road, the front right side of the vehicle—the passenger side, Petrović's side—slamming into the truck. It was later presumed he was asleep when the impact occurred and did not see the collision coming.

Szalantzy lost control of the vehicle when she saw the truck. When the Golf hit the guardrail before reaching the truck, it turned her away from the brunt of the force, and saved her life. The force left her injured enough, according to a report later published, to spend a week in the hospital before being released.[35] Edebal was in the backseat, with the impact throwing her to the

---

35 Though the extent is unknown, as Szalantzy did not reveal publicly any information of the accident nor its aftereffects.

front seat, causing serious injuries to her brain, a broken arm and right hip. She survived, but barely. Soon there was a fire crew at the site. Amid some 300 liters of diesel that had spilled out of a dent in the truck sat a crumpled Golf. The car's bonnet was pushed straight into the front right-hand side of the truck's cab, each of its front doors peeled forward. Rescue workers were able to see that the two women in the accident had signs of life, and quickly ambulances whisked them away. Edebal, her condition far more serious, was flown to the Hospital of Eichstatt; Szalantzy to the Ingolstadt clinic. "Three people in a vehicle, and three very different results," Edebal said.

At the crash site remained a young man amid the damage and the raindrops, the help working desperately to revive him before concluding that their efforts were in vain. In not wearing a seatbelt, the force threw Petrović straight in the direction of the truck, the impact causing significant head trauma. His life was taken instantly. At the time he was wearing a gold watch on his left arm, which stopped precisely when his life did—the short hand on the five, the long hand on the twenty. Dražen Petrović, just twenty-eight years old, was dead.

Biserka Petrović expected a call from her son to say that he had arrived safely in Munich, but as the night wore on that call had yet to come through. Like all parents, that naturally led to concern. Biserka spoke to her son every day that he was in Poland, and looked forward to seeing him when he returned. When the national team arrived in Zagreb, it was Stojko Vranković who had Petrović's bags. At the airport he saw Biserka. "He is on his way to

Munich," Vranković told her, handing her the bags. "But he will be back tomorrow."

As night fell she became increasingly concerned as to why her son had not called to inform her of his whereabouts. It was unusual that he had not contacted her. Very late that evening, the phone rang at the Petrović family apartment in Zagreb. Instead of hearing Petrović's deep, unmistaken voice, it was a woman with a serious, direct tone speaking German. The woman asked Biserka if they had reached the residence of Dražen Petrović. "Yes," Biserka replied. There was a pause.

"Your son is dead."

With that, the world of Biserka and Jole Petrović came crashing down. The immediate grief was so great, so devastating, that Biserka ran towards the balcony of the apartment, only to be grabbed by her husband. It was an instantaneous reaction, one that would perhaps prove that it was all just some bad dream. The parents embraced. Their youngest son, one of the world's greatest basketball players, the pride of his homeland and of their family, had been tragically taken from them.

The first call they placed was to their eldest son, Aleksandar.

The phone also rang at the Edebal household late that evening. On the other end was the Ingolstadt police. They had bad news for the parents: their daughter was involved in a harsh car accident, one that claimed a life. "Your daughter is lucky to be alive," the police officer said, "and she still may not survive." Edebal's parents were left confused. "We have two daughters here in our home, and another who lives in the United States," Edebal's father told the officer. "You have the wrong woman." But there was no mistake from the police: the lady in the back seat was Hilal Edebal. It soon became clear that Edebal, out of school for the summer, had decided to travel to Europe but failed to inform her parents. In the months and years that were to come, the severity of her brain injuries left her with scant recollection of the events leading up to and including the accident. "I was in hospital for almost one year and then to the rehab center," she said. "After the accident I couldn't remember anything. The doctor said 'Don't be surprised if you don't remember your family.' I just couldn't figure out why I was in the hospital, and why I got to meet such a great basketball player—Dražen. For a long time I couldn't remember anything. I just thought I was dreaming all the time."

Stojko Vranković flew back to Zagreb with the national team, and was staying at the Intercontinental Hotel with his wife. The two were enjoying a quiet drink in the bar with their friend, Bruno Silic, then head coach of the Croatian national water polo team. The three were interrupted some time later by a hotel employee, who told Vranković there was a call for him. On the other end was Petrović's father, Jole. Vranković was surprised to get a call from Jole Petrović, especially at that hour, and he immediately detected the urgency in his voice.

"Stojko, where is Dražen?"

When Vranković told him that Petrović was likely by now in Munich, there was a long pause, before the harrowing words. "Dražen is dead," Jole told him. Later, Vranković came to realize that Jole was seeking an alternate answer about his son's fate, with hope that it was all some great mistake. Vranković immediately called Aleksandar Petrović, the two sobbing on the phone, their shock absolute. He then drove over to Petrović's apartment, where he found the parents, inconsolable, totally overcome by the news. "It was a situation I will never forget . . ." Vranković said years later, his voice trailing off. "I will never forget it."

Mirko Novosel believes that he was the last team member to speak with Petrović. He did so at the airport in Frankfurt, and among his last words had been a wish for safe travels. Novosel traveled back to Zagreb with his group and had gone home upon arrival in the early evening. The phone rang about midnight, and on the other end was Jole Petrović. Like Vranković, a call so late from Jole was unusual and prompted thoughts of something out of the ordinary. "There has been an accident in Germany . . ." Jole began, before delivering the news that stumped Novosel.

"It was so unbelievable," Novosel remembered. "It is impossible to describe."

The flight home to Croatia was delayed for the national team, and some of its members who planned to travel on to Split decided against it, checking in to a hotel in Zagreb. Dino Radja decided to keep going anyway, and made his way to the family home. He was asleep when his mother entered his bedroom, waking him to tell him that she just received a phone call from a friend. The friend heard that Petrović was killed in a car accident. Radja's initial reaction was that it was a mistake. *I just saw him earlier today.* Radja rushed downstairs to the kitchen and called his teammate, Velimir Perasović, who was staying at a hotel in Zagreb. Perasović himself had just taken a call in his hotel room and it was true, their friend and teammate, a man with whom they had competed just twenty-four hours earlier, was dead. "When I got the information it was like you're falling off the cliff of earth into space," Radja said. "You don't know what's happening." He immediately went back to Zagreb. Perasović and other members of the national team gathered in the hotel lobby at what he estimated was three in the morning, the players standing in a circle, struggling to understand what had happened.

Neven Spahija was Dražen Petrović's closest childhood friend, and the two remained in touch even as Petrović's game and stardom lured him away from tiny Šibenik, his ambition outgrowing the small coastal city. Petrović would often return home to Šibenik in his off-seasons, usually after spending two or three days in Zagreb, and the two would catch up. Spahija was aware that Petrović was in transit from Poland to Croatia, and so he went on that Monday evening to Petrović's café in Zagreb—Amadeus—with hopes that when the team flew in Petrović would come by and they would meet for a drink and a chat. Mutual friends, however, told Spahija when he arrived that Petrović did not fly back with the team. He opted to drive instead. Spahija thought that was unusual. With that, he decided to go back to his apartment for an early night. He was in bed when the phone rang later that evening in the apartment. On the other end was the café's manager.

"Dražen Petrović is dead."

The manager had just spoken with a member of the Petrović family, who told him the news. Spahija sat for the remainder of the night on his couch, still, staring forward for what seemed like hours.

The phone rang at Warren LeGarie's Venice Beach home in the mid-evening, California time. It was another agent, Marc Fleisher, who had just taken a distraught call from his client, Dino Radja. "Dražen's been killed in an accident," Fleisher said. For LeGarie, the news made him weak. He was so stunned that his immediate thought was one he later came to be ashamed of. *Perhaps they have the wrong Petrović*, LeGarie thought, not with hope, but with desperation and confusion. *Perhaps it was Aleksandar*. Later, LeGarie hated that he had thought that instantaneously, surely a measure of the shock.

LeGarie had last spoken with Petrović in Poland the previous Friday, just three days earlier, telling him that continued talks with the Nets were sputtering. It was a very real possibility that things would not work out.

The loss devastated LeGarie, as he was very fond of Petrović— not just the player, but the person. There was a recent encounter that played on LeGarie's mind, one in which Petrović was found jogging up and down the hallway in his apartment building, reciting a name over and over to himself. When LeGarie asked

Petrović what on earth he was doing, Dražen answered he was simply trying to memorize the name of LeGarie's partner, whom he was about to meet for the first time. Because the person was important to LeGarie, she was then important to Petrović, and he wanted to make a good impression. "Where do kids like these exist?" LeGarie wondered.

The accident brought about a realization for LeGarie, that he was not long for representing players. He was too attached, too emotionally invested in Petrović, and in time he slowly moved away from player representation. Petrović was the second client of LeGarie's to be killed in a car accident. The first had been Fernando Martin.

Mario Miocic spent the day in Manhattan, and when he returned to his home that night he saw the blinking light on his answering machine. There was a message from Willis Reed, asking Miocic to come to his office in the next few days. Reed wanted to sit down and iron out details of the trip they planned to take together to Germany for the 1993 European championships later that month. It was there, Reed decided, that he would sit down with Petrović to discuss the future. Miocic would be the ace up his sleeve, the close friend there to gently nudge Petrović in the right direction, back to New Jersey.

Minutes later, Miocic took a call from a Croatian friend. The friend had heard that Petrović was in an accident in Germany, but at the same time was not sure of the outcome; the details were not certain. "Oh my God," Miocic said. The shock led to him placing his first call to Goran Ivanisevic, a good friend of both his and

Petrović, and at the time one of the world's top tennis players, who was in London preparing for Wimbledon. Then he made a call back home to Zadar, to his family. Yes, it was true, the man Miocic grew up watching torment his beloved Zadar but whom he came to love and consider a brother, was dead. That night he spoke with Vranković, then later Reed, sharing with each man his overwhelming devastation.

Rick **Carlisle was in his office at the Nets' practice facility,** the young coach staying late long after the others had gone—just as Dražen would have appreciated. He was there preparing for the off-season, when he would be coaching New Jersey's summer league team. He took a call from fellow assistant Paul Silas, who said that there was a serious car accident in Europe and that Dražen was in the vehicle. Though the details were sketchy there was one undeniable truth: it was fatal. Carlisle remembered being in a state of disbelief. Later, when he learned of the tragic set of circumstances that led to the accident—Petrović opting for the car instead of plane, that he was not driving, that there was heavy rain—he was left subdued. "Everybody's hearts and minds were spinning; it was just too much," he said.

On **the west coast, in Oregon, Nick Goyak heard a report of an accident** involving Petrović but the details were not firm.

All he knew was that it didn't sound good, and that worried him. He last spoke with Petrović twenty-four hours earlier, the day of the Slovenia game. Goyak listened as Petrović excitedly told him about being named to the All-NBA third team. It was, Petrović said, the award that had made him most proud, a validation in light of missing being selected for the All-Star Game. Petrović and Goyak rarely went more than two days without speaking, and he promised to call Goyak when he was back and settled in Zagreb in the coming days. With that, the two said good-bye.

After learning of the accident, Goyak decided to call the Petrović home, where he reached Dražen's father. "Nick," Jole began, "Dražen is dead."

In the years that followed, the sound of Jole Petrović's disheartened voice never left Goyak.

Rich **Dalatri was having difficulty sleeping** on that Monday night. There was a newborn son in his life, and with it came the usual sporadic sleeping patterns. In getting up for his son, Dalatri decided in the wee hours to wind down some in his living room. He turned to ESPN to check the scores. With the volume muted, in his fatigued daze he noticed Petrović's image appear on the screen. It was several days since Dalatri had last spoken to Petrović by phone, and he immediately assumed that the only thing possibly newsworthy in June could be related to his contract situation. Intrigued, Dalatri stayed up with hopes of catching that news again before returning to bed, so he turned the volume up and waited.

"Dražen Petrović, who with the New Jersey Nets these past two seasons had blossomed into one of the NBA's star young guards, is reported dead tonight at the age of twenty-eight, the victim of an automobile accident in Germany. Details are sketchy . . ." read Keith Olbermann on ESPN's *SportsCenter.*

The rest of the night, Dalatri sat still on his couch. It wasn't until he was greeted the following morning by his wife and child that dark turned to daylight.

Herb Turetzky was fast asleep when awakened by a telephone call from a fellow statistician with the Nets. Turetzky's friend heard overnight about Petrović's death, and with that, Turetzky sat up out of bed in shock. After hanging up the phone, he woke his wife Jane to tell her the news. The two cried together, their hearts aching in part because of the loss of a friend they came to love, but also for their fifteen year-old son, David, who idolized Petrović. *How am I going to get the strength to walk down that hallway and tell my son that his hero is dead?* Turetzky wondered to himself. David stayed home from school that day.[36]

Turetzky was a Nets lifer, and had lived through the death of another player, Wendell Ladner, who was killed in a plane accident in June of 1975. The image on the evening news of Ladner's Nets gym bag lying in the field near the crash site stayed with Turetzky. But, he thought, this went beyond the loss of a player—with Petrović's passing, he had lost a friend.

---

36 From that time forward he would scribble the name of his idol on his basketball shoes as a constant reminder.

John Brennan of the *Record* was watching the late news in his apartment when broadcaster Russ Salzberg broke the news of Petrović's accident at the tail-end of the bulletin. Brennan knew Salzberg to be not like most newsroom reporters in that he actually went to the games and had sources within the Nets organization, which led Brennan to believe that there were reportable details circulating. Brennan immediately got on the phone with his employer, the clock suddenly racing toward a midnight deadline, an enormous and heartbreaking story in need of reporting with so few details at hand. Brennan needed answers, so he made calls, including to people at the Nets. But no one seemed to be able to confirm much, there being so few avenues available to find credible details from Europe. Brennan found himself in the unenviable position of having to put together a coherent report without much printable information, while himself not yet fully able to process the shock of the story. The obvious problem was the accident details. At the time Brennan filed the story, he was under the impression that Petrović was driving the car—which was not true. Speculation and guesswork slowly seeped into the truth. It wasn't until the story was filed and more calls were made that it was established Petrović was a passenger in the vehicle.

Perhaps the most difficult journalistic task was left to Brennan's colleague at the *Record*, the late Mike Celizic. Celizic was a columnist of Croatian heritage who bonded with Petrović while covering the team. He last saw Petrović after the elimination game in Cleveland, exchanging contact details as they walked the corridor together, with a promise to speak over the summer. Celizic, too, heard the report of Petrović's death and sought about confirming it. He didn't speak Croatian, but his mother did, and she was by his side as he dialed the number Petrović had given him. Celizic instructed his mother to tell whomever answered that he was a friend of Dražen's, that he had heard there was an accident and wanted to know if his friend was okay. The call was answered by a woman. Celizic's mother did as she was told, but at the other end there was no response. The woman hung up. Celizic felt terrible, perhaps the silence saying more than any sketchy report could, and later came to suspect that it was Petrović's mother, Biserka. "To the woman who answered his phone," Celizic wrote in his column the next day, "I'm deeply sorry."

The morning after, some members of the Croatian national team gathered at Amadeus, Petrović's café in Zagreb, a stone's throw from a basketball arena that soon would carry his name. Aleksandar Petrović was there, as was Stojko Vranković, their eyes bleary and bloodshot from a sleepless night of shock and heartbreak. Veljko Mršić was one of the team's younger members, and he sat there among his sullen teammates, the room filled with an eerie quiet. "Even now, talking about this, I start to cry," Mrisc said about the morning after, being around his devastated brothers. "When I remember that we were in his bar, I just get really upset."

People shuffled past outside on the street, word still circulating of the shocking news that their hero was dead. On Wednesday, the headline on the cover of a local publication *Sportske novosti* said simply, "Impossible!"

The Nets held a press conference the following morning, Tuesday, June 8, at the Meadowlands Arena. The room was quiet. "Like a wake," wrote Brennan. Willis Reed spoke first. He got through a pre-written statement, his head leaving the paper but once or twice, his voice trailing off on occasion as he held back tears. "To me, it's like losing a son," he told the handful of reporters there. Reed fielded several questions; his answers became less and less detailed before finally his voice broke, deciding he could no longer continue.

Chuck Daly then stood forward, and Brennan noticed he looked like a man who had had the life taken out of him. "Chuck was as unflappable as anyone I ever dealt with, with basketball, with games, injuries," Brennan remembered. "But this was devastating. He sort of had the pale look of somebody who had been hit so hard in the stomach, and the wind knocked out of him." Daly spoke about how impressed he was that Petrović challenged his American team the prior summer in Barcelona, fearless and ambitious. He addressed the occasional conflicts they had, but concluded that a coach could ultimately overlook those matters due to the passion, commitment, and intent Petrović played with. "You can't get mad at a player like that, no way," Daly said. "Because he did everything for the right reasons."

Daly then reminded everyone that even for a young man with a bright future, such as Petrović, nothing was promised.

"This reminds you of how precious life is," Daly told the reporters. "And how much we take for granted."

Vassilis Skountis may not have been the last reporter to speak to Dražen Petrović, but his interview the previous week was most likely the last one of great detail that Petrović gave to any member of the media, and it would become famous for its content. When Skountis heard about Petrović's death it prompted him to look at the edition of the *Ta Nea* newspaper that had carried the interview three days earlier. There was a photo of Petrović, smiling, wearing a black shirt that carried the Nets logo. *What a shame,* Skountis thought, shaking his head. Petrović was so open, so reflective of his own life in the interview, and that proved to be an eerie coincidence.

"Are you still in love with basketball?" Skountis had asked.

"In love is an understatement," Petrović responded.

Skountis then asked about the temptations in his life, about possible avenues that could derail his pursuits. Petrović instantly began to talk about a young woman who had been a central figure in his life. It was not Klara Szalantzy, but Renata Cajić. It was his absolute devotion to the game, Petrović said, that ended their five-year relationship. Petrović confessed that Cajić floated the idea of marriage, but the timing was wrong. Petrović had just been traded to New Jersey; the new opportunity and revived dreams were the subject of his captivation. He was not ready to get married. Then, basketball consumed him, and as of June 1993 very little had changed. "It's my life and it will be my life for four more years," he told Skountis. "I've decided to play until I'm thirty-three."

Dražen Petrović sounded very much like a man with still more to achieve.

Twenty-Two

MOVING ON, POST-1993

Zagreb, Croatia

Dražen Petrović was laid to rest on Friday, June 11, 1993. It was a hot day in Zagreb, beautiful sunshine bathing the city as people lined the streets. It was later estimated that at least one hundred thousand people showed up to attend the service (equating to roughly 4 percent of tiny Croatia's population at that time). Based on footage of the service, it's a figure that doesn't seem stretched. A local television camera panned through the streets, and there was distinct commonality to the faces of the locals: sullen, the shock evident as they wiped their eyes, very clear devastation. "It was like a head of state had passed," said Chris Dudley, one of two New Jersey teammates (Chris Morris was the other) who made the trip to Croatia. "It was an unbelievable experience, just seeing the outpouring. We didn't quite get how the European players represented their countries—how big a deal that was. I didn't quite get that until I went to the funeral."

The country had collectively mourned Petrović's death since early Tuesday, in the hours after it was confirmed and the news began spreading. Just a day after the accident, a memorial service was held at Cibona's home court, a place where once upon a time in the recent past Petrović became the top attraction in Europe. Mirko Novosel stood before a crowded gymnasium and asked the people to show their appreciation for Petrović's life, and what followed was *twenty-two* minutes of applause. Various teammates took the stage to offer memories and anecdotes, with highlights playing on a big screen. Nearby a sign simply read, "Hvala ti, Dražene!" (Thank you, Dražen!)

The Petrović family remained in isolation, with Aleksandar Petrović taking his parents out of town for several days to mourn in private. It created something of a dilemma. The authorities in Ingolstadt, Germany, followed up with the family in the hours after informing them of the accident, and requested that someone make the trip to Germany to formally identify the body. It was at that point that Stojko Vranković stepped in. He had been in the presence of the family in the hours after learning the details of the accident, and he saw how distraught it left Petrović's parents. It led him to decide to take on the responsibility of retrieving Petrović's body. Vranković called Neven Spahija. "We need to go there, Neven," Vranković began. "If we don't go, then who will?"

The family gave them their blessing and with that the two men—the very first friend Dražen ever had, along with his closest at the end—took the long drive to Ingolstadt. In their travels, they passed the site of the crash. "It was a nightmare for me," Spahija remembered. Upon arriving at the morgue, they met with a staff member. Spahija asked about Petrović's injuries, and the morgue attendant outlined the extent of the head trauma before asking the men to view and identify the body. Spahija realized at that point he could not do it. *I don't want to remember that,* Spahija thought to himself at the time, the extent of Petrović's injuries deeply upsetting him. *I want to remember him smiling.*

Spahija opted to not view the body. It left Vranković, who summoned his courage. Behind a cold metal door in an empty room sat a nondescript grey casket; on it was a card with the name "Dražen Petrović."

With their duties fulfilled, Vranković and Spahija drove back to Croatia. Dražen Petrović was coming home.

The funeral was an event unto itself. The Roman Catholic Church was surrounded by rows upon rows of people. Amid the volume of the crowd was the weight of the words by the Bishop, Marko Culej. Noticing the litany of newly dug gravesites, Culej expressed sorrow to the dozens of Croatian mothers who had had to bury their sons in recent years, many as casualties of the war. In calling Petrović "a son of our nation," Culej rued the future that went unwritten: one in which Petrović would continue to glow as a basketball star and prominent Croatian, making the country proud with each pending achievement. Culej was followed shortly thereafter by a young man, Miro Juric, a native of Petrović's hometown of Šibenik and himself an aspiring basketball player. He spoke eloquently about the man he idolized. "He gave a very emotional speech, really powerful for a young man," Nick Goyak remembered. "About what Dražen meant to all them; gave them a goal, a leader. What he meant to their lives. The unspeakable taken away."

The procession then moved to the burial site. Before the casket, Spahija and Mario Miocic carried a large picture of Petrović playing for the Croatian national team. Behind them a short way was the casket, which was being wheeled by the collective national team. Among that group of brave young men was Rich Dalatri, who had helped elevate Petrović's NBA career. He made the trip to Zagreb to honor Petrović essentially on a whim, without a plan. Upon boarding the flight from the United States he spotted some familiar faces, namely the Nets' contingent of Willis

Reed, Dudley, and Morris. After landing, Reed asked Dalatri to join them at the hotel, and on arrival Dalatri was greeted in the lobby by Vranković. "Tomorrow, you come with us," Vranković told him.

So there was Dalatri, flanked by Petrović's former teammates on the Croatian national team, as well as Goyak and Petrović's agent Warren LeGarie, walking alongside the body. "The whole country stopped," Dalatri said. "There were helicopters above. It seemed like millions of people, just a wave of people." The slow walk to the cemetery brought about a realization for Dudley: it was the first time in his life that a contemporary had died. During his lifetime he had seen family members pass away, but never before had someone his age died. It was a confronting thought.

One of the enduring images of the service is the sight of Vranković. His left arm was clutched to the side of the casket, his right hung around the neck of Dino Radja. Vranković was sobbing uncontrollably as his friend's body was wheeled slowly to the burial site. Of the national team members, many of whom appeared to be still in shock, their bloodshot eyes hidden behind sunglasses, Vranković's emotion was the most expressive.

Behind them was Petrović's family. Biserka Petrović had to be held up on each arm by Jole and Aleksandar.

Petrović was then laid to rest at the Mirogoj cemetery. It is a landmark site in Zagreb, a place where presidents and prime ministers, generals, and Nobel Prize winners, come to rest. The gentle sound of "Ave Maria" played as he was lowered into the ground, his family and closest friends standing before it all, struggling to cope with the loss. "Come back, my Dražen, come back," shouted Biserka as her son was placed in his eternal resting place.

On the previous Sunday, Dražen Petrović had been playing the sport that defined his life. By Friday, he was saying good-bye forever.

There were to be reminders of his life everywhere. Dražen Petrović was not to be meteoric, his life quickly forgotten. Before game one of the 1993 NBA Finals between Chicago and Phoenix, just two days after his death, the players observed a moment of silence as a picture of Petrović, smiling, was displayed on the video screen above. "I think we judge him in terms of the international scope of the game, truly demonstrating that this was a global sport, bringing us all together," NBA commissioner David Stern said from the Finals to Jan Hubbard of *Newsday*.

Hours after the funeral, the Croatian national team headed to the airport where they boarded a flight to Montpellier, France, for the Mediterranean Games. Two days later, exactly one week since their last game—Petrović's final performance—they once again met Slovenia. Near the floor sat an oversized photo of their fallen teammate as a tribute. This time, the result would be different. Croatia won by four. Later, in the final of the tournament, Croatia was beaten by Italy. Sitting at home watching the game on television was Aleksandar Petrović, and as he observed a team whose collective spirit was affecting their on-court performance, he made the decision to re-join the team as an assistant coach. "I decided that I would come back for the [European] championships in Germany because I wanted to help them stop mourning for Dražen and start playing again," he told Christopher Clarey of *The New York Times*. "I also wanted to help myself."

Later that month the Croatian team convened in Munich, Germany, for the Eurobasket. During an off-day at the tournament, armed with a large bouquet of flowers, the players piled into a bus and ventured to the crash site some 80 kilometers (50 miles) away. As it turned out, the Croatian national team was not the first to have the idea of leaving flowers at the accident site.[37]

The Nets officially bade farewell to Dražen Petrović on November 11, just days into the 1993–94 season, retiring his number three to the sparse rafters of the Meadowlands arena. The organization came with the purpose of celebrating his life and career that evening, but in what was the first home game since his death there was still a very real sense of disbelief and difficulty in accepting the loss. Willis Reed and his staff went to great lengths to track down those close to Petrović, inviting them back for the ceremony and housing them all in a luxury box at the arena during the game.

The Petrović family was brought to the middle of the floor for the ceremony. Though neither of Petrović's parents speak English, the response and environment—the *celebration*—ensured that they were moved. Vranković and Radja were there. David Stern, the foremost purveyor of a globalized sport, was also there and spoke about the greatness Petrović had achieved at all levels of the game. With that, he turned to the parents and presented to them a plaque which signified their son's inclusion on the 1992–93 All-NBA third team. That plaque represented something far more significant than the award inscribed on it, for it confirmed an acceptance for which Petrović had worked his entire career and life. He lived just long enough to know that he had earned it.

Chuck Daly and Derrick Coleman carried a framed Petrović jersey out onto the floor, Daly, usually unshakeable, had an expression that was completely blank. He struggled to find the right words to define Petrović, and in the end he spoke of his

---

37   Munich would also host the McDonald's Open later in the year, with the tournament's most valuable player trophy, claimed by Phoenix's Charles Barkley, named in Petrović's honor and carrying his silhouette.

smile and emotion, the competitiveness and shot-making. He handed the microphone back and walked away into the darkness. Something had gone from him with Petrović's death.

Aleksandar Petrović bravely addressed the crowd, holding back the tears as the crowd welcomed him, just as they had once done for his brother. Willis Reed then spoke. In saying that he had looked forward to one day putting Petrović's number up in the rafters, he was saddened that the day had come so soon. He spoke that night as if speaking to Dražen Petrović himself, in present tense, as if unable to deal with the reality of his loss. Those close to Reed—those who knew that beneath the towering exterior and booming reputation was a very emotional, caring man—felt that Petrović's death deeply traumatized him, and pointed to his treatment of Petrović's friend, Mario Miocic, as identifiable truth. In that 1994 season, Reed made sure Miocic was permitted his usual access, allowing him to watch all Nets home games from the tunnel near the locker room. To have Mario around was to hold onto a small piece of Dražen.

New Jersey entered the 1993–94 season with a major hole in their team. Assistant coach Paul Silas passed along to Harvey Araton of *The New York Times* an exchange he had in the preseason with Chuck Daly. A compulsive worrier about his team, Daly would often say, "I don't know where the offense is going to come from." He would never mention Petrović's name to Silas, but he didn't have to. It was obvious whom he was talking about. Even with the late-season problems Petrović experienced, the players missed him. "Sure we argued, but that's just the way it is," Coleman told Araton. "Let me tell you, we respected Draz. He was a great player, and there isn't a day we don't wish he was still here."

The Nets managed to win more games in 1994, forty-five, than in Petrović's final year. It was their improved health that saw to that, with the Nets' top four scorers missing a combined five games, a far cry from the decimation of the 1993 team. Derrick Coleman and Kenny Anderson were both voted as starters for the All-Star Game, and once again the team made the playoffs. However, after taking four of five games from the Knicks during the regular season the team was set aside by New York with relative ease in the first round, losing in four games.

Things then gradually spiraled out of control. Chuck Daly resigned less than three weeks after the season, replaced by Butch Beard. He later told Araton that he considered quitting after Petrović's death, such was the perspective it brought about. He stayed on out of respect for Willis Reed, but by the end of 1994 he was fatigued and needed a break. The 1995 season quickly went sour for the Nets. Chris Morris was benched for twice showing up to game-day shootarounds with his shoelaces untied. He then asked to be traded. Derrick Coleman purposely missed practice in the season's second month, drawing Beard's ire, and then when told he was to abide by the team's dress code or be fined, he presented Beard with a blank check. Later that month, after being benched late in a game against the Knicks, Kenny Anderson skipped practice. When reporters sought comment from Coleman regarding Anderson he delivered a line that became immortal as the Nets slid to irrelevance: "Whoop de-dam-doo." In January of 1995, a *Sports Illustrated* feature chronicled the trend of young and entitled stars whose bad behavior was hurting the league's image. The publication chose Coleman for its cover, labeling him a "Petulant Prima Donna."

The Nets ended up missing the postseason in 1995, winning just thirty games, and by mid-1996 both Coleman and Anderson, players who had once joined with Petrović to form a trinity that promised to make the Nets an elite team under Daly, were both gone. In the nine seasons after Petrović's death, there were just two playoff appearances against seven losing seasons for the Nets.

They once again reverted to becoming the kind of disjointed franchise that Petrović joined in 1991.

The Croatian national team also suffered in the wake of Petrović's death, but with far less tabloid material. They finished third at each of the 1993 Eurobasket, 1994 world championships, and 1995 Eurobasket, but could not repeat as Olympic medalists at the 1996 Atlanta Games, finishing a disappointing seventh. Slowly, a glorious era of Croatian basketball began to fade. Though Toni Kukoč and Dino Radja were very good NBA players (Kukoč would win three NBA titles as a member of the Chicago Bulls, while Radja averaged just under 17 points over four seasons with Boston), they eventually succumbed to age and injury. Neither player suited up for the national team after 1999. In the twenty years after Dražen Petrović was killed, Croatia did not place any better than sixth at any of the three major tournaments—the Olympics, world championships, or the Eurobasket.

Kukoč and Radja were among a second wave of Europeans to join the NBA (both were rookies during the 1993–94 season), and the infusion brought about a gradual altering of the league's landscape. Detlef Schrempf continued his rise as an elite-level small forward when he moved to Seattle from Indiana for the 1993–94 season, and would later join Petrović as the second European to be named to an All-NBA team, making the third team in 1995. Arvydas Sabonis, whose career had first risen alongside Petrović's in the mid-eighties before diverging due to a series of debilitating injury problems, finally joined the Blazers in 1995. It was nine years after Portland had drafted him and Petrović, selections that were met at the time with some surprise and skepticism. Though age and injuries had stripped Sabonis of most of his athleticism, he was for a brief period a very good NBA player into his thirties. A specialist in the game's subtleties, his instinctive play was captivating when he came to the NBA in his athletic prime, and his greatness was yet to be measured.

Vlade Divac was able to do something Sabonis could not, and that was become an All-Star. He did so at age thirty-three while a member of the Sacramento Kings. He had built a consistent reputation with Los Angeles and Charlotte, but saw his career take a new path with the Kings. The league's most exciting team was one of movement, of unselfishness, and of creativity—not unlike the great Yugoslavian teams of the late eighties. Among Divac's teammates was Peja Stojaković, a Serbian player and one of the league's elite shooters and movers without the ball. The team's coach, a man largely credited with aiding their rise, had experience coaching a prolific European shooter. His name was Rick Adelman.

In 2002, the league's All-Star Game featured for the first time two Europeans, Stojaković and Dirk Nowitzki, a German forward. Nowitzki had previously joined Petrović and Schrempf as the third European to be named an All-NBA player (third-team in 2001) and, like Stojaković, he was at the forefront of one of the league's better teams (Dallas). Nowitzki possessed a unique style; at seven-feet tall he operated largely on the perimeter, the owner of one of the world's best shooting strokes. He perhaps best symbolized the changing attitude toward European players. Where once it would be assumed his on-court characteristics were soft, upon emphatically proving his worth he became celebrated. In time, his improvisation in shotmaking was mimicked league-wide.

Nowitzki was among the first European players to be granted league stardom and individual marketing, and in an era when European teams were now challenging the United States in international competition, he was among a group of players lauded for his emphasis on fundamentals and a professional approach. He would later win a regular season MVP in 2007, and led Dallas to a title in 2011. The development and impact of Nowitzki, of Stojaković, of Tony Parker—a Frenchman who emerged in San Antonio—led evaluators of talent to cross the seas in search of players capable of becoming NBA stars. It was a ritual first performed by Bucky Buckwalter two decades earlier.

European players had arrived as a force outside of their continent and were now universally respected. It was a dream that had been very important in the life of Dražen Petrović.

With Petrović's death, the basketball community lost a pioneering figure. Teams that he played on lost their star. The masses in Croatia, followers of basketball or not, lost a national treasure. But beyond that, something far deeper, was the loving set of parents from a quiet Croatian town who had lost their son. They absorbed the greatest tragedy that can be borne in parenthood.

With the rest of their lives still before them, they faced an unrelenting challenge. Through the spirit of their youngest son, they would save themselves and preserve the life of Dražen Petrović for all eternity.

Afterword

HE BELONGED TO ALL OF US

Zagreb, Croatia: Present Day

It wasn't until two years after the death of their son that Biserka and Jole Petrović began to see light again. It was in April of 1995, in Lausanne, Switzerland, at the official Olympic headquarters that the first step toward healing was taken. It was there that a monument of Dražen Petrović was unveiled. The idea for a monument came from Juan Antonio Samaranch, the president of the International Olympic Committee and a self-confessed Petrović admirer. Samaranch had observed Petrović at three Olympic Games and quickly fallen for the player's essence: his passion and zest, his genuine *love* for competition. To Samaranch, Petrović seemed an athlete whose approach to his craft was aligned with the Olympic spirit. He was so enamored with Petrović that, shortly after the accident in 1993, Samaranch began to conceive an idea that would commemorate all that Petrović embodied. Originally, in addition to the monument, Samaranch requested that a playground be placed alongside. He had a very clear vision as to why: perhaps other youngsters, even just one kid, could begin the pursuit of his or her own dreams there. "To emphasize the work," Biserka said of Samaranch's idea, "which best speaks about Dražen and represents him."

Though the dream of a playground would go unrealized, the monument itself is a beautiful sight. Unveiled at a ceremony at which the Petrović family was joined by Croatia's president Franjo Tudman, a silhouette of Petrović dribbling hard to his left is spread across sixteen panels. Nearby stands an eternal flame.

For the parents, the honor represented a small, gradual step to recovery. Biserka Petrović would describe the emotional pain of the initial twelve months after the accident as the brain dividing into two: one part that was unable to deal with the enormous and unrelenting heartache, while the other slowly began the process of self-protection. "You're not even aware of that," she would say of her mindset. "This is the part which somehow starts to shield yourself from that pain, to make you stop thinking that it is the end of the world, that it's all over, and that you would never live again."

For a period after Dražen's death, Biserka watched as her husband sunk into a deep depression. There were some days when Jole couldn't bring himself to leave the house. Biserka, facing obstacles of her own, also searched for a way to continue. Some months after the accident she met with Klara Szalantzy, inviting the young lady into her home with one essential goal: to learn as much as she could about the final moments of her son's life. Szalantzy was of scant help. She claimed to remember very little. The meeting had been a great emotional venture on the part of Biserka, had taken tremendous strength, and it was decided at that point that it would be best not to repeat the exercise. Up to that point she had resisted any form of medicinal assistance for the emotional burden her son's death had wrought, and it wasn't until she visited a psychologist that she finally started to find clarity. "That only through work I'd be able to help myself," she said. "He said it is the only way how to reduce the sense of loss, at least at that moment. Work saved us. Work for Dražen helped us move on. So every day we would help each other overcome the crises."

In a manner much as her teenage son had exhibited as a teenager in Šibenik, Biserka's days became regimented and consistent. It would always begin the same way: she would first go to the Mirogoj cemetery to be with her son. Some days she was okay. Others times, especially on holidays or special occasions for the family, she was not. "As if something is locked in your mind and you want to keep him only for yourself," she would say. Soon, Biserka realized that upon each visit to her son's resting place, the number of tributes or flowers or candles that were left for Dražen was increasing. Petrović's grave is all-encompassing, and as much as it was a place for the family to grieve it soon became a shrine for a steady mass of admirers. Even as the nineties played out, and as the image of Petrović's life and career moved farther back in the rearview mirror, the queue of people who would come to pay their respects—to "worship" as Biserka would say—only grew.

There was a moment shortly after the accident that deeply resonated with Biserka. One day she was at the cemetery, kneeling toward her son's grave, when all of a sudden she was approached by an elderly man and his three-year-old grandson. They laid down some flowers and paid their respects. Noticing Biserka and the obvious distress she was going through, the elderly man paused, before approaching her to deliver a simple message.

"You gave birth to him," he said. "But he belonged to all of us."

"At that moment I might not have been fully aware of the full meaning of that sentence, how deep it was," Biserka said. "Later, as the time passed by, I understand it more and more."

And then one day there came an idea. Biserka observed the people who were coming to view her son's grave. The impact that he had on these people was evident, but it played second to the *love* that emanated. This captivated her; in a way, it helped her. Soon her mind began to work. She thought back to Dražen's apartment in Zagreb, one that was overflowing with artifacts of her son's life work: medals, trophies, club and national team jerseys, photos, and letters. There they were, just sitting in his old apartment. In the years since his death, Biserka had spent a great deal of time thinking about her son and what he left behind, what his life provided in the way of lessons or meaning. She decided that his life was about hard work above all else, of the pursuit of dreams and of dedicating one's life to achieving them. People could garner something from his approach to life, she thought. "We wanted to present Dražen as an example," Biserka said. "That everything can be achieved, every goal accomplished. But with a lot of hard work, effort, love and enthusiasm—just the way Dražen was doing it."

It was then that Biserka Petrović had a dream of her own. She wanted to dedicate a museum to her son.

There was a part of Zagreb where one could still hear Dražen Petrović's heartbeat. A beautiful paved square in the middle of town carried his name. With a turn of the neck, one could still find Amadeus, Petrović's café; with another was the home of Cibona, now called the Dražen Petrović Basketball Hall. It was the perfect place for the site of a museum. So she began working.

Work saved us.

Biserka contacted the City of Zagreb to inquire about securing a site, and got in touch with the Croatian government. There was support from both parties. She fought logistics and administrative issues, planned and deliberated, and planned some more. Her fingerprints were all over the project, every detail thought through. There were dozens upon dozens of items that belonged to her son to sift through, each remnant an indicator of a life lived in full. Biserka Petrović approached the building of the museum in a way that appeared very familiar to the citizens of Zagreb, pushed by the thought of her son and the way he had lived his life. Dražen's ideals suddenly took hold in Biserka. "Despite being his parent and a person who gave birth to him, I also learned a lot from him," she said.

The process, which first began in 2000, would take six years to complete. They were long years and involved hard work, but Biserka did not divert her eyes from the end goal. There were moments—little milestones along the way—that enhanced her vision. One day, two years into development, she received a letter to say that Dražen was to be inducted into the Naismith Memorial Basketball Hall of Fame in Springfield, Massachusetts. For anyone who ever played the sport, there was no greater honor. Among the fellow inductees were Earvin "Magic" Johnson and the Harlem Globetrotters. "We were so proud of that," said Biserka. So, in September of 2002, the Petrović family flew to the United States to accept their son's induction. The family chose Willis Reed to present Petrović into the Hall. "One of the greatest honors of my life," Reed said from the stage. He talked about the void that had been left in his life with Petrović's death. He talked of Petrović's journey through Europe to the NBA, and to the Nets. It was Reed who took Petrović at a time when his prospects for NBA survival seemed somewhat uncertain. He looked out into the crowd as he spoke, spotting the Petrović family to his left. "I miss him," Reed said before taking a deep breath. "I know you miss him."

Biserka and Aleksandar Petrović took to the stage, accepting the induction medal. Then it was Aleksandar who spoke on behalf of Dražen and their parents. He spoke for two-and-a-half minutes, articulating for the audience just exactly what his brother would have felt about the honor. "Ultimate dream, there is no longer a dream," Aleksandar said of his brother reaching what he called his *destiny*, the Hall of Fame. "Ultimate tribute to his life and love of the game of basketball—the love of his life."

When the Petrović family returned to Croatia to resume life, they received a short and simple letter. The letterhead of the note said HARLEM GLOBETROTTERS. The organization had written a short note to the family saying how honored they were to be inducted alongside Dražen Petrović.

On June 7 of every year they talk about Dražen Petrović. Newspapers in Portland and New Jersey would commemorate the date with a short note, maybe an anecdote or two. At Mirogoj cemetery, people gather at his resting place, light candles and share their memories. Dražen Petrović played basketball with a smile on his face; in death, it was his devotees who smiled. On the thirteenth anniversary of his death, in 2006, the moment arrived for Biserka Petrović. The Dražen Petrović Memorial Center was officially opened in Zagreb, a beautiful modern building full of items that act as footsteps, tracing the life of her iconic son. The response was incredible, reaching outside the realm of the celebration of an athlete, appealing to anyone who possessed a dream of any description. The museum soon attracted people from all over the world. People suffering from disabilities would often come to the museum to draw inspiration. Biserka noticed that, when school groups would visit, soon those same kids would return, this time pulling their parents and grandparents along and showing them the story of Dražen Petrović.

The museum acts as the catalyst to maintain the love affair that the people of Croatia have for their fallen hero, a love affair that began in the early eighties but that has undeniably grown since his passing. Outside Cibona's home arena, just a short walk from the museum, stands a statue of Petrović shooting his world-famous jump shot. After a Cibona loss in a particularly big game, a local climbed the statue, placed a blindfold over Petrović's eyes, and left a note. *Don't look at this, Captain.* A couple of hours straight south, in Šibenik, sits another monument. It is of Petrović in adolescence, bearing all the features—mop of curly hair, long, skinny limbs, a basketball nearby—that were present when the dream began. During an unusually bad cold snap one winter, someone placed a jacket over the statue, to keep him warm. "He's always in people's memories," says Biserka. "He is absolutely present as if he walks this Earth."

There are reminders of Dražen Petrović all over this world. His name and number not only hang in the rafters of the Nets' new home arena in Brooklyn; his jersey was once spotted by Mario Miocic being worn by a young man in *Florida.* Miocic just shook his head and smiled. Not bad for a kid from Šibenik. The shoes Petrović wore the night he scored 44 points against Houston are still a treasured item in Herb Turetzky's family, and whenever Rich Dalatri is offering advice to one of his sons, Dražen is never far from his mind. "I try every day to give them the qualities, or teach and instill in him the qualities that Dražen had," Dalatri said. "You can't teach an athlete any more than what Dražen represented."

When Goran Ivanisevic finally broke through and won a Grand Slam, at Wimbledon in 2001, within minutes of the contest and with adrenaline still high, he took time to mention Petrović in his on-court speech. Ivanisevic dedicated the win to his friend. Upon returning to Croatia with a hero's welcome, Ivanisevic sported a dated, blue Nets jersey—number three. Among the first to greet him at the airport in Split was Biserka Petrović.

There was one occasion in the years after Petrović's death when Zoran Čutura, something of an icon in Zagreb after his decorated career with Cibona and now a sportswriter, was spotted by a youngster at a concert. The young man rushed up to Čutura, having recognized him from his connection to Petrović. "Do you think Dražen was a god?" the young man, quite seriously, asked Čutura, leaving Petrović's former teammate quite bemused. "The myth will live forever, as long as hearts are beating in this part of the world," Čutura said of the moment.

The Petrović narrative was reawakened in non-Europeans when ESPN released a documentary that focused on his relationship with Vlade Divac. Though largely told from Divac's perspective, with the aim at reconciling the fact that Divac never repaired his relationship with Petrović, the film was well received and was presented with emotion. The production contained lots of footage of Petrović before he came to the NBA, which gave viewers outside Europe their first true look at *Mozart*. As a result, hundreds upon thousands of people seek out clips of Dražen Petrović online.

Two years later, at the end of the 2011–12 NBA season, one that saw the Nets say good-bye to New Jersey before moving to Brooklyn, Biserka was invited back to a celebration for the final home game. There, she saw familiar faces. Derrick Coleman, Kenny Anderson, Chris Morris, relics from *Dražen's Nets*—each of them was there to greet her with smiles and hugs, posing for photos and sharing memories. His former teammates had aged now, some two decades since they had teamed in New Jersey, and it was hard not to think about how Dražen Petrović might have looked had he been there that night.

The year 2013 brought about a significant landmark: twenty years since the accident that claimed his life. Hundreds upon hundreds of candles were lit at his resting place. People converged to the museum in Zagreb, while others circled the memorial site in Šibenik. A television special featuring Aleksandar Petrović, Mirko Novosel, and Franjo Arapović aired on Croatian television, while one newspaper devoted almost a month to counting down the days until the anniversary, spinning a new story each day.

Two notable figures in Petrović's life were absent: Dino Radja and Stojko Vranković. Their lives had taken them elsewhere, yet they still think of Petrović most days. When the anniversary of Petrović's death rolls around each June, Radja opts to avoid the usual commotion. "It's always hard to think about that day," he said. Instead of focusing on his friend's premature death, Radja thinks back to the accomplishments, to the path that was laid out for him and others who followed Petrović. Vranković will speak to anyone about Dražen, and has met people from all over the world wanting to talk to him about his friend, but admits that it brings him mixed emotions. "I'm happy that I can tell people some things about him and I'm happy when I talk about him, but I am sad because he is not with us now," he said.

Radja and Vranković indeed followed Petrović to the NBA, and two full decades after Petrović last played there over ninety international players were on team rosters. It was a league record.

The Petrović family continues to endorse Dražen's memory as enthusiastically as ever, their efforts ensuring that his life—and what he stood for—will never be forgotten. Aleksandar Petrović continues as a coach in various European leagues, his surname assuring he is often approached by strangers who want to know about his younger brother. Fittingly, on the twentieth anniversary of Dražen's death, Biserka was at the forefront of the adulation heaped upon her son. She continues to build on his legacy, not only with her work in Zagreb but also in his hometown of Šibenik. There, one can visit his neighborhood, even the apartment where he was raised, where the dream began.

Nearby is a statue of the adolescent Dražen Petrović, one that readily embodies the birth of those dreams. The ball sits between the feet of the child, the eyes of the boy focused on the object, almost lost in thought. Perhaps he is dreaming of all he will become. Over his right shoulder, there sits the ultimate accompaniment: a playground.

ACKNOWLEDGMENTS

Well . . . before I began this project, I held a strong fascination for the first Europeans to arrive in the NBA. In many ways that served as the foundation for the book, as it soon was revealed to me that the perceptions held against those players—most of them genuine, one or two perhaps imagined—served as such a strong motivation in Dražen's life. That, of course, led to the origins of how one's mind was opened about getting them into the NBA, which took me straight to Bucky Buckwalter, the man who drafted both Dražen and Arvydas Sabonis in 1986. Bucky was a true visionary, and his memories of that period in league history were pivotal to the book.

I often wonder how history would have turned out had Dražen attended Notre Dame in the fall of 1984. As it turns out, he didn't. Digger Phelps was most gracious and accommodating in recalling for me his near-miss, in addition to his wonderful insight on the opinions regarding European players at the time.

The curiosity about those elite European players of the eighties, when unearthing the words written about them, makes for fascinating reading in today's age (when there are more than 100 international players in the NBA). There are three American writers, in particular, to whom I owe a debt of gratitude. Through their writing, I was challenged to explore more deeply the mentality of both the European players and also the ones who were evaluating their readiness for the NBA. Phil Hersh of the *Chicago Tribune* and Curry Kirkpatrick of *Sports Illustrated* both wrote about Dražen in 1986, the year he was drafted by Portland. And then Alexander Wolff, also of *Sports Illustrated*, himself a Petrović connoisseur, wrote a wonderfully detailed piece in 1988 that he was able to recount to me some two decades later.

Even with success in the NBA, Dražen felt as if he was trying to outrun certain misperceptions. From the great *New York Times* writer Harvey Araton, through his work and also our interview, I was exposed to the very delicate dynamic that was experienced by Dražen as he sought stardom. Even now, I'm not convinced I relayed it appropriately through this book.

A great many talented writers and reporters set the table for me with their writing on Dražen throughout his career. A select few include Vladimir Stanković; Neven Bertičević; Enrico Campana; and Vassilis Skountis, who sent me a copy of his final interview with Dražen. It was Dimitri Gonis who translated that article from Greek to English, and brought to life one of the intriguing subplots in Dražen's final days. From Dražen's time in the NBA, my thanks to Dwight Jaynes and Kerry Eggers of the *Oregonian,* and to the *Record's* John Jackson, the late Mike Celizic, and John Brennan, whose interest and support was most appreciated; Steve Popper of the *Asbury Park Press*; and Mike Freeman of *The New York Times*.

On a broader scale, the works of Jack McCallum, Bob Ryan, Michael Leahy, David Halberstam, and Araton, should be the starting points for any writer looking to capture the wonderful and varied elements of basketball. Gary Pomerantz's *Wilt, 1962* remains the model for resourcefulness in extracting the most out of things largely unseen or captured on film. It was a challenge I faced often for a biography topic who spent the first twenty-four years of his life in the former Yugoslavia.

Marshall Terrill edited my book both constructively and critically, and believed in me as I aimed to get it published. Beyond that, he provided me with wisdom and insight into the literary world, and he challenged me to make the manuscript as strong as it could be. His contributions and encouragement won't be forgotten.

Several books were helpful for particular parts of the journey. My father eagerly read Chuck Daly's memoir, *Daly Life*, and happily related to me the essence of Daly's approach to life and coaching. Rick Adelman's diary-style account of the 1990–91 Blazers, *The Long, Hot Winter*, written with Dwight Jaynes, touched on Dražen's situation during that second year in Portland and was very insightful. The reasons Dražen played so little in Portland have become muddled and twisted in hindsight, certainly prone to misinterpretation, but Rick provides a very clear explanation about his playing rotation in the book. Juan Escudero sent me a copy of his own book on Dražen that he wrote in Spanish, *La Leyenda Del Indomable*, which was also an excellent resource.

Visually, film was critically important, in many ways helping me cross language barriers. Ante Rozica directed a wonderful documentary in Croatia titled *Dražen*, which provided for me a wonderful snapshot of where Dražen grew up. Speaking of documentaries, a Spanish crew spent a week with Dražen in 1986 at the height of his fame in Europe. It was released in 1987 under the name, *Mas*. In searching for the film, I was overcome with the feeling that I'd have a better chance locating footage of

Wilt Chamberlain's 100-point game than I would finding this. It eludes not only me, but also Dražen's own family. Let me know if you have it—or simply saw it. *Once Brothers*, released by ESPN in 2010, was well received externally and has enabled a new generation to learn more about Dražen's career and relationship with Vlade Divac. Because it touches on such difficult topics, those of war and of broken friendships, it still resonates deeply with a lot of people I spoke with, some who weren't particularly fond of how Dražen was presented in the film. Regardless, it remains a meaningful and fascinating story.

I am a game-film nut and conservatively estimate that I have watched at least 90 games featuring Dražen, taking detailed notes on all. Simply put: I couldn't have written this book without them. I saw everything from Dražen's first appearance on American national television (in a 1981 exhibition game at Kentucky that aired on ESPN), to the famous 1983 Yugoslav league final, to his 40-point playoff debut with the Nets in 1992, to the very final game, against Slovenia, some twenty-four hours before his death. There are many people to thank for this. In particular, to Paul Hirschheimer and Trevor Schmid at NBA Entertainment, to Mike Pikula, Nebosja Kovacevic, and to my good friend, Adam Ryan, I say a big thanks. To the too-numerous-to-name who upload clips of Dražen to YouTube each and every week, thank you for keeping Dražen on people's minds.

Erik Dix from the University of Notre Dame archives allowed me to view a scouting film of a 1983 exhibition game between the Irish and the Yugoslav national team, which was way too much fun. Those tours of US colleges by the national team in the eighties were grueling, with a schedule so demanding, in fact, that often the players didn't know in which city they were waking up. Finding information on these tours (and Notre Dame's courtship of Dražen) was tricky, but I was aided immensely by the work of

Carol Copley from Notre Dame's media relations office. Thanks also to Kent William Brown from the University of Illinois, Jason E. Toberlin at North Carolina, Kyle Chilton of Brigham Young University, and Jeff Darby of UTEP, among others, for their help in unearthing stat sheets and other potpourri. Chuck Charnquist and Wayne Thompson, a couple of Blazer historians, were a terrific help with the Portland years. I'm also thankful to Birgitta Fella of the *Frankfurter Allgemeine* search service, who dug up an article about Dražen's accident that included new details.

One of the more intimidating elements of this project that I did not consider before diving in was the litany of Dražen historians who populate the planet. Perhaps at the head of that list is Tomislav Pakrac, who was a tremendous help in providing information on the deeper aspects of Dražen's life during the book's infancy.

What never ceased to amaze me were the emotions that were brought out in people in discussing Dražen, even two decades after he left this earth. Thanks to Spencer Ross for saying *"Petro for Three!"* on command over the phone. To Herb Turetzky for sharing personal stories and photos on behalf of both himself and his son, David. Rick Carlisle still remembers the Croatian phrases Dražen taught him, even the unflattering one he was encouraged to say to Stojko Vranković before a game one night in Boston. And Rich Dalatri didn't spare a single detail of the summer of 1991 that the two shared, one which changed Dražen's career entirely.

I have few regrets when it comes to this project. One, however, lingers with me, and that's missing the opportunity to speak with Willis Reed. I was told repeatedly by those who know him that beneath an intimidating exterior—one owing entirely to his magnificent career with the Knicks—was a caring, emotional man who had a great deal of love for Dražen. Ultimately, speaking with the necessary detail I was seeking about Dražen's life and death (coupled with the recent passing of Reed's cousin, Orlando Woolridge) was too much for him, and the several people who tried on my behalf to get Willis to speak were unsuccessful. And that's okay. I managed to find film of both the press conference held the day after the accident, and also the Nets jersey retirement, and on both occasions he spoke about Dražen as if he were still alive. I wonder if he still talks that way. I hope the young man he remembers lives in this book.

One of the true thrills for me of this writing process was getting to know some of the greats of those wonderful Yugoslav and Croatian national teams—each of whom was eager to talk about Dražen. Special mention goes to Zoran Čutura, whose detailed emails were always humorous and entertaining. No topic was off limits and he provided me a balanced perspective on those teams, even when I tried to goad him into gloating about how great they were. He was also tremendous in helping me to connect with some of the notable names of European basketball. I am also holding him to a promise he made of a tour of Zagreb when I make my way there.

No acknowledgement is complete, or could do justice, to the efforts of Nick Goyak throughout this project. Nick's love of Dražen is so very evident to this day, and his willingness to assist me in getting to the finish line will eternally be appreciated. How Nick made me comprehend the complex legal maze that freed Dražen from Real Madrid and made him a Blazer, I will never know. Thanks also to Warren LeGarie, for fighting for Dražen.

I need to reserve special place for four of Dražen's closest friends. Stojko Vranković and Dino Radja, both of the Croatian national team, shared with me their intimate memories of Dražen—friend and teammate, in the appropriate order. They miss their friend terribly, and I appreciate them sharing that with me. Neven Spahija was there at the beginning, Mario Miocic at the end, but each had a story to share. Knowing how each of these men felt about Dražen served as a great motivator when crafting the final product, if for nothing else in simply not wanting to disappoint them.

The accident, of course, was like a shadow hovering over the entire operation. It was always there. To the special young woman who spoke so willingly with me, Hilal Edebal, whose life, too, was irretrievably altered that awful day, I say thanks for your openness. Hilal gained nothing from sharing her story with me, but she did so anyway without a hint of hesitation. I wish her the very best.

Then there's Dražen's family. Firstly, to Aleksandar, for offering me his time to share memories of his life with Dražen. But beyond that, he deserves thanks for planting the seed of basketball with his younger brother. When it came to dealing with Dražen's parents, it was not unlike the scene at many of his games: Biserka was at the forefront, with Jole wandering somewhere behind, away from the action. Biserka enthusiastically shared with me the family background and anecdotes from Dražen's childhood, but it was the personal, open manner with which she delivered this to me that made the whole process so very worth it. Her letter to me describing the emotional pain experienced by both her and Jole in the years after she lost her son—emotions, mind you, that she was more than entitled to keep private—left me heartbroken. I hope they are proud of this book. Special thanks also to Aleksandra Vlatković and Miran Crnosija of the Petrović Museum in Zagreb for all their help and notes of encouragement.

On a personal level, I want to thank my parents, Leon and Helen, for showing me on a daily basis a work ethic I think would have made even Dražen envious. Their support and encouragement of me in chasing all my dreams is without limit. To Simon and Tanya, Penny and Micky, as well as Marcus, thanks for your support and love. Ditto for Roberto, Ana, and Cesar. And to my beautiful wife, Yolanda, who refused to let me quit and reassured me that I was capable of achieving this, your love means the world. And to my darling Ana Lucia, you give new meaning to my life.

BIBLIOGRAPHY

Detailed book notes found at: www.bookofdrazen.com. Page numbers correspond with print edition.

Newspapers & Magazines
Use of the following publications, including:

ABC (Spain)
Asbury Park Press
Associated Press
Baltimore Sun
Basketball Digest
Bergen Record
Boston Globe
Chicago Sun-Times
Chicago Tribune
Deseret News
Donaukurier—Ingolstadt Nach-richten (Germany)

El Mundo Deportivo (Spain)
El País (Spain)
Fort Wayne Journal Gazette
Frankfurter Allgemeine Zeitung (Germany)
HOOP magazine
Indianapolis Star
La Repubblica (Italy)
La Gazzetta dello Sport (Italy)
La Stampa (Italy)
Milwaukee Journal
New York Newsday

New York Daily News
New York Times
Notre Dame Observer
One on One (Australia)
Oregonian
Orlando Sentinel
Petersen's Pro Basketball Annual
Philadelphia Inquirer
San Francisco Examiner

South Bend Tribune
Sportske novosti (Croatia)
Sports Illustrated
Statesman Journal
Street & Smith's Pro Basketball
Annual
Ta Nea (Greece)
USA Today
Washington Post

Books

Adelman, Rick, and Dwight Jaynes, *The Long, Hot Winter*, Simon & Schuster, 1992

Araton, Harvey, *Crashing the Borders*, Free Press, 2005

Barry, Rick, and Jordan E. Cohn, *Rick Barry's Pro Basketball Scouting Report—1990–91 Edition*, Bonus Books, Inc., 1990

Bondy, Filip, *Tip Off*, Da Capo Press, 2007

Daly, Chuck, and Joe Falls, *Daly Life*, Masters Press, 1990

Daly, Chuck, and Alex Sachare, *America's Dream Team*, Turner Publishing, 1992

Escudero, Juan Francisco, *La Leyenda Del Indomable*, JC Clementine, 2006

Halberstam, David, *Playing for Keeps*, Broadway Books, 1999

Hollander, Zander (edited by), *1991 Complete Handbook of Pro Basketball*, New York, 1990

May, Peter, *The Big Three*, Simon & Schuster, 1994

McCallum, Jack, *Dream Team*, Ballantine Books, 2012

Official NBA Guide 2002–03, The Sporting News, Vulcan Sports Media, 2002

Pluto, Terry, *Loose Balls*, Simon & Schuster, 1991

Selected Sites

Basketball-Reference: www.basketball-reference.com

FIBA Basketball Archive: www.archive.fiba.com

Association for Professional Basketball Research: www.apbr.org/forum

Professional Basketball Transactions: www.prosportstransactions.com/basketball

List of Interviews (relationship to Petrović in parenthesis)

Harvey Araton (columnist, *New York Times*)

Jose Antonio Arizaga (Spanish agent)

John Brennan (Nets beat writer, *Bergen Record*)

Bucky Buckwalter (vice-president of basketball operations, Portland Trail Blazers)

Enrico Campana (writer, *La Gazzetta dello Sport)*

Rick Carlisle (assistant coach, New Jersey Nets, 1991–93)

Danko Cvjetićanin (teammate, Cibona, Yugoslavian national team, and Croatian national team)

Zoran Čutura (teammate, Cibona and Yugoslavian national team)

Rich Dalatri (strength and conditioning coach, New Jersey Nets, 1990–91 and 1991–92)

Vlado Djurović (head coach, Šibenka 1982–83)

Janez Drvaric (head coach, Cibona 1986–87)

Chris Dudley (teammate, New Jersey Nets, 1991–93)

Hilal Edebal (passenger in accident)

Kerry Eggers (Blazers beat writer, *Oregonian*)

Juan Escudero (Spanish author)

Ivan Fattorini (team physician, Cibona, Yugoslavian national team, and Croatian national team)

George Fisher (head coach, Orthez, France, and Buckwalter associate)

Harley Frankel (general manager, Portland Trail Blazers, 1986)

Bill Fitch (head coach, New Jersey Nets, 1990–91 and 1991–92)

Kenny Grant (Buckwalter associate)

Brad Greenberg (director of player personnel, Portland Trail Blazers)

Nick Goyak (friend and attorney)

Allen Israel (attorney to Portland Trail Blazers owner, Paul Allen)

Faruk Kulenović (head coach, Šibenka 1981–82)

Warren LeGarie (agent)

Clifford Luyk (assistant coach, Real Madrid 1988–89)

Mario Miocic (friend)

Veljko Mršić (teammate, Croatian national team)

Mihovil Nakić (teammate, Cibona and Yugoslavian national team)

Roger Newell (statistician to various NBA teams)

Tom Newell (assistant coach, New Jersey Nets, 1990–91 and 1991–92)

Mirko Novosel (head coach, Cibona 1984–86 and Yugoslav national team at 1984 Olympics)

David Pavao (strength and conditioning coach, New Jersey Nets, 1992–93)

Željko Pavličević (head coach, Cibona 1985–86, assistant coach 1984–85)

Velimir Perasović (teammate, Croatian national team)

Dan Peterson (head coach, Simac Milano, Italy)

Aleksandar Petrović (brother and former teammate at Cibona and Yugoslavian national team)

Biserka Petrović (mother)

Digger Phelps (University of Notre Dame head coach)

Steve Popper (Nets beat writer, *Asbury Park Press*)

Dino Radja (Yugoslavian and Croatian national team teammate)

Johnny Rogers (teammate, Real Madrid 1988–89)

Spencer Ross (television broadcaster, New Jersey Nets)
Petar Skansi (Croatian national team head coach, 1992)
Vassilis Skountis (writer, *Ta Nea*, Greece)
Zoran Slavnić (head coach and teammate, Šibenka 1979–81, and
    teammate on Yugoslavian national team, 1983)
Neven Spahija (childhood friend)
Vladimir Stanković (European basketball writer)
Brendan Suhr (assistant coach, New Jersey Nets, 1992–93)
Herb Turetzky (head scorekeeper, New Jersey Nets)
Quique Villalobos (teammate, Real Madrid 1988–89)
Stojko Vranković (teammate, Yugoslavian junior and senior
    national team and Croatian national team)
John Wetzel (assistant coach, Portland Trail Blazers, 1989–91)
Alexander Wolff (writer, *Sports Illustrated*)

ABOUT THE AUTHOR

Much as Dražen Petrović did, Australian Todd Spehr left his homeland to pursue a basketball career in the United States. After a successful collegiate playing career, by age twenty-five he was coaching at his alma mater and covering professional basketball as a writer.

Spehr graduated from Central Christian College in Kansas in 2006. His writing appears in both international and US basketball publications and prominent websites, including ESPN and *SLAM*. He currently resides in Australia with his wife, Yolanda, and daughter, Ana Lucia. *The Mozart of Basketball* is his first book.